FROM BRAIN TO MIND

FROM BRAIN TO MIND

Using Neuroscience to
Guide Change in Education

James E. Zull

1996–2011 15TH ANNIVERSARY

Stylus
PUBLISHING, LLC.

STERLING, VIRGINIA

COPYRIGHT © 2011 BY STYLUS PUBLISHING, LLC.

Published by Stylus Publishing, LLC
22883 Quicksilver Drive
Sterling, Virginia 20166-2102

Library of Congress Cataloging-in-Publication-Data
Zull, James E. (James Ellwood), 1939–
From brain to mind : using neuroscience to guide change in education / James E. Zull.—1st ed.
    p.   cm.
Includes bibliographical references and index.
ISBN 978-1-57922-461-5 (cloth : alk. paper)
ISBN 978-1-57922-462-2 (pbk. : alk. paper)
ISBN 978-1-57922-605-3 (library networkable e-edition)
ISBN 978-1-57922-606-0 (consumer e-edition)
1. Learning—Physiological aspects.   2. Learning, Psychology of. 3. Cognitive neuroscience.   I. Title.
QP408.Z85   2011
612.8′2—dc22

                                    2010044073

13-digit ISBN: 978-1-57922-461-5 (cloth)
13-digit ISBN: 978-1-57922-462-2 (paper)
13-digit ISBN: 978-1-57922-605-3 (library networkable e-edition)
13-digit ISBN: 978-1-57922-606-0 (consumer e-edition)

Printed in the United States of America

All first editions printed on acid free paper
that meets the American National Standards Institute
Z39-48 Standard.

Bulk Purchases

Quantity discounts are available for use in workshops and for staff development.
Call 1-800-232-0223

First Edition, 2011

10   9   8   7   6   5   4   3   2   1

To Ramsey, Paige, Judy, Bess,
and in memory of Rema

CONTENTS

ACKNOWLEDGMENTS

I am grateful to Hillel, Dave, Alice, Arthur, Elsie, Norm, Joe, and Susan. Each of them read either all or substantial portions of my drafts. And their reading led to significant change for the better. Their contributions are all significant, so I have listed them in alphabetical order below.

Hillel Chiel, neurobiologist, scholar, educator, and overall generally penetrating mind, never flinched when I asked him to read my drafts. As is his wont, he always pointed out something new in what I wrote (new to me that is), and even when he discovered errors or misinterpretations, he remained cheerful. This generous gift of time and talent both flattered and encouraged me. It gave me confidence to go on when the task seemed impossible. I had no illusions about the challenge I had set for myself, and it was Hillel that I trusted to keep me out of waters too deep—or at least, near the shore!

Dave and Alice are the Kolbs. It is his work that continues to provide the foundation for all my thinking about the mind. His mind fascinates and amazes me—his depth and humility. Alice makes her own contributions, often providing a perspective that both Dave and I had missed. I still remember the day we sat together on their front porch, going through the ideas, and discussing the big ideas. The fact that they felt there were any such ideas was, in itself, stimulating and encouraging. I greatly value their gifts to me.

Joe Koonce, another of my longtime friends in our Biology Department at CWRU, for a number of years my boss, and enthusiastic supporter of my earlier work, gave me honest and rigorous analysis of my last two chapters. His comments ultimately led me to rewrite the chapter on metacognition, insisting that if he could not understand what I was saying, I probably didn't either. This was invaluable in helping me realize where I was failing as a writer, and how I could address that challenge.

Arthur Lavin is my brilliant and kind pediatrician friend, whom I met and came to appreciate only recently. He understands children, their development, their brains, and their minds. He read every chapter and never failed to point out an opportunity for supporting the learner. He also told me that I should not look to him to affirm any value of fear in learning. It has none! Not even the word "challenge" pleased him. But he trusted that my heart was in the right place, and for that I thank him. He kept on reading and in general giving me the benefit of his experience, wisdom, insight, and humor.

I met Elzie Ritzenhein somewhat later in the process of writing and quickly realized how valuable her input would be. Her decades-long experience in leading the McComb Academy of Arts and Science, as well as her capabilities as a teacher, educator (writ large), consultant in all aspects of education, and contributor of her own writing, all served me well. She read every chapter, and was particularly supportive while helping me slog through the later ones. She was honest, polite, and supportive but still firm about the parts that were particularly messy—attributes that cannot be overvalued!

My long time friend and supporter, Norm Rushforth, read many of the earlier chapters, and gave me extensive, handwritten feedback on them. His attention to detail, combined with his broad knowledge of education, science, and the world in general, led me to expand and rethink my work. He didn't seem to realize that retirement implied that he didn't have to work. He just kept on reading everything I gave him, giving me the benefit of his keen and rigorous statistician's mind.

Finally, of course, there is Susan, my constant and loving wife and friend. I will not go into all the ways she helped me. That would be impossible. But of the two of us, she is the vastly better writer. And she loves the red ink! For this book she also served as editor and critic. She found those messy places where neither she nor anyone else could understand what I had written. And, at the same time she also found the missing commas! For more than 30 years, our partnership has been the foundation that I count on as I struggle to put thoughts into words. There is a path worn between our offices at home, created primarily by my back-and-forth jaunts as I sought the right word, the direct expression, and all the other clarifications and efficiencies that I knew she could provide. I can only reaffirm the recognition I tried to express in my first book. She remains the best idea I ever had!

Thanks to E. R. Kandel for permission to reprint the figure on page 182 and J. Nolte for permission to reprint the figure on page 235.

INTRODUCTION

This book has been on my mind for years. It began as an effort to fill in topics I had given short shrift in *The Art of Changing the Brain*. I felt I should have written more about very key topics such as memory, attention, or symbolic systems such as language and mathematics. I envisioned a second book entitled something like *More Art of Changing the Brain* and actually began that project in 2004.

As time went on, I realized that "filling in the gaps" was not adequate motivation for writing an entire new book. I lost my way and drifted for a few more years. The passage of time began to have an impact. I worried that I would never write again. I still felt that I had new contributions to make so I sat down at my laptop. But I remained uncertain about my message. What did I want to say? And why?

I recognized the answer, or at least a partial answer, to this question in an unexpected way and place. My wife and I were traveling in England, and it was time to return to Heathrow Airport. I noticed that our rented car had a GPS system, and it occurred to me that that we might be able to use it to find the car rental area of the airport. I had never used this technological invention before, but what better time to learn?

After fussing around a bit, I managed to get the system turned on and began to follow the directions as we entered the airport. Suddenly, I had my own guide, who, like HAL 9000 in *2001: A Space Odyssey*, took us by the hand and led us. "Turn right at the next stop," HAL instructed. "Turn left after the second red light," he went on in his sonorous voice. "Enter the tunnel using the right branch of the upcoming intersection." And so it went. We were getting information in exact, precise bits, leading us from point to point. All we had to do was follow directions.

But we had no real knowledge. So you may not be surprised at what happened next. My dear wife and I began to get very tense. We had no idea where we were. Possibly for the first time, I understood the idea of being at sea. I didn't even have a theory. You might be having that feeling yourself as you read this. Feeling lost? Worried? Overseas flights wait for no one!

Then, suddenly, the car rental offices were in front of us. The tension dissolved. But not the memory. As I remembered the experience and the feelings, slowly the nature and outcome of the technological revolution began to become clear in my mind. I began to realize that as time moved on bit by bit (literally), my life decisions might be dictated by this kind of process, one in which I followed instructions rather than working them out myself. I slowly began to understand how profound that revolution is, and how irreversible. And as I thought about education, I began to fear for children who will grow up in that technical environment. I began to realize what is at stake. It is the very heart of education itself, development of the mind.

Let me explain.

As he always has, Homo sapiens invented new tools and machines to save us the trouble and effort needed to do things ourselves. In the last century most of those inventions saved us physical labor. We invented tractors for the farmer, washing machines for the housewife, and typewriters for the writer. We are still doing that. But now we have also begun to invent machinery that does mental labor. From the handheld calculator, to the GPS, to the Droid, we now have an array of machines that carry out mental tasks of great complexity at high speeds. Children grow up surrounded by this machinery. Their minds are filled with moving images projected on screens and changing at high speed. They solve arithmetic problems by pushing buttons or keys on calculators and computers. They ask why they must memorize either the specific answers to basic multiplication problems or the algorithms that allow us to do long division. They wonder why school pays so much attention to reading and writing, when they can quickly and simply text anything to friends. If students are forced to write, grammar, spelling, and punctuation are provided by programs such as MS Word or, more subtly, WordPerfect! As I did in the airport, they can also go from place to place by taking instructions from a speaking machine, without *thought*. They can get facts instantly, directly, and in huge abundance via Google. They really don't have to remember anything. In fact, we can all know more than the experts; just give us a split second (or less). And if we have a problem with our marriage, we can have the best advice from experts posthaste! Why bother to figure it out ourselves?

In themselves, these are not necessarily bad things. I am not writing a critique of technology. It is here to stay. Anger or frustration is not a useful or appropriate response. But I believe we must respond. We must ask what kind of response is possible, but, more important, what kind of response is appropriate. Is it urgent? Are we facing some threat or danger?

I feel that we are in danger. We can begin to understand it by imagining an analogous situation experienced by the farmer and his tractor that I mentioned above. In this analogy, the farmer might start one growing season without a tractor, using a horse-drawn plow. If he were to purchase his tractor mid-season, he could then complete his plowing much faster that year riding on his new machine. How might this change affect the farmer? His physical body?

If you think that he might lose strength (physical strength) by using his body less, we are in agreement. Use it or lose it. But would you apply that reasoning to your mind? Would you agree that allowing machines to do mental work for us might weaken our mental capacities? If the brain is a physical organ of the body, will it also weaken from disuse? If you still have the mental energy needed to think about this, or even if you want to save energy, and simply Google it, I suspect that you will find the answer. And if you are still with me, I will tell you that the answer is yes.

So what is the point? Technology won't go away, and I wouldn't want it to. I would be as helpless as a newborn without my laptop. What am I trying to say?

In a word, my message is *change*. Not change in technology, but change in education. Technology has already taken over some of the mental tasks that used to be the purview of education. There will be more to come. And without some dramatic intervention, mental capabilities we attribute to the mind will be weakened or lost. If we continue to count on education for development of the mind, we need to change education itself. We must provide experiences and challenges for the brain that strengthen the mind; ones that technology does not address, or that build further on technology. The primary mission for education can no longer be just teaching the subjects in the curriculum. It must include understanding the process of learning itself. It must lead to the development of mature, independent, and thoughtful minds. Education must fill this immense gap left by technology.

What does this mean? Is cognitive neuroscience helping us form an answer to that question? What are the functions of the brain that are required to solve problems, think about experiences, develop new theories, and determine the validity or invalidity of our thoughts, theories, and ideas? Are we at a place where we can lay out an educational path that goes beyond what we can achieve directly through technology? Can we rescue the mind?

Designing such a path is the goal of this book. My hope is to identify and explain how a brain becomes a mind through experience, and to create an educational agenda that will encourage and support that goal. Technology must serve development of the mind, not the reverse. And although we may not yet know everything we need to achieve such an objective, we can begin. We can lay a foundation on which we can build for the future.

Technology is moving rapidly. It is time to get going!

*   *   *

You may be surprised by some things in this book. I suspect that most of these surprises will be related either to audience or objective. By audience, of course, I mean *who* I hope will read the book, and by objective, I mean *what* I hope will happen when they do.

Here are some ideas about audience.

If you have children, you are an educator. You are in my audience, along with all other educators in schools, businesses, and professions, or in our schools and institutions of higher education. This actually includes most adults. In fact, I hope that a significant fraction of my readers will be in that ambiguous category of the aging. I am particularly interested in reaching my own peers, especially those who are experiencing significant life changes, such as a change in profession, learning new skills, or undertaking new challenges. Perhaps one way to explain this category is to identify these people as anyone who has begun to have conversations, real or imagined, about "retiring." Development of the mind may give us much more than a good start in life; it can satisfy and energize us as we approach the end. It can accelerate at any age in response to any challenge.

The global nature of my (desired) audience is consistent with my examples and style. This book is not just about the young. I don't necessarily separate the child from the adult. To make a point, I may write about a newborn child in one paragraph and a grandparent in the next. The focus is not on maturing or "growing up" so much as it is on processes that are central to mental growth at any stage in life. It's about principles, not age.

I don't write that much about professional teachers, either. As I have already stressed, we should not assume that educators are found only in schools. To the extent that I do address school and its challenges, the goal is not to improve or deepen knowledge as much as it is to learn how we can get that improvement, and deepen that knowledge, whenever we need or want to. It's about the process, not the product.

If we are going to make development of the mind the overarching goal of education, then we must literally change the criteria for success. Our goal should be a spontaneous demonstration of habits of mind. We can claim success if learners demonstrate optimism and confidence, proceed to take actions, and ask questions when given a task. This is in contrast to getting it right. The machines will get it right if they are asked the right questions.

* * *

Throughout the book I use the metaphor of a journey. The metaphor has some advantages, but there it also has one significant drawback. A journey can often seem prescribed. It is easy to assume that journeys are linear, and that they are better journeys if they have no detours and progress is facile. They have specific beginnings and ends.

Not everyone makes assumptions like this, but they occur frequently enough to deserve this clarification. The journey I have in mind is full of uncertainty. Each traveler starts at a different place and has different ends in mind. Here, individual journeys often are highly inefficient, with a lot of backtracking and circling (great and small). These journeys also have the interesting feature of self-evaluation. Success is not determined by checking a map or reaching a location, but rather by meeting individual criteria defined by the traveler himself or herself. If we say our journey is a success, it is.

* * *

One last thing.

I hope you will recognize my role in all this. I am not working in a lab, putting electrodes into brains, or carrying out fMRI studies of people as they are reading, or thinking, or some such. I am not a practicing neuroscientist. Rather, I put my effort into identifying interesting research results obtained by other scientists, trying to understand them, and asking myself the question: "Does this mean anything for education?" When the answer is yes, I write about it.

My role in this writing is that of interpreter. I may not know everything about the research and the scientific methods used, but I do know some of the language, and I can learn more, quickly. Perhaps I can be your translator.

Not all translators are equal, however. Different ones may see different meanings. Here, you are subject to me and my meanings. This is a particularly tricky business. I am asking you to stay alert and watch for the places where I go beyond the known facts and end up putting my own theories and spin on things. I have tried to make these places obvious, but that is part of the challenge. First, I have to recognize them myself.

I have tried to do that, often reminding you in the text, but also here. A lot of what you will read represents my theories. My translation.

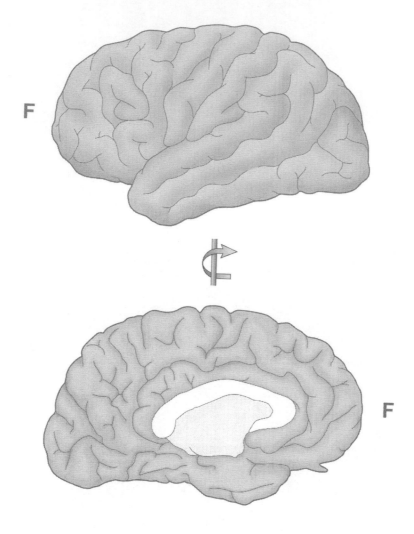

To begin, examine the brain images above. At the top, we see a lateral view of the left hemisphere. Rotating that hemisphere (not the whole brain), we see its other side, a medial view (F = front). Of course, the right hemisphere also has lateral and medial surfaces. The convoluted surface is the cortex (skin), of the brain. It entirely coats both hemispheres.

I

THE NATURAL JOURNEY
FROM BRAIN TO MIND
Brief History and Overview

It is [our] ancient and natural strength.
 —Sir William Blackstone referring
to the British navy*

We all agreed that Henry was the smartest person in our class. He always got As. So far as any of us knew, he had never gotten a single B.

It was my junior year in high school, and I was in the same study hall as Henry. In fact, he sat at the desk right next to me. Not many of us used the study hall time to actually study. We preferred to whisper and joke with our friends. But sometimes we just had to find something quiet to do until the bell rang, and that was what I was doing.

Basketball was "my thing." I would go home after school, grab the ball and shoot hoops, even in snow! It was on my mind day and night. I was trying to figure out how I could make my backyard like a basketball court; a perfect square. There were about 700 square feet of space, but it was not really square; it was more oblong. So I needed to know the square root of 700.

But I didn't know how to figure it out. I began guessing, trying to get close. This helped, but I really wanted the right answer. Then it struck me: Henry would know. He was especially smart at math! So I slipped him my question: How do you figure the square root of 700?

---

*Commentaries on the Laws of England, 1765–1769, Book 1, Chapter 13, Of the Military and Maritime States

I will never forget my shock as I watched him struggle. His face turned slightly pink as he tried different angles, and as I saw what he was writing, my surprise increased. Even I knew the general way these problems were set up; I just didn't know all the steps. But Henry didn't seem to know even as much as I did. With everything he had learned in school, he could not solve my very real, compelling, and, I believed, easy problem (easy once you know how, that is)!

This book is about a journey.

Picture a newborn child with a brain ready to learn. This is where the journey begins. Exquisitely organized for learning, this brain is destined for change as the baby grows into a child and eventually an adult. That mass of organized cells, blood vessels, and chemicals gains capacities that make it at once the most powerful yet most exquisite force in the universe. The change is so dramatic that we need a new word to define it. We call it *mind*.

This journey from brain to mind depends greatly on experience. True, biology also plays a role. The brain is a biological organ of the body, and its functioning depends on a range of biological processes from the expression of genes to even the diet. But the underlying biological structure—the neurons, their organization, and the multiple other structures—is just a foundation. It is the capacity of the brain to organize and *change itself* through experience that leads to development of the mind. By sensing, recording, and reproducing our experiences, the brain gains the capacity to think, decide, and act. It makes itself into a mind.

Different Journeys

We all begin with the same foundation and we all experience change, so the journey is something we share. But at the same time, our journeys are all different. We pass through different places, sometimes revisit those places, take different amounts of time, and expend different amounts of effort along the way. This means that each mind is unique and unpredictable; minds cannot be categorized in any reliable way. Just when we believe we understand another mind, it surprises us. And if we wait a bit, we will have more surprises.

This variability means that we can't be sure where we are headed. In fact, the idea of an ultimate destination, or a completion, does not fit into our metaphor very well. Even as we age, slow down, and wonder if we are near the end, the journey itself may provide new energy. In many ways it is self-renewing and clarifying. It may even accelerate later in life. It may reach some unexpected place and surprise us.

The journey is an adventure.

The Journey and Education

Jean Piaget is often given credit as the first to systematically study this journey. However, Charles Darwin probably is more deserving of this recognition. Darwin kept a detailed record of the development of his firstborn child (a boy), focusing particularly on "the first dawn of various expressions he exhibited." This work inspired psychologists both in his own day and up to the present time.[1]

This is not to downplay Piaget's contributions, of course. He observed children from birth into adolescence, focusing on cognitive development. Beginning with the newborn, he described the earliest behaviors, reflexes, and basic sensory-motor processes, which are ultimately followed by the appearance of formal thought. This includes but is not limited to appearance of cognitive understandings such as goal-oriented actions, object permanence, experimentation, and abstraction. With some exceptions, his work still stands as one of the major pillars in child development.

Piaget was also aware of the developmental differences in individual children, and the role of experience in either accelerating or hindering cognitive growth. In addition, he believed strongly in the importance of formal education and schooling. Following World War I and the subsequent collapse of major economies, Piaget wrote, "[O]nly education is capable of saving our societies from possible collapse, whether violent or gradual."[2]

This increasing awareness of the importance of education in society was greatly influenced by John Dewey. Dewey was arguably the first to describe the powerful and broad connection between education and experience suggested by Piaget.[3] He focused particularly on formal education of children in schools, but also used the idea of a journey, of growth and development. Dewey criticized the rigid models of schooling that were widespread in his time and wrote extensively about creating schools with a positive environment that would lead to student growth and to intrinsic motivation for learning. He believed that the development of the mind would progress naturally if school experiences were supportive and positive.

The notion that education and experience are intimately linked catalyzed a new and essential contribution by David Kolb. Dewey told us about this connection, but Kolb provided us with a theory to explain it. Kolb began to ask key questions about the nature of the learning phenomenon itself and turned our attention to education as a *process*, one that continues beyond the walls of any institution and has no defined content. In particular, he stressed individual differences in approaching learning and the idea that education should be adapted to the personal strengths and attributes of the learner. Further, his ideas were not limited to school, but rather extended our understanding of experience as the basis of lifelong learning, at work and in school.

Dewey focused on school years, while Piaget and Kolb were concerned with preschool and postschool experience and development, respectively. The overall result was a growing realization that while school is important, the experiential journey encompasses an entire life span. When we speak of education, we must include all of our experience. In some ways, school is just an interlude.

A Personal Journey

Kolb's major work, *Experiential Learning*, was published in 1983. At the time, the discipline of cognitive neuroscience was beginning to open up, and methods for directly examining brain engagement in cognition were appearing. This led to the notion of a "decade of the brain" in the 1990s, and by the turn of the new millennium, it was apparent that research on brain processes and structure was exposing new vistas of learning itself. There was a hope that new and heretofore unrecognized insights about the actual processes of learning would revolutionize formal education.

At this time I began to explore this new area from my perspective as a biologist and educator at a research university. Fortunately, I discovered Kolb's work and realized that in many ways his theory of learning ran parallel with the fundamental processes by which all nervous systems work, biologically. This led to *The Art of Changing the Brain* in 2002, in which I pointed out that the parallel between a learning theory and the structure of nervous systems provided a context and a pathway for deep learning, in both formal practice and lifelong learning.

However, my earlier work had major gaps. In fact, it did not address questions that one might say are of greatest interest—questions about the mind. I acknowledged this at the time and, in fact, consciously refrained from discussing the topic. Although I realized that growth of the mind is arguably the most fundamental goal of all education, I felt that I was not yet ready to address it. In fact, I was not sure that I would ever be ready!

My own brain had begun a longer and more complicated journey.

Challenge

At this time, I found myself challenged by an unexpected development. I learned that not everyone thought it was possible to link neuroscience and education. There was a claim that the gap between them was (is) too great. It is just a bridge too far.[4]

As is often the case, the challenge triggered a reaction. Suddenly I found myself energized to get back to work on the mind thing. My reasons were simple. In my life as a biochemist, I had always focused on trying to find out how things work. How does DNA work? How do vitamins work? And I had never found that this questioning was a waste. I couldn't predict the outcome or benefit, but as the work progressed, new connections and research directions always opened up. Ergo, I should find out how brains work, if I could. And if we began to understand learning, could education be far behind? Then we could see if the bridge *was* too far.

There are other arguments for examining possible connections of education to neuroscience, of course. From the biological point of view, learning is fundamentally a function of an organ, the brain, working in the body. Biologists have always explored how organs work. We should no more turn our backs on the relationships between learning and brain function than we should deny those between the beating heart and blood pressure.

Then there was the question of motivation. Educators are just naturally motivated to learn about the brain. We want to know, and despite uncertainties, that curiosity persists. How can we state that there is no bridge if we do not look for it ourselves? We are going to look. It is inevitable!

Finally, I believe it is our duty to look. Educators face great challenges. The need for change and improvement is deep and troubling. We should look at any serious opportunity to address those challenges. And we are free to do so! Nothing prevents us. Given that freedom, how can we justify ignoring a potentially fundamental source of new and deeper understanding, on either practical or ethical grounds? Isn't that what the cardinals asked of Galileo?

Yes, there are pitfalls. We may find ourselves tempted to oversimplify or overinterpret new findings about the brain and learning, and we should be cautious and remain aware of that possibility. We should not be looking for instant remedies, clever pedagogical tricks, sudden breakthroughs, or isolated facts. Rather, we should seek a deeper understanding of the "learning organ" and how the journey toward mind can be facilitated.

Our objective should be conceptual, not technical.

Education

In the brief discussion of Dewey and Kolb I stressed the idea that we are all being educated and have many educators throughout life. This is why I wrote earlier, "life is learning, life is teaching."[5] I could as well have written, "life is education, life is educating."

It is important that we keep that notion in our discussion of the journey from brain to mind. The journey includes formal schooling and professional teaching, but that is not what I mean by "education" and "educating." A deeper and more complete concept of education is lifelong learning built on experience. When I speak of education, I mean all experience, not just school.

One reason I stress this point is because schooling itself is such a mixed experience. It contains much that is helpful for progress toward mind, but also much that does not help and may even impede us. Just going to school or just studying the curriculum does not guarantee progress. We may learn more from experiences outside school than those inside.

The story about Henry and me is an example of this. My education had begun to extend from school subjects out to my life experiences. Progress in my journey toward mind was accelerating. There were no horizons. But Henry was stalled. At least with mathematics, he had learned that there is an end to knowledge; it ends when the course does. Then we can box it up and close the lid. School experience actually reduced his learning through life experience.

Schooling is part of education, but not all—or even most—of it. So, yes, I will write specifically about schooling, but not *just* about schooling.

Plan for a Book

My feelings about taking on this project were complex. I was excited but also intimidated. Writing about the mind is nothing if not daunting. However, it turned out that the brain perspective is also a help. It allows us to begin with concrete structures and functions (brain) before following them in the more abstract direction of mind. For example, memory is the result of physical connections between neurons, but using memories to think and solve problems is a property of the mind. If we start with the first, we may discover more about the second.

I had discovered this advantage while writing *The Art of Changing the Brain*, and I decided to approach this new work that way. The plan was to begin with a short list of brain functions that are either missing or not adequately addressed in that earlier work. However, the new work must be more than unfinished business. It should also have its own logic and lead to new ideas. Those new directions were unpredictable, but I had faith that they would make themselves apparent. The journey from brain to mind would lead where it will.

That plan, applied to development of the mind, goes as follows. We will begin where it seems learning begins—not that it is possible to precisely define that point, but simply because we must begin somewhere. I have chosen sensory-motor learning to serve that role. This very early learning leads to discovery, and the discovery to joy. I then follow with a sequence of chapters describing how deeper learning develops, how symbolic systems such as language and numbers emerge as tools for thought, how memory builds a knowledge base consciously and subconsciously, and how memory is then used to create ideas and solve problems. The journey leads, then, to the possibility of designing new education approaches very early in life as well as in schools. And, ultimately, we discover a link that ties everything together: metacognition. The ultimate outcome of the journey is to understand our own understanding.

Other Plans

Individual chapters also have their rationale. Each one begins with a story that illustrates a central idea or example of the topic being discussed. Consistent with the idea that the journey toward mind is not just about schooling, the stories are not always school stories. To a great extent, the stories are about my own journey, including experiences that are memorable to me, that changed me.

In the rationale of the individual chapters, these stories are followed by the main idea or topic in layman's terms, a description of some neuroscience research that gives us insights into that idea, and, last, a direct discussion of schooling.

Here are the chapter topics in sequence—my list:

Transformation. Our first proposition, and the focus of chapter 2, is that the brain is a natural transformation machine. It is that way at birth. Specifically, the brain transforms information into action. Data collected in sensory parts of the brain are changed into actions expressed by the motor, or action, parts. This is why biologists divide the brain into *sensory* and *motor* regions. In some other animals (non-human), these two regions make up nearly the entire brain.

Very early in the journey, transformation expresses itself as mimicry. The brain contains the machinery for mimicry, and that machinery leads to action. We might argue that action is the whole purpose of the brain. Indeed, in his book, *The Brain*, Richard Thompson comes close to that claim when he writes that "the purpose of the brain is to produce behavior."[6] Behavior is action. It is what we *do*, frequently unconsciously, in response to experiences and environment.

Action is an often-neglected partner in education. We are used to thinking of learning as "getting" information (sensory), but not so used to thinking about "doing." But, ultimately, action is the entire point. Our actions can reveal our thoughts, sometimes to others and potentially to ourselves, if we pay attention to them. Even babies express their "thoughts" with their actions.[7]

Appropriately, then, transformation is at the heart of the story about Henry and me. I wanted to transform knowledge (information about square roots) into action (designing a basketball court). Transformation is application. It goes beyond receiving information and beyond remembering experiences and data. It is changing the passive into the active. It was what I wanted when I asked Henry for information. I didn't just want to *have* the information, I wanted to *use* it.

Emotion—focus on the joy. Contrary to common belief, the concept of mind includes emotion. The transforming, integrating, and "imaging" regions of the cortex are awash in chemicals that we associate with emotion; the brain is an organ of emotion. We come to understand this as we progress in our journey. Often we are warned to avoid emotion because it leads to mistakes and bad decisions. But as the journey continues, we also realize that all thought is emotional. We can't get rid of emotion. The trick is to use emotion as an aid to deeper understanding and more effective action, while avoiding the errors. This is a major part of the journey.

A great deal has been written elsewhere about negative emotion and the brain. But here I focus on the positive emotion systems and the intrinsic rewards. In chapter 3, I propose that action and exploration as discussed in chapter 2, lead to discovery, and discovery leads to joy. My Henry story illustrates this implicitly. It was all about my love of basketball. This was the source of all my thoughts and actions. But that love led to the discovery that a school subject, math, could also be joyful. Ultimately, I came to love math because I saw it as a way to achieve other goals and desires in my life such as my experiences with smart students in college and my theories about intelligence and school. The emotional entanglement was inevitable, unending, and joyful.

Emotional links generate motivation. They keep us going. But emotion is also implicit in the direction our minds take. Emotions direct our choices, even when those choices are based on reasoning. We favor the reasoned choice because it feels right, because it is based on good emotions. It achieves something that we trust. And it is the trust that we value—that we *feel* best about!

The brain rewards itself with joy.

Integration. As the journey continues, we begin to go beyond mimicry. Instead of transforming sensory input directly into action, we use a less direct, but far more powerful, approach. The transformation process becomes more complex. It begins to engage more regions of cortex, connecting sensory perceptions to one another.

"Connecting," or associating, is not a totally satisfying image for this process. I use the term "integration" to describe it. We learn not only to connect things, but also to put them in a specific place; we seek the right place to put them. An example of integration is a single piece of a jigsaw puzzle that might associate (connect) at several different places, but only truly integrates in one of them.

Language is another example of integration. We can connect sounds with images in different ways, but each way has its own particular meaning. Words and images must be integrated if we are to know the difference between "he hit the ball" and "the ball hit him." We must not only comprehend this difference when we hear language, but we also must know how to create meaningful language ourselves by *intentionally* integrating sounds and images. Comprehension of language and creation of language both require integration.

Integration is the subject of chapter 4. It is often missing in schooling, and this omission shows up in different ways. In my story, Henry may well never have integrated his knowledge of square roots with anything outside the classroom. Sometimes school subjects and curriculum divide the world into unnatural categories, which makes integration difficult. It can seem as if there is no natural meaning, and so we memorize. I believe this is often the case with algebra. For many, it is hard to see how it integrates into real life before, during, or even after the school years.

Images. In the processes of transformation and integration, we begin to accumulate more complete representations, which we call images. This is a key aspect of the journey toward mind. We come to depend heavily on the ability of our mind to analyze and manipulate images. In many ways, images are the vehicle of comprehension, thought, and action. In thinking about thinking, we find ourselves continually returning to images. The brain makes consistent images of the real world. Images are used or implied for most if not all other functions one might identify with mind. We integrate parts of images, we remember images, we manipulate images, we color images, we transform images, we create symbols for images, we create our own unique images, we leap from image to image, we build new images and forget old ones, we constantly change our images, and we predict and invent new images. These ideas are discussed in chapter 5.

Images are, in fact, the core of my story about Henry. I had an image of a basketball court in my mind, compared it to an image of a real half-court in my memory, recalled an image of Henry in a math class, created a new image of Henry calculating square roots, and took actions designed to make reality conform to my mental image.

Symbolizing. The ubiquity of images in thought ultimately leads to shorthand approaches in our thinking. We make up symbols for ideas.

Developing this symbolic capacity represents key aspects of the history of the human intellect, and in individual development of the mind.

Symbols are an example of integration. We have the ability to create abbreviations and symbols for objects, actions, and relationships. For example, the = sign is a symbol for a complex and emotional idea that has various associations (algebra, money, even democracy through equality). Development of symbolic systems might be the most important step along the journey toward mind.

The symbolic power of the mind also is intimately related to transformation, integration, images, and emotion. We use symbols for objects, meanings, ideas, and actions. The use of sounds with specific phonetic features, such as "oh!" "ow!" "wow!" "yes!" and "##**#*^!!," is an important way of symbolizing emotions and feelings. Symbols are vehicles and tools of thought. They are images of images.

My story is full of symbols. The use of numbers to define a basketball court, the rules for manipulation of symbols in mathematical calculations, and the representation of good performance in school with single letter symbols (grades) are all examples.

These ideas and their significance for education are central themes in chapter 6.

Making memory. One day my fellow professors and I were talking about how some students learn more quickly than others. Then, one of my colleagues interrupted us. "I am not so interested in how fast they learn," he said. "I want to talk about how long it lasts. How can we make learning last? How can we make it permanent?"

This is a natural longing, especially for educators, but as we will see, it is not a productive question. Very few, if any, memories are permanent, and the more we use any particular memory, the more it changes. Memory is a biological phenomenon, which means that it is alive, never static, and subject to continual modification. Memories change as they are consolidated, continue to change when they are recalled, and change again when they are "reconsolidated."

Memories consist of networks of neurons, and certainly the brain contains such networks and adds to them from its very conception. In that sense, we might argue that formation of memories is more a function of brain than of mind. But the dynamic image of memory described above strongly suggests mind. Also, formation of strong memories seems to be delayed in the child until the age of four or five, again suggesting that memory formation is the outcome of earlier processes in the brain. Our increased ability to remember things, and to be aware of the *process* of memory formation, is progress in our journey toward mind. It is the awareness and the conscious manipulation of memories that is mind-like.

As mind develops, memory becomes more and more central in every-thing we do. Knowledge of the past is essential for thought, development, and growth. The ability to remember allows us to establish our identity. As we grow physically, our memory of experiences does as well. Those memo-ries give us a sense of our self, our likes, our beliefs, and our personality.[8] This is why Alzheimer's disease is so devastating. People are lost and alone in a profound way. Not only do they lose their place and get lost in the physical world, but they also lose themselves internally. This maturation of memory capability and its role in our journey toward mind is the central theme of chapter 7.

Using memory. The model of memory described above points out the purpose of memory—what it is and what it is not. Memories are of value when they are used; they are not inert recorded information. And learning how to use our memory to solve problems, get new ideas, and predict what will happen next is a major step in the development of the mind. Using memory is the basis of thought, logic, and invention, and it fits best near the end of this book. It requires a developed mind, one that has moved far beyond the copying brain. This is the topic of chapter 8.

The memories we need to solve a problem do not necessarily appear in a particular sequence. One reason for this is that we do not attend to our experiences in an organized way. The brain evolved to scan the world, not to attend to just one aspect of it. Each new scan may gather cues for memo-ries. This is how we survived throughout evolution, and it makes a satisfying explanation for why we are so attracted to novel events or objects. Anything that is not part of our former experience can be a danger *or* an opportunity. It is important to constantly examine the world for the new. In fact, we look forward to these interruptions and discoveries, so we scan and remember. If what we see is not in our memory—if it is novel—it gains special signifi-cance. We identify the new by discovering that we don't remember it!

Perhaps the most impressive use of memory is its role in prediction. Our memory of what has happened in the past allows us to guess what will hap-pen in the future. We need to predict that if we perform such and such an action, the outcome will be such and such. We need to *use* our memories.

In our story about Henry, my goals and motives were based on a prediction that came from a memory. I was working toward an image that only existed in my mind, and my prediction was that I would be able to convert it to reality. In my effort to find out how to calculate square roots, I did not follow any particular plan. At first I was fiddling with the problem by myself, but then it suddenly occurred to me that there was a better way. Henry was right next to me, so I changed direction, abruptly. Straight lines and logical progressions are relatively un-biological concepts. Our mind just isn't that way.

Plasticity. The concept of a dynamic journey from brain to mind might not have been acceptable a few decades ago. The brain does get larger as we mature, and that is change, but the sticking point might have been that, in development, the brain also changes its *capabilities*. In a baby, a kidney is a kidney; at maturity it is just a larger kidney. But the brain of a baby is structurally and functionally different from the brain of the adult.

The brain's ability to change with experience is often called *plasticity*, and we use this term throughout the book. It is a relatively new term in neuroscience, and it means that the brain is molded by its experience—by the sensory input it receives, by the problems it has solved, and by the emotions it has experienced. This change can involve a very few neurons, or in some cases of disease or injury, millions or even billions of neurons.

Plasticity does not usually imply large-scale physical rearrangement of regions of brain tissue. For example, sensory cortex doesn't become motor cortex. And it is important to examine what doesn't change. What remains constant? What can we count on as the journey progresses? To discuss change we need reference points, things that don't change. This realization will be an important part of our discussion of curriculum in schools, in chapter 9.

An example from my story is the way my mind changed about school, Henry, and myself. My whole image of learning changed, and so did my behavior. I became much more self-reliant, less impressed by credentials, and more skeptical. Perhaps the greatest impact was emotional; I can still feel the change!

Some of the most interesting research on how the brain changes as we develop from a child to a young adult suggests that the best minds are those that have had a dynamic history. By dynamic history I literally mean a history of physical change. In this research the physical change was directly observed as a change in thickness in the cortex (bark of the brain). Over this time some brains experience much more change in cortical thickness than do others, and that characteristic is correlated with intelligence.

Dynamic physical change correlates with a dynamic mind.

The integrated mind-self knowledge. One of my main objectives is to develop a biological model of the mind. If development of the mind is our overarching objective, it is necessary to discuss how we define mind. How will we know when we have reached our goal? Addressing this question will require using some recent brain research, together with the ideas in the preceding chapters, to explain the role of self-knowledge as the culmination of our journey. We reach this point when we not only understand the preceding stages, but also know that we understand because we can consciously apply our understanding. This is called *metacognition*. As I write, this model of the mind is still only a kernel of an idea, and I will not attempt to describe or summarize it here. But if you can't wait, you will find it in chapter 10.

Linear? Parallel?

The actual development of the capabilities I have just described is not necessarily as linear as it may seem. I don't want to imply that each of these stages is absolutely dependent on the ones that precede it in this chapter. A more helpful image is that many of them develop in parallel. They also "feed back" to each other. For example, as we begin to integrate sensory data into images, we also use those images to facilitate new integration. This is one reason that the brain is so powerful and amazing. Each of the 10 functions above supports and influences the others. Cognitive development by experience leads to a mind characterized by increasing complexity, flexibility, and non-linearity

In some ways, writing a book about this dynamic process is, itself, a trap. It cannot be described in a sequence of numbered chapters, but any discussion of biological structures or processes faces that challenge. Life itself is dynamic and flowing, and at some level, any effort to describe it accurately with words and sentences is doomed. Each stage influences all of the others.

At the same time, the implied sequence is not useless. Often, we organize things in a specific sequence, not because it is accurate, but because it helps us think. It forces us to make decisions. "What comes before what?" turns into "What supports what?" or "What influences what?" The goal is not to provide an exact, correct sequence, but to explore and sometimes clarify underlying complexity.

The *sequence* of chapters here should be viewed in this light. I am trying it out. Maybe it will be useful, or maybe we will have to rearrange it in the future. It is our theory of the moment, part of my proposal about how experiential learning builds a complex brain—one that looks more and more like a "mind."

The Rest of the Story

I do not want you to believe that my momentary disillusionment with Henry is the end of the story. We might say that schooling failed Henry, but I don't know that. However, I can tell you the rest of *my* story.

This particular event had a long-lasting and positive outcome for me. I didn't get the exact answer to my square root question that day. In fact, I ended up estimating it as well as I could and being content with that answer. I still played basketball nearly every day, and I almost made the varsity team in my senior year.

But the more important outcome came during my first year in college when I learned more about exponents, discovered logarithms, and finally knew how to find the square root of any number. It was my personal experience with Henry that I thought of first when we came to these topics in the college class, and with that motivation I found myself paying very close attention as I finally learned how to solve my basketball problem. It was that unique experience in my personal life that gave me meaningful connections to an abstract area of math. Integration worked! The connections I made between this highly individual experience and abstract thought gave me deeper understanding of and greater energy for math and science. All the characteristics of my natural mind came into play.

So this is how it goes. By chance, by personal engagement, and by individual meaning, our brain begins as nascent mind and travels along a path that has no apparent end, but rather leads simply to unexplored territory. Our natural mind takes over, and learning goes on throughout our lives. It is not an end but a process. And it is "our ancient and natural strength."

Notes

1. Volkmar, F. R., (2005), *American Journal of Psychiatry*, 162, p. 249.

2. Huitt, W., & Hummel, J. (2003). Piaget's Theory of Cognitive Development. *Educational Psychology Interactive*. Valdosta, GA: Valdosta State University. Retrieved from http://www.edpsycinteractive.org/topics/cogsys/piaget.html

3. Dewey, J. (1938), *Experience and Education*, Simon and Schuster, New York, NY; Kolb, D. (1983), *Experiential Learning*, John Wiley Co., New York, NY.

4. Bruer, John T. (1997), Education and the Brain: A Bridge Too Far, *Educational Researcher*, pp. 4–16.

5. Zull, J. E. (2002), *The Art of Changing the Brain*, Stylus, Sterling, VA.

6. Thompson, R. T. (2000), *The Brain*, Worth Publishers, New York, NY, p. 285.

7. This idea is presented in a video prepared for preschool teachers and daycare workers by the Hannah-Perkins Foundation, Cleveland, OH. It stresses the importance of understanding that babies do have language; their behavior is their language. It is of great importance that we respond to this language with actions of our own, rather than reacting to the behavior. So, if a baby cries when her mother leaves in the morning, the baby is saying, "I miss my mother." In the video, a suggested response to this language is to let the baby "talk" to her mother on the phone for a minute or two, rather than trying to stop the crying.

8. This notion of the brain basis for development of the self is the key theme in Quartz and Sejknowski's (2002), *Liars, Lovers, and Heros*, Harper Collins Publishers, New York, NY.

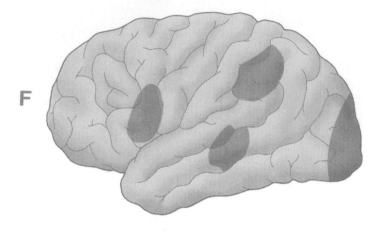

F

Regions of cortex involved in mimicry. Visual perceptions originate in the back, are processed further forward, and activate mimicry behavior in the area furthest toward the front. This transformation of perception into action is described in the next chapter.

2

THE GREAT TRANSFORMATION

Changing Perception to Action:
The Beginning of Mind

The great end of life is not knowledge, but
action.

—Thomas Henry Huxley

It was a basketball game with our archrival. The game had been tense and close, and now it was in overtime. We were ahead by one point with only 30 seconds to go, so our best player began to dribble the ball, stalling for time. As the seconds ticked down, players from the other team surrounded him, reaching and pressing close, trying desperately to steal the ball. Both our hero and the ball seemed to disappear among a tangle of legs and arms. Then suddenly he reappeared, dribbling low and fast, free and clear as the buzzer went off to end the game.

I was just starting my first year in junior high and had never seen anything like that game. I slept poorly that night as I replayed this dramatic moment over and over in my mind. I had a ball of my own and had spent hours learning to shoot, but I had never paid attention to dribbling. So the next day, early in the morning, I went to our basement and began to bounce the ball on the cement floor. Visualizing my hero, I had great confidence that I could mimic his skills. Of course, the ball immediately bounced off my foot and into the corner. As I tried over and over, I realized slowly that my remembered image was not enough. I would have to practice.

And practice I did. For days! But I was disappointed with my progress. I made mistakes over and over. In a way, I was practicing my mistakes. Then one day I had an idea. Maybe I could watch myself in a mirror. Then I could see my mistakes and correct them.

And it worked! I began to improve rapidly.

Eventually my parents had had enough. They were tired of the incessant "thump, thump, thump" in the basement. "Aren't you bored?" my mother shouted down to me. "No!" I shouted back. "Come down and see what I can do!" So she did. But after a few minutes, she just shook her head and went back upstairs. And I kept on dribbling. It was second nature. I had mastered dribbling, and I enjoyed it. I never got bored, even though everyone else did!

A s I said in chapter 1, not all of my stories are about schooling. But they *are* about education. Sometimes they are about experiences that I had when I was of school age and going to school, but still they had nothing to do with school. This is true of my dribbling story.

I have used this story here because it seems to have lessons about discovery and action, which are important features of learning at the very early stages of mental development. I discovered new things, tried to mimic them, encountered difficulties, met them with new actions, and ultimately mastered a new skill, without any formal program or teaching. The timing of this learning experience was not predetermined or planned in any way. Things just happened.

Action in Experiential Learning

The way our mind develops is through use of the raw capacities of our brain. We try things out and learn from errors. Without trying there will be no progress in the journey toward mind. Experiential learning centers on action. It is action that makes it so powerful. We learn by doing; *doing* is the experience!

As previously discussed, neuroscientist Richard Thompson wrote, "The purpose of the brain is to produce behavior." He goes on to say that behavior is action: "[V]irtually all behavior consists of movements resulting from the actions of the skeletal muscles."[1] Action is where the rubber hits the road. Just gathering sensory information or processing that information is of little value without action. We can produce clever ideas, but they are not useful if we don't try them out. Our thoughts and ideas must be tested against the facts of the real world.

At the beginning of any new experience, our actions are not necessarily a product of planning or thought, but are accidental or even random. In that case, they are driven by the brain, but they are *mindless*. We can see this in my dribbling story. It begins with an unplanned action that led to a discovery. I discovered dribbling, but I did not set out with that purpose. In fact, it was totally accidental. A friend asked me if I wanted to go to the game, and with nothing else to do I agreed.

Unplanned action can lead to learning at any time and any place.

Discarding the Randomness

The value of mindless action depends on chance. Our actions may lead us to something that we will think about and explore further, or they may lead nowhere. The dribbling story is one example. Another example is the way babies learn language. Many sounds that a baby hears or produces lead nowhere with regard to language. A door bangs, a car drives by, a spoon falls on the floor, or the baby bumps the crib, all sounds that have no meaning in language. But other sounds have great meaning. The mother says a name, or the baby accidentally says something close to "mama." Those language sounds are repeated over and over, and they begin to have meaning. So-called statistical learning begins. Things happen in patterns that are far beyond random in nature.

The kind of learning I just described could be considered the beginnings of mind. Discarding infrequent or meaningless experiences and retaining frequent or meaningful ones puts experiential learning into gear. The journey has begun!

The next step is to discard the randomness. Rather than hitting on good learning experiences randomly, we begin to select and copy specific actions. We begin to mimic. For example, in the dribbling story, I had a picture in my mind, and I wanted to copy it. I wanted to change my perceptions into goal-specific and purposeful actions. This is what I call the great transformation—*changing sensory experience into action experience.*

Simple as it seems, action is the cause, vehicle, and outcome of education. Perceptions, thoughts, ideas, memories, and intentions are important, but they are not the end product. As we see in the next chapters, they are just middlemen in the transactions of the mind.

Action Is for the Learner

Before we proceed with our discussion of action, I want to be sure there is no misunderstanding. Quite often my colleagues agree with me when I talk about the importance of action in learning, but for the wrong reason. They may nod their heads and say something like, "You are right. I know my students are learning by what they do, and how they perform on tests or in discussions." These colleagues think the action part is for *their* benefit, because it allows them to decide whether students have learned.

I am not thinking of it that way. In fact, student actions, especially performance on tests, can be misleading to educators. Students may learn or even memorize the actions their teachers want them to. This may allow them to do what the teacher requires, but without their own understanding. Or they may refuse to risk demonstrating their knowledge out of insecurity. The value of action is not in what observers perceive, but in what the learner perceives about his or her own actions. Action is a test of learning, but only the learner can know the motive or the outcome of the tests. I knew how my dribbling education was going by evaluating my own actions.

Beginnings

I would like to step back a bit and think more about the beginnings of learning through action. Let's focus on the process, look at some more examples, and examine learning's biological basis.

The earliest aspect of learning in babies has been called the "reflex phase." At first, babies appear to have no learned actions. The things they do might more appropriately be called "movements." Driven primarily by reflexes, these include head turns, leg kicks, arm movements, body twists, and, importantly, eye movements. While these are all apparently random, they turn out to have value.

Actions like these produce the first encounters with the environment. For example, as the eyes and head move randomly, the baby might begin to see light from different perspectives. Action produces perception. If the perceptions are consistent, for example, if the light comes from a window in the corner, memory begins to form.[2] Subconsciously, the baby connects turning his or her head toward the corner (action), with seeing the window (perception.). The randomness begins to diminish. The baby begins to look at the window more often, or longer, than can be explained by chance.

We can understand the neuronal basis for this transformation by looking at reflexes. An example is the test of our nervous system that a physician performs as we sit in his or her office, relaxed, with our leg crossed. The physician taps the front of our knee with a small rubber mallet, and our foot swings out gently in response. If our nervous system is normal, we are relaxed, and if the tap is in the right place, this response is always the result.

In this reflex, only two kinds of neurons are involved: sensing neurons and action (motor) neurons. Sensing neurons extend from the tendon below the knee (where the mallet strikes) to the spinal column. There they connect with the motor neuron, which in turn extends directly back out into the muscles in our thigh. The first neurons are for sensing the tap, and the second are for moving the leg.

Although this reflex is very simple, it is still impressive. There is debate about its normal function, but it is probably part of the complicated combination of sensation and muscle contraction that helps us stand upright rather than falling over. If we begin to lean back a little while we are standing, the tendons at the front of the knee stretch, and, reflexively, the muscles in the thigh tighten, straightening the leg. This simple reflex is part of a more demanding and complicated behavior of standing and keeping our balance.

It is a direct demonstration of the "great transformation."

Action and Mind

In some ways, this reflex is a model for our brain. Of course, the brain is far more complex, but still we find that sensory information flows into specific regions of the cortex, generating new signals that are sent on to a different cortical region to produce action. I have illustrated this way of describing the brain in the figure on page 32.

As this figure shows, the flow of information in the brain is the same as in the reflex: from sensation (back cortex) to action (front cortex). This general pattern is dramatically oversimplified and is not meant to imply that there are not other routes for neuron signaling. In fact, different parts of the

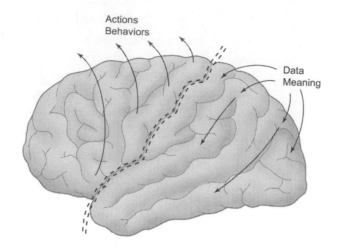

brain communicate with each other in many ways. Still, the brain's overarching job is to take in sensory data and generate actions from that data. The overall flow of signals is from the back portions of the cortex toward the front portions. Even simple images activate the back cortex first and, in a fraction of a second, move on to the front. Data from our experiences are rapidly delivered to the parts of the brain that produce actions, and the meaning of that information is shown in how we act—what we do.

It is easy to see the importance of this. Be it a simple reflex or more complex pathways that engage the brain itself, the useful expression of nervous system functions requires physical movement of the body. Action is also the expression of thought. Even apparently mundane actions can require complicated thinking. They require a continuing process of getting new sensory input and generating effective actions from that input. Their effectiveness reveals the thinking.

As I write, I am observing an example of this going on across the street. There a young man is breaking up a damaged section of the sidewalk to replace it with new cement. He has a power saw to cut through concrete, a sledgehammer, and a metal pry bar as his tools. As I watch, he has finished cutting across the old cement in a neat line to separate the damaged part from the rest. Now he is pounding on the damaged old cement with the heavy hammer. He hits the cement in strategic places, hoping to break it at its weak points. As fragments break free, he strikes again in another vulnerable spot, and so on. However, this pounding drives the cement deeper into the ground, so to loosen the fragments, he now takes the pry bar, jabs it at a cracked area where it seems as though he might gain some leverage, and pries the piece loose. Finally, he lifts pieces of the cement free and throws them into the back of his small truck parked nearby.

This apparently simple physical action is deceptive. It is full of mental challenges. The young man must first envision his ultimate goal. In his mind he must have an image of a new piece of sidewalk with a straight edge, and then plan where he will cut. He must judge which parts of the cement will break most easily with a well-placed blow with the sledgehammer. He must also recognize what points provide him the greatest leverage to pry the pieces free, at what angle the pry bar should be, and how much force to use in each of his movements. His brain is estimating physical quantities while applying the basic laws of physics, but everything is done naturally without consulting any books or mathematical theories.

Thinking of these actions is only part of the complexity. In fact, to carry out each part of each action, he must contract and relax specific muscles in effective proportions and to specific extents. Not just one or two muscles, but dozens of them. He must balance hard, quick contractions with longer, smoother ones. And he must adjust all of these parameters for all of these muscles with each movement he makes. He must continually re-perceive the cement pieces as they shatter, visualize the way he wants them to change, conceive the actions he wants to do next, and convert these mental goals into new patterns of muscle contraction that will produce the needed actions. And all this perception, coordination, estimation, and judgment are applied without conscious thought.

Our workman is a master—an *artiste*.

Setting Goals for Actions

Sometimes our understanding of the word "action" is too limited. When we speak of the motor brain and control of muscles, it helps to have a more sophisticated understanding of them. For example, action is not just muscle *contraction*; it also requires muscle *relaxation*. In any intentional action, the brain must generate both. We realize this requirement if we think about lifting a weight in the classic "curl." We must not only contract the biceps but also relax the muscle at the back of the upper arm (triceps). If we contract both, the two muscles work against each other, and the arm cannot move. No action.

Action does not have to be dramatic or even obvious. The simple (and usually unconscious) movements of our eyes as we survey the room or the subconscious shuffling of our feet to relieve tension are actions. They are all the net result of multiple muscles contracting and relaxing in a remembered and predetermined way, producing the set of movements that puts our body into the right arrangements for the desired outcome.

Not the least of these coordinated muscle movements are those required for language: talking, writing, gesturing, body movements, and facial expressions. In this sense, intellectual expression through language is the same as breaking cement.

Organizing Action

How does the brain produce action? Yes, it triggers muscle contractions and relaxations, but how does it know the way to organize them to achieve a specific outcome? How do we know what actions we should carry out and when? Actions imply goals, either consciously or unconsciously. How do we set goals?

This remains one of the central unanswered questions in neuroscience. But in order not to leave you without any idea, I will make a proposal that seems consistent with what we know at this time. My proposal is that setting a goal requires, at a minimum, two perceptions: one is what exists at the moment, either in our immediate perceptions or in our memory, and the other is how we want it to be—the image we desire to produce (or reproduce). Action changes the first perception into the second.

I illustrate this in the figure on page 35. Imagine you want to pick up a pencil from your desk. The goal-setting part of this is shown in the two images, one with your hand open and one in which it is grasping the pencil.

The muscles that need to contract to turn the first image into the second must move your thumb and index finger toward each other. This becomes easy as we practice it, but for a baby it is not a simple task. In fact, while learning and experimenting, the baby may engage millions of front cortex neurons. These are the neurons that regulate and control the movement of thumb and finger in the right direction, at the right speed, in the right location, with the right pressure, at the right time. And there are neurons that stop and start movements.

The firing of all these neurons is the "motor program" for grasping. As I explain later, it does get more efficient and require fewer neurons with practice, and eventually this efficient and precise sequence of neuron firing becomes part of our subconscious memory. We do it without thought or awareness.

The parts of action consist not only of muscle movements but also of the regulation of those movements to bring things into alignment with the imagined image. The specific combination of a mental perception with muscle contractions of the body is an elementary example of problem solving. We define the problem by imagining a goal, and then we solve it through muscle contractions, through action.

Ultimately, this grasping process is of more use than we might think. We use it to achieve all sorts of goals, from tying our shoes to writing to unlocking doors. We also use it as a metaphor for mental and psychological actions such as "grasping" an idea or "seizing" the moment.

It represents progress from brain to mind.

Copying and Mastering

Mimicry comes from the existing wiring in the brain. Perception neurons automatically send their signals to action neurons. This is part of the forward flow of information I illustrated in the diagram above.

Recognition of the specific neurons that are directly involved in mimicry led neuroscientists to coin the term "mirror neurons." These neurons fire both when an action is perceived and when that action is planned. They are a dramatic example of the "great transformation." And as we would expect, those neurons are in the front regions of cortex—the action cortex.[3]

Mirror neurons are responsible for "matching" observations with actions.[4] And, of great interest, their location in the cortex is very similar to a region called Broca's area, the area we use to construct and actually produce language. This neuroscience connection between mimicry and language suggests interesting ideas about how we learn and remember, which I discuss in later chapters. Here, however, I would like to draw your attention to the role that mirror neurons play in what we call "mastery."

When we have repeated them many times, combinations of sensory perception and motor actions such as those described above become automatic. We master them. They are inserted into our daily lives and used continually but unconsciously. If we look, we can find them in the flow of action that makes up our waking hours and in the flow of language in the form of metaphors such as "grasping." We carry them out perfectly, without conscious thought.

How does this work? What happens in our brains when we master things?

A recent neurobiology experiment conducted with monkeys addresses this question. I won't explain all the details, but there are a few key points that will help us understand the experiment. The animals were shown two lights on a computer screen for a few seconds, then the screen went blank. The task for the monkeys was to move the cursor from one spot to the other by memory. While they were attempting this, the frontal regions of cortex were monitored for the amount of neuronal firing that was associated with the action of moving the cursor. The monkeys had great difficulty with this assignment, moving the cursor generally in the right direction but with many errors, including starts and stops, and even moving it in the opposite direction at times. But if the monkeys were allowed to observe the cursor movement visually, they quickly mastered the task and eventually could do it completely from memory.

The important discovery for us is that when the animals attempted the task from memory, they engaged many thousands of motor and premotor neurons. All the errors were associated with unproductive neuron firing! But once they could follow the cursor movement visually, the number of motor neurons engaged dropped to a few dozen! Incorporating visual information converted complicated and inefficient motor neuron firing into a much simpler and more efficient "motor program."[5]

This may seem hardly worth mentioning. Of course, we can move the cursor any place we want to, if we can see where it is! But the way we do this isn't necessarily obvious or simple. As I said earlier, the visual data are actually used to prevent, or inhibit, unnecessary movements. They *reduce* firing of large numbers of motor neurons. In this experiment, it appears that mastery is not so much a matter of repeated firing of the correct (effective) neurons, as it is inhibiting all the others.

Mastery comes by reducing neuron firing, by eliminating the *un*helpful![6]

Action and Vision

The experiment I described above suggested a direct engagement of a visual (sensory) area of the cortex in carrying out an action (motor brain). This particular observation may not surprise you. Indeed, of the cognitive senses (touch, body perception, sound, and vision)[7], vision seems to be the most fundamental. That is not to say that other senses are not important, but there is increasing evidence that other senses either strengthen the visual or are subservient to it. We tend to check everything with our eyes.

Here are a couple of examples: Owls make accurate maps of space to succeed in hunting. These maps use both hearing and vision. However, it appears that the auditory sense is a slave to the visual sense. When auditory information does not agree with visual information, the owl brain creates a *new auditory map* that does agree. Visual information is actually channeled into the part of the brain that normally receives only auditory information.[8]

A second example suggests a direct influence of vision on touch in the human species. Visual acuity seems to be enhanced if, in addition to looking at an object, we actually touch that object. This suggests that the sensation of touch somehow interacts with the sensation of vision. However, touch and vision are localized in separate regions of the cortex, and they are far enough apart that a direct interaction between them seems unlikely. But as you may have guessed, further research revealed that such a pathway—an actual physical connection—does exist.[9]

Our species tends to check everything with our eyes. We are always looking out for ourselves.

Why Vision?

What makes vision so important?

The cognitive senses (vision, hearing, touch) gain much of their power by virtue of the "spatial maps" they generate in the cortex.[10] Physical and factual information about the world ultimately is mapped on the cortex. The information content of these maps depends on the nature of the original signals: light, sound, and pressure (through touch). Of these, light has the greatest potential for providing information. Touch is good for determining shape, but it is limited by how far we can reach. Sound can distinguish general spatial location, but light is much more precise. If we try to grasp something we hear, we grope, but if we see it, we grab it instantly and exactly.

It is true that some animals live in the dark—for example, different species of moles—and the visual sense is not important for them. But for all animals that live primarily in the light, it is very understandable why vision has become the dominant sense for cognition. Through natural selection, our brains have adapted in ways that provide the most information from a particular environment.

This centrality of the visual in both cognition and memory is proven by many different experiments. Let me give you two examples, which are instructive in our discussions of education. First, studies of illusions show that people believe what they see with their eyes, even though it contradicts actions that they, themselves, do and remember. In fact, recall of the visual representation of actions engages a different part of the cortex from recall of the movements themselves. Our mind separates memory of movement from memory of image, and if the two conflict, memory of the image dominates.[11] This suggests that it may be helpful, possibly even essential, to have an accurate visual image of actions we take. This enhances accurate recall and also provides information helpful in refining our actions as we work toward mastery.

Second, the importance of the visual brain for learning actions is suggested by brain imaging studies in humans who learned to juggle.[12] MRI images were obtained of their brains before and after they learned, and the only change in the brain that could be found was an increase in the density of the sensory cortex devoted to visual detection of motion. A key aspect of learning to juggle is the ability to follow the balls visually and sense their position and movement .

Learning a motor skill changes the sensory brain!

Two Learning Lessons

The fact that learning to juggle produced an *increase* in the density of a specific region in the visual cortex is not surprising. It is what we have come to expect in experiments of this sort. We tend to think of learning as an addition to or an increase in our knowledge, so adding more knowledge has to show up as an increase in something in the brain! On the other hand, you may recall the monkey experiment with the dots on the computer screen in which learning led to a *decrease* in brain response—the opposite effect!

These two examples illustrate an important difference between sensory and motor learning. In the former, the brain gathers and records information and details of increasing complexity, which shows up as more complexity and density of connections in sensory cortex (juggling). But in motor learning (cursor movement in monkeys), the actual use of neurons becomes focused, efficient, and *less* complex as skills increase.

Learning is two-sided; we need both complexity and efficiency.[13]

Back to Action

Now I return to our discussion of action—the main point!

We have seen evidence that sensory experience, especially vision, may be more fundamental than action. If we are to use biology as a guide, we can do our best if we find ways to visualize what we want to do and see how it is progressing. As I have claimed, learners should see images of what we want them to learn. A great deal of teaching is showing.

However, if we look more deeply into the role of vision and the sensory systems in learning, we find our attention drawn back to action (motor). Vision itself is based on action. Without action (muscle contraction), we cannot gather information visually. This is because neurons in an ancient part of our brain, the brain stem itself, are specialized for triggering and remembering eye movements. If we cannot carry out or remember the actions of moving our eyes and focusing them on a particular region of space, we cannot gather information visually; we cannot perceive. To produce useful visual maps of space in the cortex, we must have information about the position of our eyes. Are they looking right or left, up or down, and how far?

We move our eyes (action), to gather visual information (sensory).

Where are we, then, in this back and forth between motor and sensory brain? We started with the notion of the "great transformation," the conversion of sensory information into action, as a key to learning. But we ended with the discovery that sensory perception itself originates in action. Ultimately, action generates more action—new action. We might call this an "even greater transformation."

This suggests three things. First, since we always end up with action when we try to trace brain activities back to their origins, our main thesis regarding the centrality of action is growing stronger. Second, the primary function of eye movements is exploration, not mimicry. Everything begins with exploration. This is true for the new baby, but is just as true throughout our adult life. For example, as I explained at the beginning of this chapter in my story about dribbling a basketball, we could add the *exploratory* step at the very beginning. I had to go to the game. I had to put myself in a place and situation where I could perceive dribbling.

The third suggestion has to do with mastery. The biological pathway to mastery requires us to repeatedly use and recycle the action-perception transformations. We see, we do, we see what we do, we do something new, et cetera, et cetera, et cetera!

Action, Mastery, and Comprehension

I have drawn your attention primarily to two categories of action: *exploration* and *mimicry*. I also pointed out that even apparently simple actions can be shown to have cognitive content, and I return to that idea soon as well as later in the book.

First, however, let's look at what can be achieved by combining exploration and mimicry, but leaving out cognitive actions. This might seem like a strange approach, but it does occur, probably more often than we suspect. It appears that a great deal of our early learning (but not *just* early learning) can actually lead to mastery with very little cognitive content. Often we master things without actually understanding them.

There are many examples of this. In fact it seems to be the norm in both learning language and mathematics. Children discover new sounds, words, scripts, and grammar, repeating them primarily from memory at first. They also learn times tables and algorithms for manipulating numbers such as division and multiplication the same way. In fact, we may never get beyond the discovery-copy method of learning and solving problems. For example, I know how to do long division, but I have no ideas why it works.

The Pyramid of Mastery

To bring some of these ideas together, I have invented a pyramid model for mastery. It brings five concepts together: exploration, discovery, mimicry, complexity, and efficiency, but you will notice it does not include comprehension or cognition. As I mentioned in my earlier discussion of random movement, mastery achieved in this way is mindless. It is based on asking sensory questions such as what, when, and where, but not why. It is completely sensory-motor.

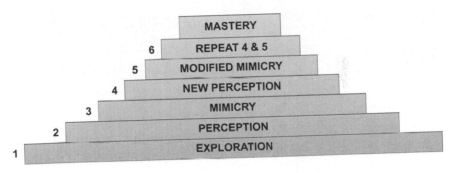

The base of the pyramid is exploration, but not directed, or intentional, exploration. While exploring in such a mindless way, we may discover a great deal without actually understanding. We may perceive fact but not understand origin or cause. In my story, I perceived dribbling but did not understand it. I knew facts about it.

In the pyramid, then, the mirror neuron system in the brain kicks in, resulting in the first crude efforts at mimicry. This leads to repeated cycles of perceiving errors and correcting them through new actions. Again, however, the corrections are simple changes based only on perception, not on true comprehension. We perceive only in the most elementary sense of the word.

The pyramid model seems apt because it begins with a very complex and broad perceptual base obtained by chance, but ends with a very efficient process. Each stage reduces the complexity and increases efficiency. The pyramid narrows. Biologically, this means that very large numbers of neurons are engaged at first, but a large percentage of those are eliminated when efficiency is very great. The unhelpful is removed. And the outcome is action, not reasons!

In sum, then, the pyramid is an operational model, a sequence of operations. It is "brain-derived" rather than "mind-derived," and does not provide much help in the journey toward mind.

It warns us that mastery is not necessarily evidence of growth of the mind.

Mastery and Schooling

Earlier, I said we would begin to discuss formal education (schooling) as we approached the end of this chapter. We are at that point now. The topic of mastery gives us an appropriate nudge in that direction. It provides some specific examples and ultimately brings us back to our theme of the journey toward mind.

The sensory-motor or mechanical kind of mastery described above plays a major role in schooling. For example, we expect students to master what we call "the basics," such as the sounds of letters in the alphabet or the multiplication tables. Even though it does not necessarily lead to development of the mind, this type of mimicry is not a bad thing. In fact, it gives us an opportunity to examine the nature of the more "brain-related" functions and how they may serve as precursors to growth of mind.

We discussed mimicry earlier in this chapter, but there is more to say about exploration. We can begin with the fact that this type of action is not necessarily planned. More often, exploration is spontaneous and inclusive, by which I mean that it can take in any feature of any experience. The human species is an exploring species. Exploration may lead to new learning at any time. Movement of the eyes continually reveals new things, even when we don't change our location. We also have new experiences all the time, even in a classroom where a teacher is attempting to control the experience within the boundaries of a particular subject. Student attention wanders. We explore.

Instead of trying to control this wandering, educators might take advantage of it in school. Mind wandering is a biological fact, and schools are just a particular part of the big, wide world open for exploration. In my own childhood, I attended a one-room school for grades K–8. This provided an excellent environment for discovery. I could explore what the older and younger students were doing as they had their "lessons" at the front of the room. I was fascinated by what I saw and heard. I continually discovered new things about other children and about the world. I often wonder if we should go back to such schools.

Gardner has drawn our attention to the central purposes of education; it should be about truth, beauty, and goodness.[14] The point here is that schools should be a place where students can discover those things. In addition, and also beyond traditional academic subjects, students might discover the useful and the significant. If we want students to read, they should discover reading. If we want them to calculate the strength of a bridge span, they should discover calculus. They should discover problems, skills, behaviors, and ideas.

I am not saying that we should instruct students to act in certain ways or compel them to certain behaviors, only that we should give a great deal of thought to creating opportunities for them to discover what we want them to. A very important example is teacher behavior. The way a teacher behaves has more impact on students than how much a teacher knows. School changes people when they discover behaviors and ideas they admire. And, coming full circle, if we want people to discover, then we should model curiosity, which is the foundation of discovery.

Curious teachers will have curious students.

Experts and Modeling

I am proposing that schools create environments that provide examples of the values and behaviors we believe are of great importance. At the same time, we also want students to discover the disciplines—the subjects. We want them to see expertise.

At this point, I am not thinking of the expertise involved in knowing a school subject. That is essential for a teacher, but in this book I am also going to stress expertise in a more specific context. The expertise of a banker is one example. The connection between such an important person in the "real world" and the subjects taught in school must become apparent to students. We need specialists, and sometimes the specialty may be one that is not part of the standard curriculum. It is important for people (young and old) to see that educational subjects are used in the "real life" of experts. They need models.

This might be accomplished if children become aware early in their schooling of businesses, civic institutions, legal work, and so forth operating each day in the community. At a minimum, students can learn where these experts are found. If this were so, schools would be viewed as "boundary-free." They would be less a place and more a range of opportunities. The entire community should be available for discovering what experts actually do, what they care about, and how they work and learn. Apprenticeships and co-op activities might be the norm rather than the exception. All members of the community can serve as teachers and all buildings as schools.

The point is not necessarily to expose students to more teaching and explaining, but to more experience and discovery. Experts are not necessarily good teachers or explainers, but they can provide opportunity for mimicry and stimulate exploration.

Cognitive Action

Our pyramid of mastery is based on very basic brain functions. It is remarkable in that it does not mention cognition or mind. I created this separation of brain from mind to talk about a journey from one to the other, but this divide is somewhat artificial and problematic. To address some of the problems, let's examine whether the mastery pyramid excludes the mind to the extent that I suggest above.

In my earlier story about the young man breaking cement, I pointed out that what appear to be simple actions may actually be rich in cognitive content. Perhaps we can apply that way of thinking to the pyramid. One aspect of cognitive action apparent in the pyramid is the notion of improvement. Improvement is based on perceiving the flaws in our images, imagining what changes can be made to eliminate such flaws, and developing plans and ideas about how to make those changes. This is problem solving, clearly going beyond simply copying actions and involving cognitive undertakings such as making choices, noticing details, and getting ideas. Less brain and more mind.

We can also think of problem solving as a combination of exploration and copying, but not limit our actions in the narrow way implied by "copying." We can generate new images, rather than relying on the ones given to us. Problem solving challenges us to take *creative* actions.

There are also different kinds of problems to solve. For example, there are problems with exact answers, such as calculating the profit for a day's work, and problems without defined answers, such as settling a dispute between employees. These are not as different as they might seem. Whether the problem requires a mathematical relationship or understanding the relationship between two people, it is essential to see the central elements involved and how they relate to each other. This kind of action is a specific example of combining discovery and copying. We take action to discover relationships, and when they are discovered, we recognize the similarity to something we might be able to copy.

Another problem-solving action is defining objectives. When we have a problem, we need to decide how far we want to pursue it. What will be a satisfactory final image? Do we need a number, a definition, an approximation, an intermediate state, or some other objective? And defining objectives requires judgment. We need to balance things (notice the physical metaphor) and estimate how long the action may take or how far it may lead us. Mastery might not even be the objective; simply progressing toward mastery may fill our needs.

But I am ahead of my story. These cognitive actions require us to go beyond the perception-action transformation that is the focus of this chapter. They are farther along in the journey from brain to mind. To continue, it is necessary to expand our discussion of the brain beyond the sensory-motor elements. That happens in the next chapter.

Talk to Learn

So far I have focused on discovery, mimicry, and problem solving as examples of incorporating action into education. There is an aspect of action that is possibly the most fundamental of all, but one that I have hardly mentioned. That aspect is *talking*. Let me tell you another story to illustrate this point.

> We needed a carpenter. The cabinets and shelves in our living room were warped and the paint had been peeling for years. We couldn't stand it any more! So Chris, the carpenter, entered our lives.
> As the new shelves began to take form, I realized that Chris was a master of his trade. There are infinite possibilities for mistakes in carpentry.

One shelf at a slight angle can destroy the whole effect; every cut, every nail, and every hinge is important. But Chris never seemed to make a mistake.

And soon I found out his secret. It can be stated in two words: Chris talked!

The moment he entered the house in the morning, he walked up to the shelves and began talking. He explained what he saw, what he would try next, and what tools he needed. It almost seemed that he was talking to the shelves, explaining what he would do to them.

But, of course, Chris was mainly talking to himself. He explained his images out loud to himself.

One day while he was taking a break, I mentioned this to him. It seemed that the talking was such a habit that he was unaware of it, but when I brought it up, he knew exactly why he talked and what it accomplished. Although his ultimate action would be constructing the shelves, that was not his first action. Talking was. He talked to discover flaws in his images and plans. (Another great transformation: changing sound waves into mental images!) The image became real, and he could improve it though the action of talking. And, finally, he could remember it. He could hear what he had said, in his memory.

It may be that each of us can incorporate Chris's approach in our individual education, but could it be used in school? Could we think of ways to encourage problem-solving talk without utter chaos? Perhaps our schools should have spaces where students can talk about their work to themselves without interfering with the work of others, something like the practice rooms found in music departments. Another example is an active learning classroom where small groups of students talk intensely and sometimes quite loudly, but each group is completely focused on its own specific challenges. Or, in an example taken from my own childhood experience in a one-room school, students were expected to work on their assignments while, at the front of the room, the teacher was having a "class" with several other students, asking questions, and listening to the lessons prepared by individual students. This school was considered "traditional," but what happened there was more "progressive."

Talk is engaging, and we actually do not need silence for effective learning. But the one essential condition is that the talking should be useful talk.

Talk that explains, that questions, that invents new ideas, that motivates—"*Chris* talk!"

And Write

One reason I have stressed talking is that it is the opposite of what we tend to assume about school. School is where you listen! Of course, another way to encourage and nurture problem solving and critical thinking is writing. I propose that learners should write for the explicit purpose of thinking. They might write like Chris talked. And in case that sounds too different or extreme, we should remember that writing also has advantages that talking doesn't. It is quiet. It is permanent. It can be reconsidered later, when we might forget the talk. And it is slower. It facilitates more reflection and more careful thought.

Action and Us

We have developed a number of ideas based on the centrality of action in learning. I included specific suggestions as we went along, but you might make your own list. To get you started, let me pose three questions that may help guide your thoughts.

First, what ideas in this chapter challenged you the most? Perhaps you could make a list first, and then sort out the ideas' relevance for you in your particular situation. The list will be helpful in itself, and it may also lead you to wonder *why* certain things are at the bottom, as well as the top.

Second, what steps can you take to address these challenges? What "action-centered" questions might you use in your own role as educator, be it as teacher, school leader, learner, or parent? For example, would it help you to begin the day by asking yourself, "What are my learners going to *do* today?"

Third, and perhaps most interesting, "What action-related ideas were *not* mentioned?" What would you add if you were going to rewrite this chapter? What is missing, and why is it so important for you? How could you institute those missing ideas, even though they were not discussed in this particular book?

Of course, I am trying to provoke you to think about your own actions when I ask these questions. And, believe it or not, to provoke myself the same way!

Beginnings of Mind

As we come to a close, let's remember the big picture. We are still talking about education, writ large—more than just school. Our topic is the journey toward mind through experience. As I explained in the introduction, we are asking whether formal education can be constructed in a way that goes beyond the "subjects," that leads the developing brain toward the challenging and the difficult—beyond technology!

How have we progressed toward that goal so far? To develop our answer, let's remind ourselves what the "mindless" state looks like: a newborn baby, sleeping, eating, crying, and frequently making random movements. These movements are a type of exploration. By chance the baby begins to learn about his or her environment. Within a few months the baby starts mimicking, and before we know it the little one is mastering some things. The baby's brain has wiring for exploration and mimicry, but we probably are not yet ready to call it a mind.

As we have discussed, further progress depends on action. Those actions will lead to new challenges that cannot be met by pure sensory-motor brain. The baby must bring new capabilities of his or her brain into play. As we discussed above, those new capabilities begin to develop through both increased complexity and increased efficiency.

Another change is also occurring. Action and discovery begin to create a new mental environment that is essential for further growth of the mind. The key element in this new environment is satisfaction, or even joy. Successful actions or new discoveries not only enhance the cognitive process for building a more complex and powerful mind, but they also trigger the brain structures involved in the internal reward system. These structures have evolved to respond in situations where cognitive efforts produce success. Discovery and action both make us happy. The brain rewards itself during successful use and continuing development of the mind.

Thus, as we move ahead in the journey, we should expect that, with new cognitive development, will often come feelings of fulfillment—of joy. In fact, every following chapter, when examined carefully, may be found to rest on this foundation. We begin to examine this idea in the next chapter.

Notes

1. Thompson, R. T. (2000), *The Brain: A Neuroscience Primer*, W. H. Freeman, New York, NY.

2. Development of vision in newborns occurs slowly over the first months after birth. However, research shows that a baby's visual responsiveness begins to improve *within hours* after surgical removal of cataracts.

3. A great deal has been made of mirror neurons, in both the neuroscience literature and the popular press. But those of you who have read *The Art of Changing the Brain* may not find the mirror neuron concept as novel. In the learning cycle, the activation of frontal cortex neurons (premotor and motor) by back cortex neurons (perception and comprehension) appears to be the same process as the mirror behavior. This term can be viewed as another name for the frontal cortex neurons that fire both in initiation of an action and in perception of that action. Neurons with those properties are predicted from the learning cycle.

4. Iacoboni, S., et al. (1999), Cortical Mechanisms of Human Imitation, *Science*, 286, pp. 2526–2528.

5. Taylor, D. M., Tillery, S. L. H., and Schwartz, A. B. (2002), *Science*, 296, p. 1829; also see review of this work in the same volume by P. Konig and P. F. M. J. Verschure.

6. These results suggest an explanation for earlier research that showed a reduction in cortex engagement after learning. In other words, the *learning* itself took more brain effort than did *executing* the learned skills. If motor programs become simpler with learning, then instead of using large amounts of energy and numbers of neurons to achieve imperfect results, they will require far fewer neurons and less energy to achieve a greatly improved result (images of mind, reduction of brain activity after learning). Posner, M. and Raichle, M. (1994), *Images of Mind*, Scientific American Library, New York, NY, p. 127.

7. The term "cognitive senses" refers to the senses that give us information about form, structure, and category. Smell and taste are omitted from the cognitive senses because of the qualitative nature of the information they provide. We become aware of these "qualities" by strongly engaging the emotional brain, much of which is non-cortical. Thus there is a biological difference between these qualitative, feeling-based senses, and the cortical ones that map out cognitive aspects of our sensory input. Gutfreund, Y., Zheng, W., and Knudsen, E. I. (2002), *Science*, 297, p. 1556; also see summary of this work by M. Barinaga in the same volume, p. 1462.

9. Mascaluso, E., Frith, C. D., and Driver, J. (2000), *Science*, 289, p. 1206; also see comments on this article by B. deGelder on p. 1148 of the same issue.

10. The basis for this statement is developed in *The Art of Changing the Brain*.

11. Schwartz, A. B., Moran, D. W., and Reina, G.A. (2004), *Science*, 303, p. 380.

12. Draganski, B., Gaser, C., Busch, V., Schuierer, G., Bogdahn, U., and May, A., *Nature*, 427, p. 311.

13. As we will see in chapter 7, there are also two aspects of memory that point to this two-sided nature of learning: enhanced memory brought about by the creation of new and stronger synapses, and selective reduction in memory brought about by elimination or weakening of synapses.

14. Gardner, H. (2000), *The Disciplined Mind: Beyond Facts and Standardized Tests, the K–12 Education that Every Child Deserves*, Penguin, New York, NY.

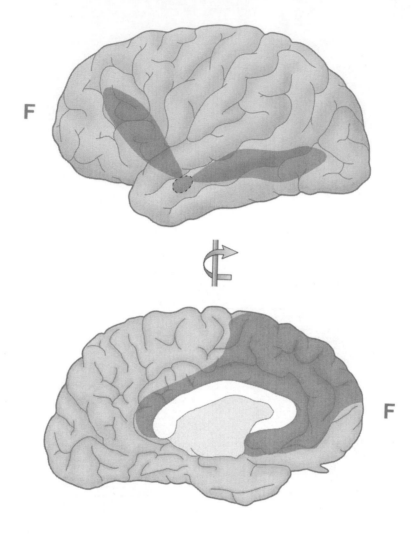

Some cortex regions for emotion. The lateral left perspective (top) shows the amygdala and regions it influences (negative emotion). The medial left (bottom) shows areas influenced by dopamine (positive emotion) and the limbic lobe. A right cortex view would be similar.

3

FINDING THE FREEDOM,
FINDING THE JOY

Emotion and Progress Toward Mind

The joy of learning is as indispensible in study
as breathing is in running.
—Simone Weil

One of my colleagues had to miss his class, so he asked me to fill in for him. Without much thought, I agreed. All I had to do was explain one of the methods I used in my research. It would be a snap.

But when I sat down to plan the class, I began to get nervous. I realized that, although I used that method almost every day, my actual understanding of it was shallow. I understood the ideas, but not the theory. There were equations for predicting the outcome of experiments, but I didn't actually know where those equations came from. Did I dare just present the equations to the students without actually explaining them? More to the point, would I be happy doing that?

I decided that I would have to work through the theory.

I will never forget that evening in the library. I found some books that I hoped would be helpful, but they weren't. I began to think things through starting from the beginning, which is where my students would start!

As I worked, I found my insecurity being replaced with some confidence. But progress was slow, and I began to worry that I had started preparing too late. Maybe I would have to work through the night. Maybe I wouldn't get it done by the time the class met!

Then I recognized a key point. I wrote down the steps that had led to that point and began to feel exhilarated. Yes! This would work. My

53

students would be able to start at the very beginning, with things they already knew, and I could lead them to the answers from there. That was exciting, but my exhilaration did not come from this realization. Rather, it came from the excitement of actually understanding things myself! I felt a surge of power and control over this little tiny bit of the world, and I had reached those feelings through my own work—not simply by being told!

No one could duplicate that feeling of excitement by leading me along; it was all mine. I had escaped dependency. I was free!

In addition to action, I frequently mentioned feelings and emotion in chapter 2. Very early in our journey we begin to feel the excitement and joy of discovery. We look forward to exploration. The imitative sensory-motor actions of chapter 2 are also driven by emotion. Emotion impels action. In fact, emotion itself has been defined as a "tendency to act."[1] In *Slaughterhouse-Five*, when Billy Pilgrim says, "Everybody has to do exactly what he does,"[2] it seems likely that he is referring to the underlying emotion and feelings that drive us to all our actions. Our emotions tell us what we "have to do." Learning takes place through action, but it is driven by emotion.

The story above is an example of this from my own life. I had never consciously recognized the freedom that understanding brings. But this particular experience was so powerful that it worked its way through all of my mind's cognitive layers and broke into the sunshine of my own awareness. I was joyful!

Keeping the Joy

Joy is an integral part of any learning experience. It is what keeps us going on our journey. We discuss some of those pleasures in following chapters, but I want to introduce this subject now because this joy is what drives everything discussed in those chapters. Virtually from the beginning, the journey—the education—has the potential to be joyful.

Notice that I say, "has the potential." However, as we move into more formal educational environments, we can begin to lose the joy. We start to feel pressure to "learn." Everyone feels it: students, teachers, administrators, and even parents can become anxious and frustrated. Everything is tested, and if the results don't meet expectations, we may become fearful or angry. We lose track of the journey and begin to focus more and more on the destination. We develop negative ideas about learning and studying. We forget that the joy is an essential part of the learning—the development of mind.

This loss may not be irreversible. We may regain the joy later in life when we become engaged in a profession, hobby, or some other challenge of our own making. When schooling is finished, we may begin to search, and often find, what we enjoy. But for many, the joy never returns.

The Price of the Loss

There is a serious price to pay for losing the joy; it has a profound impact. Dissatisfaction extends from the sense of loss itself to frustration and anger. Ultimately, we may begin to encounter difficulties with student behaviors in school settings. This can happen at *all levels*, even in graduate and professional schools.[3] In the worst cases, teaching becomes policing and punishing in an effort to control behaviors, or to persuade students to do assignments. It can be a daily and debilitating struggle; often, just keeping order becomes the main goal and the measure of success of each day. The positive feelings I described in my story seem distant from the reality of daily experience in school.

To emphasize the point, we return to Billy Pilgrim. Students will just keep doing what they "have to do." So will teachers, administrators, and parents. That being the case, the challenge is to arrange things so that more of us "have to" experience satisfaction and freedom in our learning. We are searching for environments, activities, and techniques that naturally generate positive feelings and that automatically lead students to say, "I have to learn."

Somatic Markers[4]

One way to think about this challenge is provided by Antonio Damasio, who has written extensively about the brain, emotion, and consciousness. He divides feelings into three categories: primary feelings (Darwin's six universal expressions—fear, anger, sorrow, disgust, surprise, happiness); secondary feelings (a wide range of complex social feelings); and background feelings

(feelings of bodily state). Primary and secondary feelings are strong, and we are generally conscious of them, although that consciousness may not be expressed in language or specific images. Nonetheless, when asked, we have little difficulty in recognizing that we are angry or happy (for example).

Damasio argues that these strong responses are linked to consciousness. The primary and secondary feelings reach our awareness exactly because they are strong. As Damasio says, "In organisms equipped to sense emotions, that is, to have feelings, emotions also have an impact on the mind, as they occur, in the here and now." He continues: "Consciousness allows feelings to be known . . . and allows emotion to permeate the thought process, through the agency of feeling."

What about the third category, "background feelings"?

The proposal is that these feelings are always present. They go with experiences of the moment. For example, we may feel mildly energized but still relaxed as we look out a window on a snowy winter afternoon. Or we may feel a bit uneasy as we leave the house, unconsciously leaving our keys behind. Damasio calls feelings such as these "somatic markers." They are the low-intensity feelings in the body (the *somatic*) that accompany particular experiences. We may be unaware of them, but as the term says, those feelings are body (somatic) labels (markers) for moment-to-moment experience. They are in the background; some might say they are intuitions, or that they lead to intuitions. To identify them we have to make an effort; we have to pay attention. The primary emotions reveal themselves, but we have to look for the somatic markers.

It makes great biological sense to believe in somatic markers. If a primary emotion such as fear is marked by the feelings associated with elevated levels of stress hormones in the body (sweating, increased heart rate), it is no great leap to believe that a complicated mix of small amounts of emotion chemicals—for example, adrenalin and dopamine—will produce lower-level feelings in the body. An example might be a touch of fear mixed in with a bit of pleasure. That chemical process will lead to complex body responses that we sense and that "mark" the experience. For example, right now I am aware of a body response as I type quickly to capture a pleasing idea in words, before I forget it! This complicated feeling is a mix of small amounts of excitement, joy, fear, and anxiety, all produced by an ill-defined mix of small amounts of stress hormones and reward hormones.

I might not put a conscious label on this body feeling, but I still type quickly.

Feelings, Consciousness, and Reasoning

We might argue that we always have such background feelings; they come with everything we do. And if we can become conscious of them, they might be of value in reasoning and problem solving. Furthermore, if recognizing our background feelings improves problem solving, this will lead to the types of positive feelings I described in my story at the beginning of this chapter.

Damasio places feelings at the interface between the conscious and unconscious aspects of mind.[5] Strong feelings can demand our attention, thus producing consciousness. In turn, consciousness can illuminate feelings. When that occurs, we may be better able to apply what Damasio calls "high reason," which involves the pursuit of wise application of our energies in solving problems and making plans. When that occurs, it leads to action-responses to problems, which we call *behavior*.

This line of thought suggests that reasoning can alter feelings and seems to contradict the notion that we cannot control how we feel. However, both are true. Our emotional responses of the moment are difficult to control or even predict. They arise in the experience. But if we improve our ability to consciously identify and think about those feelings, we may gain more control than we expect. If we get to the feelings before they drive us to action—that is, if we discover our own feelings and understand their origins—our actions may be greatly modified. By *understanding feelings, we open the path to "high reason" and the most effective action.*

The most effective education!

In the Here and Now

The quotations above contain the phrase, "emotions have an impact on the mind, as they occur in the here and now."[6] This raises an issue that came up in my earlier work.[7] I divided back cortex and front cortex in the dimension of time: back cortex is about the past, and front cortex is about the future. This is not to suggest a sharp boundary, or any lack of communication between back and front, but rather an overall functional outcome of these regions of cortex. My point here is that this earlier perspective is enhanced by thinking of the time implications. In particular it makes us wonder about the "here and now," the *present*.

When one puts things in terms of synapses and neuronal wiring, the present hardly exists. There is only past (memory) and future (planning). The present is simply represented as the interface between them. Even as you read, you are moving across that interface. The words to come next are in the future, and once you have read them they are in the past. In neuronal terms, the present exists only for some milliseconds, which is the order of magnitude for the time required when signals pass from one group of neurons (for example, sensory) to another group (for example, motor.)

When we realize that human experience is about more than just networks of neurons, that is, it also includes the emotion systems, we can see another perspective on this issue of the "present." Perhaps the best way to perceive and define the present is through our feelings; maybe it is the *only* way. Often, our feelings last much longer than the time required for synapses to fire. This is not always true, as I discuss below with regard to rapid responses to threats mediated by the amygdala. But the firing of neuronal pathways via existing synapses and the impact of dopamine or adrenalin through modulation of those synapses are distinct from one another. They work through different physical mechanisms. Synapse firing is a fast transfer of electrical energy directly from one neuron to another, while modulation of the synapses proceeds through much slower processes of chemical secretion and diffusion. To see this difference, think of the electrical event at the synapse as the passage of a spark from one wire to another, while the impact of the emotion chemicals is more like pouring heavy cream into your coffee.

Thus, we experience emotion in our bodies through the surge of a feeling and its slow dissipation over a period of seconds to minutes. So, if someone asks me how I feel, they use the present tense: "How am I at the moment?" Although I may embellish and modify my reply to include how I felt before this moment, or how I want to feel in the future, I still refer to the present when I try to produce the most accurate response to the question.

The neuroscience basis for this is that feelings are caused by changes in the chemical environment of neurons and neuron-muscular connections. For example, feelings of tension and preparation for aggression arise in our body when adrenalin increases in the bloodstream. But it takes a little time for the adrenalin to reach the places in the body where actions are exerted; it takes time for the feelings to change. Dissipation of our fear does not happen instantly. This is part of the reason we put the emotion chemicals in a category called "slow neurotransmitters." Given the longer time it takes for these emotion chemicals to act in our body and our brain, the sense of the "present" becomes more meaningful.

Amygdala

We are going to begin the biological discussion of positive emotion by looking at a brain structure that is actually associated with negative emotion, the amygdala. We will gain insight into positive emotion by analyzing brain aspects of negative emotion.

The amygdala processes sensory information and takes part in judging whether it represents a possible threat to survival. Below is a figure that outlines how this information flows. Sensory data are channeled first to a structure called the thalamus. They then split into two pathways.[8] In one pathway, a small amount of the data goes directly to the amygdala. It is then passed directly to the brain stem and then out to the muscles of the body, generating rapid but crude actions somewhat like reflexes. This has been called the "lower pathway" because the amygdala is known to be older (evolutionarily) than the cortex, and thus has more direct but less refined actions. It is crude, hence low.[9]

$$\textbf{Cortex} \Rightarrow \quad \textbf{Amygdala} \Rightarrow \textbf{Action}$$
$$\Uparrow$$
$$\textbf{Sensory event} \Rightarrow \textbf{Thalamus}$$
$$\Downarrow$$
$$\textbf{Amygdala} \Rightarrow \textbf{Action}$$

In the upper but less direct route, sensory data flow from the thalamus to the cortex before reaching the amygdala. In this path, both short-term and long-term memory systems of the brain are engaged. Since the cortex is part of this pathway, it is thought of as the "higher" path[10], a path involving Damasio's "high reason." The involvement of the cortex draws in more complex and potentially modulating data and memories, which allows for a less reflexive and slower response to the sensory data, and a deeper understanding of its significance and meaning. The upper route has the potential to bring emotions into new experience, and those emotions allow us to judge the experience and to analyze whether it is truly dangerous, or whether it might in fact have positive implications.

This amygdala-cortex complex is one place in the brain where emotion and cognition both enter into our understanding of experience, and our judgments of actions that are appropriate and helpful. In this way, the amygdala can be a part of positive emotion.

The Lower Pathway

The small amount of initial information that skips the cortex, reaching the amygdala directly, has a very rapid impact. It goes to the brain stem and the hypothalamus, both of which send direct signals to the body. The brain stem sends electrical signals through the spinal column to the muscles, producing almost instantaneous behaviors such as the "startle reflex," which manifests itself in humans by jumping back, ducking, or freezing. The hypothalamus responds by secreting chemicals into the bloodstream, and those chemicals trigger more slowly developing yet powerful feelings throughout the body. We begin to feel fearful, sick, angry, embarrassed, or other powerful negative body responses to this brain activity.

The increased activity of the amygdala can be produced not only by the specific negative stimuli[11], but also by the environment in which those stimuli have been experienced. For example, mice that learn to respond to a tone or a light by associating it with an electrical shock give the same response when simply placed in the cage that is used for such experiments.

We know from our own experience that people are the same. Some students (we hope not many) freeze in fear when they find themselves in the "cage" used for our experiments in education: the classroom.

A Positive Perspective of the Negative

But back to joy. The upper pathway can lead to cognitive analysis of experiences that initially seem dangerous, but actually turn out to be harmless or even healthy and helpful. This can be the outcome when we engage the cerebral cortex because it has the power to provide more accurate and deeper understandings of experience.

Another way to include the amygdala in this story is more direct. We can think of joy as the opposite of fear; if fear is negative, joy is positive. The amygdala also responds to positive stimuli, the only difference being that this kind of response is a *reduction* in activity. For example, when people look at happy faces, their amygdala becomes less active. Emotion can always be thought of in this way. Less fear means more happiness, and vice versa. The amygdala is like a thermometer, responding to both heat and cold. Thus both negative emotion and positive emotion have an impact on the amygdala. "Normal" is somewhere in the middle.

The action output of the amygdala triggered through the lower pathway will decrease when the sensory environment is positive. On the other hand, receptivity, openness, and thoughtful reactions will increase. Thus, in education, using threat and punishments in an attempt to achieve positive goals seems bound to fail. Behaviors may change temporarily, but the emotions and amygdala activity actually increase. Ultimately this increase will produce negative emotional outcomes expressed in actions, one way or another. When negative responses are triggered by the environment, positive outcomes are unlikely.

These properties of the amygdala lead to a logical conclusion. Educators may be able to enforce certain behaviors with threats or punishments, but these approaches probably will not alter lifetime attitudes or produce true learning. The only way negative experiences can become positive is through cognitive processing that actually changes our comprehension of a given experience from negative to positive.

The Rewarding Brain

We can think of the amygdala as the defensive component of our emotion system. Its function is to reduce or eliminate threat. The goal is reduction. The other end of the emotion spectrum is linked to brain structures that are part of what we call the reward system. This system is attractive, not defensive; its goal is acquisition.

We can identify three aspects of the reward system. First, there is a process of analyzing sensory data to determine whether they are likely to generate reward. Second, there is the initiation of "reward-seeking" behaviors. Third, there is the experience of the reward itself. An example of these three can be found in voluntary physical movement (sports, dance, etc). We consider the anticipated behavior and conclude that it will be (or may be) pleasurable, begin the behavior and find that progress toward the reward is, indeed, pleasurable. Finally, we reach the reward (which we often consider to be the main point).

Similarly, mental movement that we sense in stories or in solving problems is also rewarding. There is reward in the process, and in the end point. Often the three aspects of reward can be integrated into what we identify as a single rewarding experience.

In time, a rewarding experience is remembered through the feelings it generates. Those feelings can be anticipated, experienced, and remembered as one thing, or we may analyze them in greater detail and see the different aspects of reward separately. In any case, as we noted earlier, reward extends over a longer time frame than that of the instant. We can legitimately claim that we feel happy, in the present tense. The present becomes identified through the time span of our feelings.

This process can apply both to concrete and abstract (imagined) experiences. For example, it is fun to anticipate playing a game, actually play the game, and win the game. All very concrete. But people also enjoy and feel rewarded when they create mental goals, make mental progress, and finally attain the goal—for example, when they experience a desire to learn calculus, work through the concept of differential equations, and feel success when the basic idea becomes clear.

Problem solving engages the reward system in a similar way. It is fun to figure out exactly what the problem is (Aha! I see the problem!). Then we begin to work toward a solution, and finally solve it. We can extend this idea to the process of moving from one image to another, which is described in chapter 4. This type of mental movement will also trigger our reward system.

Another rather simple example might be students' classroom assignments. If a student has an image of a paper that has been assigned but not yet written, some elements of that image could include empty sheets of paper and a tense, anxious self. On the other hand, an image of the pages covered with fine prose and a self that is relaxed and satisfied is one that the student can create in his or her mind. Moving from the first image toward the second one is the pleasurable part. In fact, if a student can create the second image in his or her mind, the student may actually begin to *want* to write the paper. The student may be motivated in the best way possible: the intrinsic motivation of enjoyment of the process itself, and reaching the goals that he or she has set by the learner!

The Biology of Motivation

What is being learned about the biology of satisfaction and enjoyment? What actually is going on in the nervous system?

Let's begin with research on an ancient animal, the sea slug. This example deals with primitive behavior, but nonetheless behavior that the slug might be said to *want* to do—to be motivated to do. This behavior is eating: specifically, biting and swallowing.

The biological processes associated with this primitive but rewarding behavior turn out to be directly related to the reward chemical, dopamine. In fact, when dopamine is sprayed on a specific neuron that is known to cause the biting action, the animal bites more often and enthusiastically, even when there is no food.[12]

We have no real measure of "enjoyment," no "enjoyment meter," so we can't prove that the slug "enjoys" eating. But we do know that dopamine is a significant component of the reward system, not only in slugs, but also in more complicated animals like us. The fact that the same chemicals are involved with the behavior of simple *and* complex creatures suggests that if we did have an "enjoyment detector," it might well start beeping when the slug eats. We might even argue that the slug truly "wants" to eat, using the same terms that we use for our own species.

This apparent ubiquity of the connection between dopamine and the reward system suggests that, if we want to understand motivation and reward, we should look for the regions of the human brain that are naturally exposed to dopamine or that have receptors for dopamine. If we locate such regions, we may also find clues for new ideas about motivation and reward in education.[13]

But even before we go hunting for dopamine, we should remind ourselves that the brain always reacts to the environment. The reaction can be fear and escape, boredom and disengagement, interest and enthusiasm, or anything in between. Perhaps rather than saying the brain "reacts," we might better say that our environment always influences the "state" of our mind. These "states of mind" depend on our experience, and thus will be different in detail for each of us. But the potential for engagement and motivation is a feature of every brain. In education, the challenge is not to create emotions, but to unearth them.

They are always there.

Front Cortex and the Rewarding Brain

In simple animals, the dopamine system is ancient and direct. But, as with the fear systems of the amygdala, things are more complex in the human brain. This complexity can be traced to the neocortex, not all regions of cortex but rather the cognitively most powerful one, the front integrative cortex! That is primarily where the dopamine is delivered. There is a strong connection between the ancient brain stem neurons that make dopamine and the most evolutionarily recent and analytically powerful part of the human brain, the frontal cortex.

Of the emotion-related neurotransmitters, this front cortex delivery appears to be unique. Other modulating neurotransmitters such as adrenalin or serotonin are released throughout the entire neocortex, but there is little or no dopamine delivery to the back. This is illustrated in the figure below,[14] which shows the locations of the dopamine-producing neurons, and the regions of cortex they reach and to which they deliver this neurotransmitter (the arrows.) This is the same perspective as shown at the beginning of this chapter (left, medial). The point is that the arrows *do not* extend to the back regions (right side of the image) of the cerebrum.

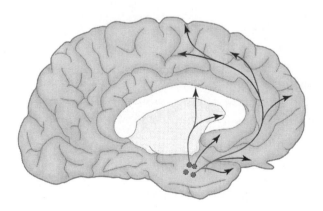

Even though, at the level of the intact organism, the functions of dopamine remain poorly defined, the fact that front cortical regions can receive more of this modulatory neurotransmitter than can the back regions is thought provoking. The impact of dopamine on changing synapse function is greater in front than in back. And if, indeed, dopamine is an obligatory component of the reward system, then the front cortex is more associated with reward than is the back. This idea meshes with our experience that front cortex functions such as using working memory to solve problems, intentional recall of facts and stories, and decision making, are all rewarding, satisfying, and even exhilarating. That is not to say that back cortex activities cannot be pleasurable and satisfying, but natural selection clearly has responded to pressures to provide more dopamine in front, whatever the selective pressure may be.

In our context, this striking difference between back and front cortical regions illustrates the fact that these regions of cortex are different from each other, biochemically and thus functionally. That difference draws attention to the suggestions that education should engage the entire cortex. Front and back are different, so we must use both to get the full package.

This speculation goes beyond what I proposed in earlier work. Reward is related not only to voluntary movement—either primitive physical movement such as biting and swallowing, or imagined movement toward a goal—but also from the most *advanced* cognitive functions that characterize our brain: functions identified with the front integrative cortex.

Thinking is rewarding. It is work, but also fun—as long as there is movement and progress toward a goal.[15]

A Reward Center: Name and Function

In the past, I have referred to pleasure centers in the brain as "basal structures." I created this term because it seemed unnecessary to list the extensive, highly complex, specific structures to which that term refers. Also, less was known about these structures than about the amygdala. Since then, a great deal of new work has been done on the positive emotion centers. It will be helpful now to identify and discuss one important structure by its correct name, the *nucleus accumbens*. It is located in the lower center regions of the two hemispheres and is one of the aforementioned "basal structures."

The nucleus accumbens is rich in dopamine receptors, suggesting that it has a major role in the positive emotion pathways of the brain. It also receives strong signals from the amygdala, the movement centers, and, ultimately, the action centers. Metaphorically, the nucleus accumbens is the linchpin of emotion.

Here is an example from some recent research about the interactions among amygdala, nucleus accumbens, and front cortex. I will not describe the experiments themselves, just summarize the idea that emerged from them. Quoting the authors of this research, this summary is as follows: the prefrontal cortex can "modulate the consequences of amygdala activity by suppressing dopamine release in the nucleus accumbens."[16] This summary is also illustrated in the figure below, which brings back integrative cortex, front integrative cortex, nucleus accumbens, amygdala, and motor cortex into a sequence that ultimately prevents actions driven by the reward system. This occurs because front cortex predicts the possibility of negative outcomes to imagined future actions, thus instructing the amygdala to block dopamine actions in the nucleus accumbens (the "blocking" is indicated by the black inverted triangle).

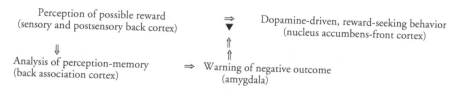

In the absence of these signals from the amygdala, we are not aware of the danger and plunge ahead toward the immediate reward, as shown in the top line of the diagram. Given additional time for cortical processing, we sense some danger and slow down or even totally stop our instinctive reward-seeking behavior, through the action of the amygdala on the nucleus accumbens.

Given the time and opportunity, our cortex can tell our amygdala to warn our reward system that mindless actions, "going for the gusto," may not always be the best idea. The reward system can be regulated by the cortex-amygdala team. Reasoning alters feelings and, thus, action.

Two New Players in the Game of Feelings

I have stressed the role of the slow neurotransmitters as major players in negative and positive emotion. However, many other chemical regulators are important in such processes. These include the morphine-like natural chemicals such as endorphins, and two other physiologically important hormones, vasopressin and oxytocin. The latter two have been the subject of highly interesting research on control of emotion and feeling in the amygdala.

Vasopressin is an important hormone in the regulation of salt, water balance, and blood pressure. It also initiates negative and aggressive behaviors by triggering stress, anxiety, and fear-related memories. The exact relationship between the physiological actions on blood pressure and the behavioral actions is not understood. However, parts of the amygdala have an abundance of vasopressin receptors, and when vasopressin interacts with these receptors, negative and aggressive behaviors are increased.

Oxytocin is similar to vasopressin in that it has both physiological and behavioral effects. Physiologically it is involved in uterine contraction during birth and stimulation of milk release in new mothers. In addition, both males and females respond to oxytocin with mating and positive social behaviors. This hormone decreases anxiety and stress while facilitating social encounters and inhibiting avoidance behaviors. It is the one chemical we could most count on if we wanted to follow the advice of the hippies in the 1960s and '70s and "make love, not war."

The Devil Made Me Do It

Some of you may remember Flip Wilson's (a comedian in the 1960s and 1970s) skits about decision making. Faced with a choice—perhaps between deceiving a friend to get even for some real or imagined insult, and forgiving the friend—Flip would work out the conflict he felt by consulting an angel on his right shoulder and the devil on his left. He would debate the issue back and forth, turning his head toward the devil to listen to negative "evil" advice, then toward the angel to hear positive "good" advice. If he decided to make the "evil" choice, he would shrug and say, "The devil made me do it!"

One reason this scenario was humorous was that it came so close to the truth. It seems like we are always debating our choices, second-guessing them, defending them, even blaming them on something or someone else. But, in any case, moving from the ridiculous to the sublime, we encounter new research that suggests something very much akin to the Flip Wilson gig. In fact, the neurons in the amygdala that respond to vasopressin to produce negative feelings and aggressive actions (devil on the left) are inhibited by neurons that respond to oxytocin (angel on the right). At least part of the battle between Flip Wilson's devil and angel occurs at the vasopressin receptor in the amygdala.

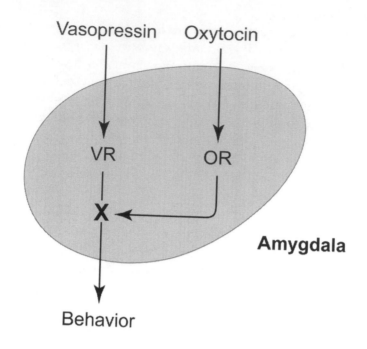

This connection is shown in the schematic figure of the amygdala, above, which shows the receptor systems for both hormones (OR and VR) and how they affect each other.[17] There are synapses between the neurons that respond to oxytocin and others that respond to vasopressin; the two systems are directly and physically connected. The result is that oxytocin blocks the action of vasoporessin in the amygdala (shown by the X crossing the arrow from the vasopressin system.) Thus, our behaviors are strongly influenced by whether the vasopressin receptors are more effective or are reduced in activity by oxytocin. A direct, physical link between the two systems seems to be one likely source of our right-shoulder, left-shoulder behaviors.

I am stressing this neuroscience discovery, not because it gives us unexpected or unpredicted ideas about behavior, but because it allows us to understand our sense of emotion, feelings, and behaviors as physical and explainable functions of neurons rather than as mysterious and/or "character issues." This knowledge can influence our values and judgments. It may make us less likely to judge or criticize behaviors that displease us, and to help us remember that any feelings and behaviors may be found in any person under the right conditions. We all have these connections.

These discoveries also give us the hope that, instead of generating more discomfort and negative feelings by trying to control behaviors through force, we might discover ways to stimulate the oxytocin pathways for positive behaviors and use nature's balancing system in the mind. Ultimately, oxytocin rules!

Oxytocin inhibits the vasopressin system directly, particularly reducing consolidation of fear memories and avoidance behaviors. Education environments that have oxytocin-enriching characteristics could have a major impact on the negative behaviors we sometimes see in schools. These behaviors frequently appear early and, indeed, may be a direct result of negative experiences that occur in formalized education. We should also remember that they are not limited to children, but often are observed in educators and administrators themselves. The biology of the amygdala tells us that in behavior, negatives accumulate and lead to more negatives, but positives can and do block out the negatives.

Revisiting the Upper and Lower Pathways

The vasopressin/oxytocin system in the amygdala is strongly reminiscent of the "upper and lower" pathway for sensory information that we discussed earlier in this chapter. The vasopressin system directly transfers action signals to the body through the brain stem[18], so it seems likely that this pathway is at least partially responsible for negative body language and other defensive responses that do not require planning or thought. On the other hand, the oxytocin-responsive system appears to originate primarily in the cerebral *cortex* and may well be a component of the upper, high-reason pathway.

Thus, the modulating actions of oxytocin may depend on cognition, while the vasopressin system may be more instinctive. The drawing above suggests that the upper pathway controls the lower one, rather than vice versa. Biology suggests that positive emotion can win out over negative emotion.

The journey toward mind is supported by the positive emotion systems.[19]

Intrinsic Reward

Earlier I suggested the existence of three components of the reward system: identification of reward, progress toward reward, and reaching reward. I emphasized progress more than actually reaching a goal. If we accept the assumption that release of dopamine, or the presence of large amounts of dopamine receptors, is indicative of intrinsic reward, we can look to neuroscience for information about this subjective aspect of mind.

New research confirms this general assertion and also identifies new and more specific aspects of intrinsic reward. As I said earlier, this research indicates that dopamine release in the brain is not dependent on receiving the reward itself. This is suggested by studies with mice, using a new and highly sensitive method for measurement of dopamine. The first cue that a reward will be forthcoming, that is, the expectation of a reward first develops (or even the reminder that the reward exists), causes nearly as much dopamine release as does the actual receipt of the reward itself. It produces an anticipatory burst of dopamine, not a sustained release, strongly suggesting that the expectation of doing well and being rewarded is a powerful neurological event in itself.[20]

Beyond anticipation, actually organizing and executing actions is also rewarding. Psychologists call carrying out actions designed specifically to achieve certain goals "instrumental conditioning." We take actions because they are associated with intrinsic reward, and this behavior produces learning. Doing things we have learned produces results that please us.

Some psychology researchers divide the process of instrumental conditioning into two sub-functions: the "critic" and the "actor." The critic makes judgments about what behaviors (actions) will generate the greatest reward or the least punishment, while the actor initiates the behaviors and modifies them to carry out the judgments of the critic.

These two functions engage brain structures associated with the nucleus accumbens. The critic function is associated with one such structure (one physically below the other), and the actor function is associated with the dorsal (upper) regions. Of interest, the critic region has significantly greater numbers of dopamine receptors than does the actor region, suggesting that the critic function may be the more rewarding of the two. Making judgments and decisions may be more rewarding than putting them into action.[21]

So What About Education?

My objective in this chapter is to suggest ways to activate the elements of the brain's intrinsic reward systems in educational settings. Doing this effectively is an important aspect of my views about our journey from brain to mind.

It appears that the more negative aspects of behavior derive from the evolutionarily older functions of "survival brain." They are the unreflective and instinctive elements of emotion. However, the reward systems take us to the ideas of self-awareness, reflection, thought, and conscious control; We associate these ideas with *mind*. Moving from the instinctive lower path in the amygdala to the more cognitive upper path epitomizes this idea.

To the extent that our journey takes place in schools, it is obvious that this is a tough assignment. Educational environments often seek to remove control from the student. This mentality extends throughout all organized education. Teachers may spend most of their time and effort keeping students "under control." Administrators may believe they should control what teachers do in classrooms, and watching over the entire scene are parents and boards of education. This control pyramid discourages the freedom that is so essential for intrinsic motivation. It reduces the freedom of students, teachers, and administrators.

Throughout this book, starting with the first story about Henry and square roots, I have tried to stress the relationship between freedom and effective education. When we are free to dream and to anticipate, when we know we are in control of our own learning, and when we actually begin to do more than just imagine and dream, when we are free to act, we will discover the joy!

Our question is: Can this happen in educational environments?

Can Fear Lead to Joy?

Often educators try to eliminate fear in learners. This has not always been the case, and by no means is it universal in our modern educational environments. We realize that fear can be paralyzing or pathological. At the same time, challenge is an important part of learning. In fact, overcoming challenge is part of the joy. How can we have positive feelings about success if we don't respect the task? In addition, there probably is no way to eliminate the concern, and even worry, inherent in learning new things. If they are new, we cannot predict the outcome, or even assess our progress, with confidence.

As we have discussed, natural selection has given us brain-machinery for dealing with challenge. Our amygdala continually scans sensory information and evaluates whether it is safe. Awareness of danger and alertness to its possibility are part of our neurological condition. But nature has also given us the tools to deal with challenges. We can learn what we should fear and how to respond to pressure. The answer is in overcoming the challenge, not in avoiding it.

What are the elements of "overcoming?" As I have implied, one of these elements is confronting it. Ignoring the reality of threat, or even searching blindly for ways to stress the positive, are not solutions. For one thing, the lower pathway in the amygdala is fast. Its direct wiring to the brain stem and the body means that the signals begin to exert their effects more quickly than does the upper pathway through the cortex. When challenged, we may well react before we think. In fact, this early response may be necessary to give us the signal that processing is needed. It activates our more-conscious awareness.

In addition, it is important to consciously recognize that challenge is valuable. There are often very real dangers that cannot be avoided. They may even be essential content of what is to be learned. Those dangers may be part of the truth. An example of this from my own experience is the behavior of college students. As freshmen, many of these students are uncertain, if not actually fearful. But different students respond to this fear in different ways. Some view it as useless and distracting. They seek escape rather than under-standing, and they do not see their discomfort as valuable. They are locked into the more primitive brain functions of survival; their journey toward mind is blocked.

Other students react very differently. They use their experience to gather information about themselves. They see it as part of the truth. So they may be disappointed when a "C" shows up on their grade report, but their response is simply that they are learning where their talents lie. The "C" is information, not failure. And in some cases, this produces intense joy. Free-dom is increased. Such students can then follow paths they have defined for themselves! Part of this joy comes from their continued progress on the jour-ney toward mind. They process the fear.

The route to joy must include the truth. Our amygdala helps us find it.

Mistakes and Joyful Education

The route from brain to mind has many detours and dead-ends. These can make us fearful, but as we just discussed, they often are inevitable and ulti-mately can enhance our growth and increase both our knowledge and cour-age. Often they become part of the rich and joyful experience that characterizes progress in the journey toward mind.

Particularly in formal education, we may think that fear and mistakes are bad and should be avoided, but I am suggesting that a "mistake rich" environment is preferable. It produces a better education and leads to more insight and more truth. Mistakes are expected and become information. It is a cause for worry if a student does not make any mistakes.

When the value of every outcome is determined by whether it is right or wrong, pressure and high stakes become an integral part of the school experience. It turns the focus from learning and understanding to fear, tension, and crisis. It produces the primitive fear and tension of the primal brain rather than the joy found in growth, freedom, and development of mind.

Pay Attention to Feelings

Neuroscience has given the world important information by delineating the difference between the upper and lower route through the amygdala, and the ability of oxytocin to override the more primitive aggression and fear behaviors. Our belief that there is value in retaining awareness of our emotions is reinforced by defining the neurosystem responsible for that conclusion. Awareness of this information engages cortical processes that alter behavior of individuals and, eventually, of cultures. Knowledge that there are different routes through which information can be channeled in the brain, and that we can consciously decide which route to use, provides a way to deal with some of the most difficult moments in our lives. These are moments that otherwise may lead to conflict and even wars, or, alternatively, to taking a deep breath and analyzing how we feel and why. The outcomes can be dramatically different.

The journey toward mind must include experiences that challenge us. Meeting such challenges is an integral part of gaining knowledge and wisdom. Treating emotions as tools rather than as enemies should become a primary goal of education. To use them as tools, we must have control and self-awareness. This awareness of our own feelings is central to development of mind. From the earliest childhood through adult life, it is of great benefit to ask ourselves continually, "How am I feeling?"

Do Front Cortex Things

As we saw above, the region of cortex innervated by dopamine neurons in the human species, the front cortical regions, is primarily responsible for the creative and directing functions that are so characteristic of human activity and behavior. Among others, these functions include creating images, solving problems, making decisions, planning actions, generating language, evaluating options, predicting events, and directing the body's actions.

These front cortex functions can be motivating and rewarding for children and adults. If education is to be joyful, the freedom and control associated with front cortex activity must be part of the experience of students, teachers, and administrators. Not that everyone associated with education can be in charge at once. In fact, too much choice creates confusion and actually reduces our ability to choose. Further, our decisions and choices are based on experiences and things we know about, so it is actually impossible for every person to have equal say in every problem.

A practical goal in education is to acknowledge that all of us have some experiences in which we can take control and feel ownership. This can only happen in a culture that acknowledges the necessity of freedom in learning. This freedom can be expressed in many ways, and those expressions are part of the freedom. The key is choice—not an infinite range of choices, but choices within an existing knowledge framework.

I suggest that this can be achieved in all subjects, at least to some extent. Let's take the subject of arithmetic. Everyone agrees that this subject is of great importance, but how does choice enter the picture? Arithmetic is arithmetic, after all. Answers are either right or wrong!

Nevertheless, making choice a component of learning arithmetic is not a matter of right or wrong, even in schools. There can be choice of assignments and what learners actually do to learn arithmetic. And keep in mind that this approach can be used in college-level teaching in philosophy or physics, for example. This is possible in spite of the established structure in most schools where teachers control students, administrators control teachers, and a formal board controls the administrators. Each of these three stakeholders can have points of control and choice if they agree to give up choice in other aspects. To illustrate this, imagine a school where the following categories of choice exist:

- Student's choice. Students use arithmetic to explore any subject that interests them: money, distances, sports, populations, etc. Students choose the kind of problems they will work on. In this category, students are free of teacher control.

- Teacher's choice. Teachers regularly choose additional specific assignments as well as pedagogical approaches (how students will be taught). In this category, teachers are free of administrative control.
- Administrator's choice. Administrators choose the big picture in arithmetic instruction. They set the overall philosophy and educational goals. In this category, an administrator can be independent of the board.

I choose these examples, not because they are free of complications, but as illustrations only. They are meant to stimulate discussion about how formal education can create more freedom of choice within a hierarchical structure. I believe that such freedom can play a major role in creating more joy at all levels in the system. It may actually be essential!

The Value of Past Success

One of the neuroscience findings discussed earlier in this chapter demonstrated that the mind rewards more than the experience itself. It rewards *anticipation* of the experience. If affective neuroscience is our guide, and if increased dopamine levels are evidence of reward, then the image or anticipation of enjoyable experiences is a reward in itself.

Is it possible to create an environment in the classroom in which *everyone* associated with it can either remember or imagine the experience of success? Everyone should have the experience of setting goals and achieving them. It is the success that matters, not the subject. Our goal should be to find some area of success for everyone. For example, if a teacher remembered a time in his or her life when he or she succeeded in a sporting event, it might generate the dopamine pulse associated with visualizing success and provide new energy and motivation for a new task such as working with a difficult student. If success is its own reward, then remembering success might become a reward for trying new endeavors. The trick would be to remember and revisualize *any* success when faced with a frustrating or new challenge.

This is not a novel idea, but the neuroscience perspective might lead us back to it.

The Group

Up to this point, we have primarily discussed feelings derived from individual experiences of students. However, education is almost always experienced in a social setting. Indeed, the most powerful feelings students experience are driven by the social environment. Being part of the group, having friends, being approved or disapproved of by the teacher, and being aware that such approval/disapproval is apparent to the group are the kinds of feelings students carry home with them most strongly and most often.

There is a growing body of research examining how the brain responds to pain or pleasure generated by the social environment itself, and some of this work may encourage us to invent new ways to educate. One example is new research on the pain of social loss. The suffering that is generated by exclusion from the group is one of the most common and damaging negative experiences in school. In these experiments, neuroimaging studies were conducted with people who were rejected by a group playing a virtual ball-tossing game. The most striking finding was that the areas of the brain associated with this social rejection were remarkably similar to those areas that are activated when physical pain is experienced.

Rejection hurts—literally![22]

The Deepest Joy

Beyond avoiding the pain of exclusion, the social nature of learning itself, the experiences of joint discovery, teamwork, and participation are all of great importance for success in education. They have been stressed repeatedly, and a great deal of pedagogical theory and practice has been directed toward them in the past decade. I do not downplay them in any way.

I do, however, feel a need to nudge the pendulum back the other way. Ultimately, understanding and learning are highly personal experiences. Each of us builds on our own neuronal networks, and for that reason the social aspects of schooling are not, by themselves, adequate to lead us far along the route from brain to mind. Their impact is to provide an environment in which fear is reduced and spontaneity is more likely. However, that in no way assures developing deep insights or satisfying new ideas. For that kind of progress toward mind, I suspect that individual reflection and hard work are necessary. As happened in my story at the beginning of this chapter, we are most likely to experience this "deepest" joy when we work alone, are immersed in our thoughts, and are struggling in serious and individual battles with ideas and skills. In chapter 2, this is illustrated by my need to practice dribbling, by myself, intensely and repeatedly. In experiences like that, it will not do to discover someone else's answers. This growth of mind is selfish; we want to own it.

In this view, experience is broadened to include both social interactions and private, deep experience. Both are essential. At times we travel alone in our journey from brain to mind, but we are not lonely or sad. We have ourselves and the joy inside us.

New Questions for Educators

Emotion is probably the most important factor for learning. Our feelings determine the energy with which we begin new challenges and where we will direct that energy. The actions we take are determined by how we feel and how we believe those actions will make us feel. Not that we only seek out experiences that look easy or even joyful; we also respond to challenge and often are motivated by confidence and pride. We may want to show how good we are. A challenged student has a better chance of successful learning than does a bored one. It is important to balance confidence and challenge. This balance is one key to the art of educating.

What questions might we ask ourselves about keeping the joy in this emotional experience? One possibility focuses on understanding and using the difference between the upper and lower pathway in the amygdala. The question this raises might go something like this: "Can educators enhance the probability that learners will recognize the value of channeling their experiences toward the upper path? Can they realize how important that is?" And asking that question will lead us to think seriously about it for our own purposes. We will begin to wonder how we can stress this upper path, and how we can help learners view it as an explicit goal. The way our brains work suggests that learning this skill as a child may be as important as learning to read.

Second, but related to the above, let's ask how we can design the experiences of learners in ways that minimize the negative. An example would be the question, "How can I generate a mistake-rich environment." Our own awareness of this goal will enhance the experience of our learners and ultimately create opportunities for them to become more self-aware. They will begin to think about how their own bodies are feeling, and how their own "somatic markers" can help them learn. Learned early in life, when everything seems so easy, this skill will be invaluable. Stressing the positive, using the upper path in the amygdala, will lead us to reflect on successes rather than failures. Learners may develop the habit of taking frequent inventory of successes, asking themselves questions such as, "What did I do well today?" or "What were my greatest successes?"

Third, we should educate and reeducate ourselves about the capabilities of our front cortex. We should remember what it evolved to do and stress those things. We all should have more choices, more creative challenges, and more opportunities for problem solving. We will feel rewarded already when we have choice, and that reward may be greater than any we could gain through "acting out." A question, then, that directs our thoughts along those lines might be, "What aspects of front cortex am I going to emphasize to help my learners understand my goals today?"

Toward Making Meaning

Finding the joy happens very early in our journey. And, as I argued both in this chapter and in chapter 2, once it happens we will continue to make discoveries, all the while feeling more and less fearful. We are prepared for new steps along the journey. In fact, we are eager for them!

In the narrative of this book, the next stage of our journey leads to comprehension of our experiences. Moving from the sensory-motor way of learning, we begin to process what has happened. This includes what we have seen, heard, touched, smelled, tasted, and understood about own actions and how to carry them out. Our interpretation of this information is personal, involving our individual experiences and bringing them together to produce an integrated picture of our world and our experience in it. I call this "making meaning," and it heavily involves a region of cortex that we have not yet discussed extensively.

Notes

1. This phrase is found in discussions of emotion over the past century, possibly beginning with William James, and continually showing up in modern scholarly work.

2. Vonnegut, K. (1969), *Slaughterhouse Five*, chapter 9.

3. Some readers may question whether these problems are also found in advanced education environments such as medical or graduate schools. I claim they are because of my experience with education at this level. Often, when trying to

work seriously with these students, I find that they turn to idle chatter and go "off task" as soon as they believe I am not watching or listening to them. Also, medical educators tell me that students retain their obsession with grades, even when trying to learn things that are essential for their professional practice. If they receive an evaluation that is less than excellent, they will pay more attention to the evaluation than to the errors they made. I have come to believe that it is the school setting itself, with its accompanying threats and rewards, that generates problems of this sort. I discuss this more in later parts of this chapter.

4. In this section I quote extensively from Antonio Damasio's book *Descartes' Error*. Forced to use one sentence to define the message of this book, we might say that the message is "emotion is necessary for reason."

5. These relationships between feelings and consciousness are the main theme of Damasio's second book, *The Feeling of What Happens*, Harcourt, San Diego, CA, 2000.

6. The quotes in this paragraph come from *The Feeling of What Happens*, p. 56.

7. Zull, J. E. (2002), *The Art of Changing the Brain*, Stylus, Sterling, VA.

8. I have not previously mentioned the thalamus, because until now it didn't seem necessary. However, I have been uncomfortable with the omission, so here I would like to draw your attention to the sensory elements of the body that send their signals through this structure, where they are routed to the correct parts of the cortex. In general, the thalamus is involved in forwarding information from the sense organs to different regions of cortex as well as from one region of cortex to another.

9. This model is based on a similar one presented by Joseph LeDoux in his book, *Synaptic Self*, Viking, New York, NY, 2002, p. 123. This low route has been studied with both the auditory and the visual sensory systems.

10. Cortex is considered "higher" since it is the area of brain most engaged in the more advanced functions and is the most recent to appear in evolution. Thus, creative, cognitive, and analytical functions characteristic of human thought are "higher" than reflexes, or more ancient behaviors such as fight-or-flight or reproduction.

11. The notion of the amygdala as a detection system for negative sensory information has recently been complicated by a report of a patient (SM) with bilateral lesions of the amygdala. SM does not respond to pictures of fearful faces, as is expected in such patients, but the defect turns out to be that SM simply does not focus on the eyes in a face. This is in contrast to the normal behavior of looking frequently at the eye regions in a face. An explanation for this abnormal behavior and its relationship to amygdala function is not currently available. See: Adolphs, R., et al. (2005), *Nature*, 433, pp. 68–72.

12. Brembs, B., et al. (2002), *Science*, 296, pp. 1706–1708.

13. Recent work by Hnasko, Sotak, and Palmiter (*Nature*, 438, 2005, pp. 854–857) suggests that dopamine itself may not be responsible for the "hedonic" or "wanting" experience, but that it is necessary for the actions associated with these feelings. This

work provides a warning for research that demonstrates behaviors (actions) indicative of internal motivating feelings, when we have no direct measure of the feelings themselves.

14. Nolte, J., (2002), *The Human Brain*, 5th edition, Mosby, St. Louis, MO, pg 283.

15. A link between the reward system and positive emotion was identified in *The Art of Changing the Brain*, p. 61.

16. Jackson, M. E., and Mohagddam, B. (2001), *Journal of Neuroscience*, 621, pp. 676–681.

17. This is a modified drawing taken from Huber, D., Veinante, P., and Stoop, R. (2005), *Science*, 308, pp. 245–248.

18. LeDoux, J. (2002,) *Synaptic Self*, Viking (Penguin), New York, NY, pp. 121–123; the "quick and dirty" term refers to the fastest but least accurate pathway with regard to content. A "dirty" pathway is one that contains basic information but that appears "smudged" through lack of detail and clarity.

19. Positive behaviors seem to be more learned, and thus are strongly associated with growth and development. We revisit these ideas in chapter 7, which focuses on that topic.

20. Phillips, P. E. M., et al. (2003), *Nature*, 422, pp. 614–617; also see the review of this work by David Self in the same issue of *Nature*.

21. This research is described in O'Doherty, J., et al. (2004), *Science*, 304, pp. 452–454.

22. Eisenberger, N. I., et al. (2003), *Science*, 302, pp. 290–292; also see commentary on this research by Jack Panksepp in the same issue of *Science*.

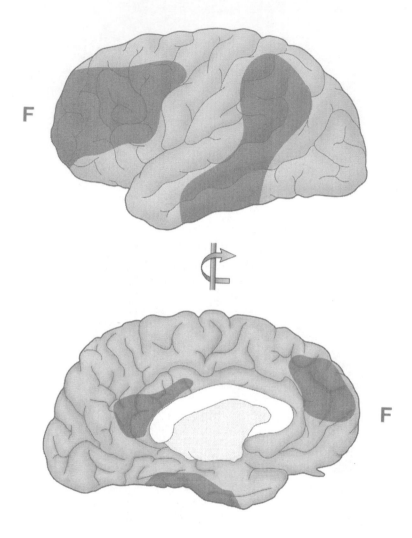

General areas of integrative cortex seen from left lateral (top) and left medial (bottom) perspective. These regions and their functions are discussed next.

4

DEEPER LEARNING
THROUGH INTEGRATION

Growth of Mind by Making
Meaning and Creating New Ideas

We pass the word around; we ponder how different people put the case; we read the poetry;
we meditate over the literature; we play the
music; we change our minds; we reach an
understanding.

— Lewis Thomas

*I was 10 years old and in fifth grade. My school consisted of a single room
with children in grades K–8. There were two students in my grade, and
the largest number in any grade was four. All the children were our
neighbors; some we liked and some we didn't.*

*Our school days were spent alternatively working on assignments
and going to the front of the room for lessons. When it was time for a
lesson, the teacher would ask us questions or ask us to read aloud. Sometimes we would work problems on the blackboard. If we wanted to, we
could watch and listen to the lessons for the other grades.*

*One day, the first graders were having their reading lesson and I
was watching them. It was interesting to see the little kids learning to
read or do arithmetic. It reminded me of when I was that age and how
excited I was when I realized that I was a good reader.*

*Most of the first graders could read, but some still struggled. They
would stop between sentences, take a deep breath, and then plunge into
the next sentence if they could.*

One day I noticed something I hadn't realized before. My little friend, Mike, wasn't reading. I knew Mike and his family well. His mother was very smart and often read from the Bible in our church, so Mike's trouble surprised and fascinated me.

As I watched, the teacher asked Mike to read. His response was just a long silence. The other students began to fidget and snicker. The teacher tried to help Mike by sounding out words, and he did repeat them after her, but then the long silence began again, and so did the snickering.

Then I realized that Mike was looking at the floor, and his face was getting red. Still, what happened next surprised me. He just burst into tears and, sobbing, cried out, "I can't read!"

In chapter 2 I wrote about a "great transformation." By "great" I meant wonderful, essential, big, and even surprising. In chapter 3 we examined the emotional aspect of that transformation, the idea that these more rudimentary and ancient aspects of the brain can be influenced by regions of neocortex, and that such an influence can increase the chance for positive emotions and feelings.

However, we have not yet discussed the functions of either back or front cortex in enough detail to reach some understanding of terms such as "making meaning" or "creating ideas" that I used in those earlier chapters.

Generally, sensory-motor experiences and mimicry (chapter 2) are what we expect from a child. As we mature and develop complexity and individuality, those child-like behaviors lessen, but when faced with new experiences, we may return to them, perhaps more often than we like to admit. Still, in the right environment and with the right experiences, we continue to work toward more mature behavior, making our own interpretations of our experiences and responding in unique and complicated ways. As Lewis Thomas says, we approach and reapproach our experience from many different perspectives. Ultimately, "we reach an understanding."

This growth of mind is what we hope will happen in education. We want learners to go beyond borrowed knowledge and skills and develop their own thoughts and ideas. That is how they become able to make informed, creative, and responsible decisions. It is also how they prepare for roles as contributing members and leaders of society.

It is the theme of this chapter.

The Pathway

Although we will move away from mimicry now, we are still discussing a process that begins with experience and leads to action. Action is still the "bottom line." It is how we get to action that interests us now. Rather than taking one giant leap, we look at a pathway that has intermediate steps.

This pathway is shown in the figure below. As with mimicry, it begins with sensing and ends with action, but along the way, brain processes that help us generate meaning and new ideas come into play. This is shown in step 2. It involves making interpretations of our experience and manipulating those interpretations to create ideas of our own. These two processes (making meaning and creating ideas) are keys for cognition, and they direct our thoughts toward the most interesting capabilities of the human brain.

$$\underset{\textbf{Sensing}}{(1)} \Rightarrow \underset{\textbf{Meaning (Facts/Interpretations)}}{(2)} \Leftrightarrow \underset{\textbf{Manipulate/Create (Ideas/Plans)}}{(3)} \Rightarrow \textbf{Action}$$

This might seem arbitrary at first, but it actually comes from the structure of the brain itself. Referring to the model we discussed in chapter 2, the first step deeply engages the back cortex, and the last engages the front cortex. But the intermediate stage shown in step 2, engages *both* sensory and motor cortex. Also, I indicate that this stage is reversible, using the double-headed arrow. Unlike sensory experience and motor actions, which cannot be reversed (we cannot un-sense, or undo, things), we can discard a meaning or an idea. In fact, analyzing our ideas often leads to discarding them, and discarding them opens the way to new ones. This dynamic nature of step 2 partially characterizes what we call "thinking."

With the brain, the overall flow, from sensory experience to action, is forward. But when we add stage 2, that flow now includes large regions of what has been called association cortex. In the human brain, these regions take up far more area than any other part, and it is the ability to examine their activity and function that has led to our understanding of what I am calling the "deeper" path. Scientific study of these regions of cortex was nearly impossible until the last few decades. It was much easier to manipulate sensory input and measure motor output than to either manipulate or measure internal associations. Now, new techniques have made it possible to more directly examine the processes of thought, itself and, to some extent, emotion.

Integration Cortex

Although the term *association* is still commonly used, at this point I am replacing it with the word *integration*, and with the symbol "I" as shown below. I first got this idea when I read William Calvin's *How Brains Think* and came to believe that *integration* is more accurate. It implies combining things together in a way that generates a complex pattern or structure to create a new unified whole. For example, a "skylight" associates sky and light, but it also makes a new whole out of the two separate parts, which are integrated.

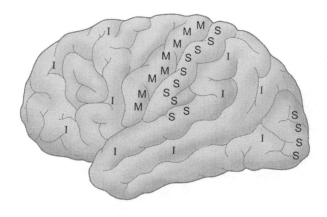

In the figure above, I have indicated areas of cortex that have sensory function (S), motor function (M), and this integrative function (I). As shown, the integrative cortex is spread out over both back and front regions of cortex. Also, it takes up much more cortical surface than does either the sensory or the motor cortex. This distribution of cortical function makes sense when we remember the sensory-motor kind of learning discussed in chapter 2. Very early in life, these regions of cortex are the primary ones involved in experiences, even preceding mimicry. They are primarily involved in the earliest steps of the journey toward mind. But they are primitive and limited in their functions, just as they are in the amount of cortex allotted to them. It is the integrative regions that provide the resources for development of complex human intelligence. That is, through the much greater amount of cortex allotted to them, those regions have the nascent capacity to extend the journey toward mind.

These regions of the integrative cortex are heavily involved in step 2 of our model, above, the part that seems most like mind. Clearly, they are critical for progress in our journey from brain to mind.

Back Cortex Integration: What About Mike?

I will discuss the back integrative cortex and front integrative cortex separately, beginning with the back and its function of creating meaning from experience.

An example of back integration that creates meaning is the process of "naming." We use this process to encode our sensory experiences in language. This naming phenomenon can be understood as an integration of an auditory process (hearing the name) with another sensory process (visualizing the face) Eventually the two components (the name and the image) come together in the mind. This integrative process becomes ubiquitous, and eventually we develop labels for almost everything.[1]

The story about my friend Mike gives us another example. He could not integrate letters to form words. It wasn't that he didn't know the words. He used them in his speech, and he recognized them when someone else used them. He had no trouble sensing the letters on the page, although we don't know if he could distinguish some of them from others, as sometimes happens in dyslexia. But whatever the cause, Mike just couldn't integrate combinations of letters into his existing understanding of language or his memory of specific sounds and letters.

Although I still do not know the cause, I do have some thoughts about it. One comes from the discovery that the visual cortex is able to integrate the *edges* of objects. These edges create an outline of what we are seeing and areas of strong contrast; they give us its *form*. With written language, those edges differ for each letter, and when we integrate them we recognize each intact letter itself. For example, the letter X consists of two edges crossing each other in the middle. Mike may not have been able to integrate the edges that form the letters. Maybe he couldn't distinguish the letter X from the letter T. Maybe AX and AT looked the same to him.

A second aspect of back cortex integration that is central to reading is the perception of the spatial relationships between the letters in words. This kind of integration might also explain Mike's difficulties. An example would be the difference between "bat" and "tab," with "b" at the beginning or end of the word, and vice versa for "t." Mike may have been unable to see the key difference in the location (spatial relationship) of the "b" and the "t." If so, he may not have been able to integrate the three letters into a single word.

Integration, Category, and Relationship

In the preceding example of back cortex integration, we can see two very fundamental ideas. The brain separates our ability to recognize *what* things are (is it a *b* or a *d*?) from recognition of *where* things are (where are the *b* and the *t* located?). It turns out that there are actually specific regions of cortex for *what* and *where*.

The *what* region is the area that responds to physical form defined by the edges of things and also to color. Important examples are faces and objects. Beyond this, the integrative function in this part of the cortex also allows for generalizations. Things that have similar edges are lumped together in categories. For example, human faces, four legged domestic pets (cats or dogs?), or different kinds of furniture (tables or chairs). Creating such categories, or generalizations, is one of the most useful abilities the brain develops with experience. It is essential for success in school.

The same is true for the kind of integration that defines spatial relationships: *where* things are. Telling *bat* from *tab* requires us to identify the location of the letters, to see where the *t* and the *b* are in relation to the *a*. Beyond recognizing written words, this capability applies to objects and their relationship to other objects (a fence in the backyard—an object in a place), and even metaphorical relationships such as sequences (one thing comes before another), size (an elephant is larger than a man, which is larger than a cricket), motion (the car is moving, it drives past us, and up the hill beyond; its spatial location is changing), and even value.[2] In the last example, judging what is *of more value* engages the spatial region of the back integrative cortex. Its physical meaning is that item 1 is of more value than item 2 (the spatial metaphor is that 1 is in front of 2).

What (category) and *where* (relationship) are cornerstones of mind.

Integration Takes a Slower Path

The quotation by Lewis Thomas at the beginning of this chapter, an eloquent description of making meaning, vividly describes the process of integration. To paraphrase Thomas: "We gather new information, think about it, identify categories and relationships, engage with it in creative ways, and eventually we understand."

This integration processes contains many elements that contribute to our idea of "mind." One of the more important elements is time. There is a sense of reflection and deliberate pace in this image. There is no rush to understanding; it cannot be forced or accelerated. Rather, almost unconsciously, we grasp new parts of the whole, and one day we understand. Things come together; they are integrated. This may take time, and we cannot predict when, if ever, the process begins or ends.

It is easy to overlook this time factor. It seems to have gone out of style since technology has evolved as a primary tool for education. But the fact remains that, for development of the mind, we must have time to reflect on the sensory data and to recall relevant memories.[3] We recognize new insights suddenly and unexpectedly at some point after an experience, but we can't predict when that will happen. Often it happens when we are focused on something else, not paying strict attention to much of anything, hardly using our mind at all. In fact, speed may be counterproductive. Trying to speed up comprehension may distract us and obscure important aspects of both *what* and *where*.

Subconscious Reflection

I hinted above that reflection times are not necessarily times of mental inactivity. In fact, from the beginning of its cellular life, each neuron in our brain appears to send out signals at least occasionally, even when it is not activated by specific input. This "background" activity of neurons is probably necessary for their continued survival, since developing neurons often die when they fail to make functional connections with other neurons. Truly "quiet" neurons can become dead neurons.

This background firing is not necessarily random; whole pathways may fire. For example, in research with mice, brain neurons kept firing even when the animal was anesthetized. Although sensory input is virtually zero (unconscious mouse), cortical sensory neurons still send out signals. In the visual cortex, the patterns of such unconscious neuronal activity resemble those that typify waking visual experience.[4] In the absence of new experience, the representations of past experience are replayed.

A mind is restless. Rest-less!

Sleep: Time for Integration?

This restless nature of mind makes us wonder what is going on when we sleep. We spend roughly one third of our time sleeping. Is it possible that this is one way nature gains time for learning? Is the mind awake when we sleep?[5]

Many experiments suggest that sleep may enhance learning. For example, it has been observed that people who are learning a new game, and are interrupted by falling asleep, perform better at the game right after they wake up. However, the improved skill that is evident after waking is fragile. If we do not practice again soon after awaking, the gains made through sleep are at least partially lost.[6]

Monitoring activity in the integrative cortex has shown that when we first fall asleep, the specific regions of cortex that were most active when awake continue to fire. At this initial time in sleep, other regions quiet down. Then, remarkably, as time passes, the active areas of cortex begin to fall into deep sleep patterns, eventually giving signs of sleeping even more soundly than the rest of the cortex ("local sleep").[7] The region that is most active when playing the game eventually becomes least active; it sleeps the soundest!

Since it focuses on what we call *procedural* learning (learning a skill), this particular example of learning a game may not seem highly relevant to school subjects or to development of abstractions that are more typical of the curriculum. But sleep also facilitates development of insight. For example, the recognition of patterns that are inherent in repeated tasks—what we might call "shortcuts" or "hidden rules"—are enhanced by sleep. In the research describing these results, the authors say, "[S]leep, by restructuring new memory representations, facilitates extraction of explicit knowledge and insightful behavior."[8] The "memory representations" are networks of neurons in the brain, and the "extraction" process is the awareness of these networks that facilitate the shortcuts.

Sleep can be "time used," rather than "time lost."

Child to Adult: Maturation of Mind

As a last point about the back integrative cortex and "meaning making," let's revisit the example in chapter 2 of a baby becoming aware of light coming from a window. First, the baby perceives a distinct line of contrast at the edges of the window (notice the *what* and *where* in window edge) in her room. Later, the edges that enclose the window define a new object, the window itself. Even later, the spatial location of the window (it is in the wall separating inside from outside) leads the child to understand the window better: it lets light into the house. The child learns to move things closer to the window to see them better. Later, the child may realize that seeing things better reveals physical relationships better, and from there it is a small step to the metaphor of casting light on ideas or *shining light on a subject* so we can understand it better and become *enlightened*. Even later, in college perhaps, the young adult may encounter the term *enlightenment*, and connect his or her original insight with understanding a historical period in philosophy. As adults, we become aware of more complex ideas, identify new categories, and see new relationships throughout a lifetime of personal growth and development, as we construct our own "enlightened" philosophy of life.[9]

Back integrative cortex lays the foundation for insight and understanding. It plays an essential role in the journey toward mind.

Changing Gears: A New Kind of Integration

This is a good spot to pause and become consciously aware that we have reached a major turning point in this discussion of integration. Now we will turn to the kind of integration that characterizes the *front* integrative cortex. This integration involves the *intentional* combination of separate networks of neurons to solve a problem.[10] Here is a mundane example:

> I recently bought a small pickup truck with four-wheel drive. I didn't think much about it at first, but when I tried to shift from two-wheel to four-wheel drive I discovered that I didn't know how. So I taught myself.
>
> First, I thought about shifting a car with a standard transmission. I already knew how to do that, so I just activated a network of neurons already in my brain. I then examined the lever on the floor of my truck that was labeled "4W." Since I had never seen such a lever before, examining this one generated a new network of neurons that mapped out the structure of the 4W shift lever and the direction I wanted to move it (from 2W to 4W). Then I tried to combine the old network (how to shift with a standard transmission) with the new (the 4W drive lever.) While the truck

was rolling along, I put my foot on the clutch and pushed the 4W lever the way I would with a standard transmission.

It didn't work.

I then envisioned a new scenario in which the truck was stopped while I shifted. Eventually, putting together all these old networks and parts of networks, I discovered the answer. I learned how to shift from two- to four-wheel drive smoothly and without paying much attention at all. All I had to do was bring the truck to a stop, move the shift lever from 2W to 4W, and then take off again.

Do you see how this is different from back cortex integration? If not, let me try another example.

This purposeful kind of integration is also used to create language. It must occur when we write or speak. We intentionally recall appropriate words and scripts (meanings) from memory and organize them in new ways to create sentences and paragraphs. If those sentences do not quite fit the images we are trying to convey, we manipulate them more by adding explanatory language or perhaps removing words. As far as we know, this is a continuing process of creative integration that occurs only in the human mind.

As you can see, the capabilities of the frontal integrative cortex are significantly different from those of the back cortex. In fact, the front cortex's capabilities begin to explain key parts of the mystery of thought, cognition, and even intention. Here are a few of these differences and capabilities: Creative integration does not involve working with large amounts of data at a time. In general we can mentally hold and manipulate an average of seven distinct elements (words, images, numbers, etc.) simultaneously. This may seem like a drawback, but it is also an advantage in that we are not required to work with highly complex scenarios during creative integration. The process only requires us to remember this limited number of specific aspects that are part of each problem or task. (I provide more information and examples of this highly important subject later in this chapter when we discuss *working memory*.)

Another fascinating capability of front integrative cortex is that it can be driven deliberately by our desires; we use it to achieve our goals and objectives. It is driven by need and intent, rather than by chance. Creative integration is an active, rather than reflective, process. This means that we can change our purpose at any time. We can change our reasons for thinking, which will then change the content of our thoughts. We can discard specific facts and ideas and replace them with others. We can choose what we want to think about and what problems we want to work on and play with them in our mind. We can identify the elements that make up our thoughts and move them around in our mental pictures as we work toward a specific goal or purpose. We can discard things that do not serve our purpose and add things that do.

All this freedom! All this choice! This is what makes creative integration creative. And it is what we value! It is central to the human species.

Origins of Creative Integration: Making Plans

For our species, creative integration is what gives us our great advantage in natural selection. Although today, in our advanced culture, we may think of creative integration as a tool for modern activities, such as inventing new devices, playing mental games, or dealing with academic challenges, over evolutionary time, the most important capability it provided was simply the ability to make practical plans. The purpose was survival, so we made plans for hunting, for keeping warm, and for escaping danger. Eventually, as agriculture emerged and developed, we made plans for next year and plans for the crops. The better our plans, the better our chances for survival.

Although the challenges are different, the task of making a plan still serves as a useful model for understanding front integrative cortex. Let's look at an example.

How do we make a plan? Let's presume that fate has decided the purpose of our plan. We find that we have a flat tire, so our purpose is clear. We want to fix it and drive home. We can turn to the two aspects of creative integration I mentioned above: selection and manipulation. We must *select* specific memories and facts that are essential parts of our plan, and we must *manipulate* the sequence of actions we will perform to solve our problem. We try to recall specific facts and experiences that are part of changing a tire. Such facts might include the image of the tools needed (jack, wheel wrench, spare tire) and their location (in the trunk of the car). Relevant experiences would be remembering the last time we changed a tire or watched someone else do so. These are all parts of the solution; they are the things we need to solve our problem. We must know what they are if we are to solve the problem.

Manipulation involves arranging these parts of the problem into a sequence that will allow us achieve our purpose. The plan is basically the idea of how to change a tire, the sequence of steps. First, get the jack and tire out of the trunk. Then loosen the bolts holding the wheel to the car, but just a little bit. Then jack up the car so the tire can be completely removed. Then put on the spare tire and tighten the bolts. Finally, lower the car back to the ground.

This process is a concrete example of creative integration. We can do the same thing with more abstract challenges. We can imagine how to solve a math problem by selecting the right equation, identifying the key bits of information that must be part of the solution, and then proceeding through the steps of placing key facts into the correct place in the equation.

In all this, however, we must remember that our plans are not actually true solutions. We will only know whether they work when we put them into practice and test them by action. Until then, they are just abstractions of solutions that exist only in our mind. They are just ideas and plans. Predictions are products of the mind, but their value can only be proven by action!

Machinery for Planning: Working Memory

The primary machinery used for actually carrying out this "purpose setting" and planning is that of working memory.

I discuss memory in general in a later chapter. Here I focus not on the memory part, but on the *working* part. The front integrative cortex contains neurons that behave in a unique and suggestive way. They fire when stimulated, but continue firing for at least a short time after the stimulus is gone.[11] Because they keep firing without a stimulus, we say that they remember the stimulus.

This firing is not just in single neurons, since all neurons are connected to others. Rather, it is a network of neurons that represents the memory of the stimulus. The firing does not last a long time. It may continue for a few seconds to a few minutes, but eventually it disappears. Furthermore, the effect of the "remembered" stimulus can disappear instantly if a second stimulus interferes. This behavior is highly suggestive of what happens with short-term memory in general. For example, if we are trying to remember a phone number when our spouse begins to talk to us about something else, we may forget the number.

Different working memory cells in front integrative cortex respond to different stimuli. On average, as shown in the figure below, those in the upper area of this cortical region respond to stimuli related to spatial information, just as in the back integrative cortex. Those in the lower part of front integrative cortex respond to stimuli related to object information and category, just as in the back. That is, the front cortical regions that are engaged when *working* with category or relationship are the same as those in the back integrative cortex engaged when *perceiving* category or relationship.[12]

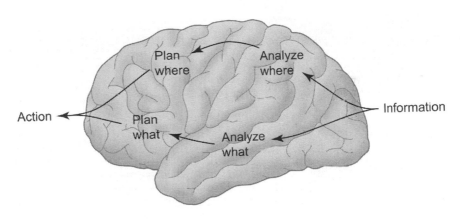

The actual planning process involves attention to objects (*what?*) that are in a useful category (tires and jacks for changing tires) and manipulating the relationship (*where?*) between those objects in time and space (jack before spare tire, spare replacing flat) such that the plan achieves its purpose through action.

We solve problems by integrating and manipulating *what* and *where.*

More About Working Memory

With our model for flow of information from the back to the front of the cerebrum (ending in action), we must remember that for most pathways in the cortex, signals go in both directions. This is especially important when we are trying to solve a problem or searching for an idea. These tasks engage working memory in front integrative cortex, which dynamically communicates with memories and information in back integrative cortex. This exchange is essential in problem solving and idea generation. It is all part of the work.

One reason why remembering is work is that it requires attention. As mentioned above, since working memory is limited in the number of items it can hold at any one time, it is susceptible to distractions. If we are suddenly challenged by a diversion, we may even change or lose the contents of working memory. Bringing in something new can drive out something already in place. We can prevent this if we pay attention to the central aspects of the tasks we undertake, keeping out distractions.

The contents of working memory are fragile. We may be able to control them by paying close attention and refusing to let in distracters, but when we do that, we may alter the perceptual processes that are disrupted by the distractors. For example, if we are trying to remember a random sequence of seven numbers, we have to work. We rehearse the numbers periodically by saying them to ourselves. If someone interrupts, for example, by showing us a picture of a friend, we either have to take our attention away from the picture or focus especially hard on retaining the number sequence. The image of the friend and the number sequence *compete* for space in working memory, and when the image is displaced temporarily, the visual cortex becomes more active. It is as if the cortex is literally getting full; when the image of the face is pushed out of working memory (in front), it begins to fill up the visual cortex (in back). It becomes more difficult to remember the number sequence.[13]

This research clearly suggests applications in education and learning. When we are trying to solve a problem, we heavily engage our working memory, put it to work, and dynamically replace its contents with new information as we create the solution. In that case, we need new information in working memory. It appears that we turn not only to memory, but also to increased use of sensory cortex in searching for additional information in the environment.

To solve problems, we can use *all possible sources of new information*: working memory itself, long-term memory, and exploring the immediate environment with sensory and perception areas of cortex. When a student (or anyone else) is struggling with a problem on the blackboard, we see the student's eyes continually looking back at the board for new clues. When we find ourselves unable to figure out how to change a tire, we go back to the trunk of the car and look for tools or other clues about how to proceed.

Thinking engages multiple areas of cerebral cortex—a characteristic of mind!

Front Integrative Cortex and Ownership

Until now, we have focused on *mechanisms* of thought—the mechanics. Cognition also has strong affective elements, and the emotional aspects of learning and problem solving are as important as the mechanistic ones. An example of this is the sense of ownership. Learning is greatly enhanced when a student takes ownership. In fact, it is almost guaranteed!

Perhaps the strongest feelings of ownership come from our belief that we own our own bodies. It is *my* body! However, damage to the *where* region of the back cortex can prevent us from recognizing our own body. For example, we may not understand where our legs are. Oliver Sacks writes about such a case in *The Man Who Mistook His Wife for a Hat.* Sacks describes a man who threw himself out of bed because he was convinced that the leg he saw in bed was not his own. He was very upset that someone else's leg was taking up his space, and he literally fell out of bed trying to remove the alien leg, which turned out to be attached to his own body.

This condition comes from brain damage. However, we may simply be fooled about ownership of body parts. A recent neuroscience experiment[14] used this fact to examine which parts of the brain are most active when we decide we own something. In what is called the "rubber hand illusion," people become convinced that a rubber facsimile of a hand is actually their own hand.[15] The moment the illusion takes over, a small region of front integrative cortex increases its activity. The specific part of the front cortex that becomes more active was the general region we would expect would be involved in organizing hand movements. In action!

Where does this lead? Is there a connection between ownership and action?

Our actions are the way we reach our goals, and our goals are created in our mind. We own our goals, they are ours, so voluntary movement of our body is at the core of ownership. It is the *voluntary* part that makes this so. As noted above, the integrative front cortex uses working memory to organize a sequence of movements to accomplish a goal. This planning precedes the actual movements, although we are normally not aware of the planning phase (the *idea* phase) in such movements. Thus, in every sense of the word, we own our plans for action. If we can generate the ideas for purposeful movements, develop them, and carry them out, we must own them!

Integrating Education and Life

Let's now turn our thoughts to education. To begin, let's go back to the challenge of integrating schooling and "real life." The failure of this integration is strongly related to the idea of ownership. Some students and their families do not take ownership of their schooling. In their mind, formal education belongs to the teachers and principals or other authority figures, or maybe even the other students. Parents, particularly, may separate themselves from their child's school or college, even expecting teachers to take on parenting.

This is a category problem. We put the process of education in a different category from "real life."

Forming categories like this is one of the important capabilities of the mind, but sometimes the categories are misleading or unhelpful. They create a separation and obscure potential opportunities for enrichment of the learner; opportunities for seeing connections and new directions. Sometimes it is important to break down or at least blur boundaries of this sort.

We may be able to do that with school when everyone feels ownership. The emphasis is on *everyone*. Some students and families do take ownership, but there are also those who feel excluded. It is very important to identify those excluded students and their families and make special efforts to draw them into the school community and integrate their lives with their school. This kind of integration deepens the personal meaning for such families and provides opportunities for educators to reach the students who otherwise might become the most problematic.

This challenge arises more in grades K–12 than in preschool or college, graduate, and professional school. It is in the K–12 years that students begin to realize that they are being sent *off* to school, where they categorize *school* subjects as distinct from *real* life, and where they learn *school* behaviors. It is where the idea of separateness is established, and where school begins to be dis-integrated from the rest of life.

We may only begin to reintegrate school with life when we enter graduate or professional school and are allowed to follow our own interests and focus our energies on learning that relates to our own goals. Even there, certain aspects of school often remain dis-integrated. For example, medical students may not see the connection between the basic science part of their curriculum and what they view as the true practice of medicine.

The image of school as *separate* is powerful and long-lasting. It is a major barrier to development of the mind, leads to simplistic thinking, and discourages depth and complexity of thought.

What and *Where* in Education

There are physical barriers to better integration of education into our lives. These barriers start as physical, but soon become mental. By design, school buildings are separate from the buildings where we live and work. Students are walled into their grade at first, and then into their subject. First grade is physically different from fourth grade. Rather than an integrated story, the model of education becomes one of leaping from one mental space into another.

When things are physically separate, they also become mentally separate. It is easier to view the group "over there" as different from ourselves, even to decide that they are the enemy. The enemy is in the next room, the chemistry lab. We are defeated the minute we enter that space. Rather than a flow of experience that might take us through several different, but related mental "spaces," we may break up the flow because we have constructed separate categories of knowledge. This fragmentation disrupts the story of learning.

An example of this dis-integration, and the value of reintegrating school and life, is apparent in a story one of my friends (we'll call her Sally) told me. She teaches elementary students in a city public school, and in one class she encountered a student (we'll call him David) who was smart but never completed his homework. One day it occurred to Sally that since it is called "homework," she would try to get David to see the connection by walking home with him and meeting his mother. Sally realized that it might not be enough just to talk to David's mother; David would have to be part of the discussion, too. So the three of them had a conversation about school in David's home. For the first time, his school experience was integrated with his home experience. On his turf! The school had come to his home.

I know this is not a unique example. Creative teachers find many ways to make better connections with their students' parents and even their homes. But the brain's perspective, in which school and "real life" are separate categories, may make this challenge more evident. There are real barriers in the mind that must be overcome if school is to be meaningful. Overcoming the barriers will take planning and energy.

But once the barriers are breached, the term "breakthrough" may also take on concrete meaning. This was true for David, his mother, and Sandy. All three of them developed new understanding that would not have been possible any other way. His mother connected with the school; she began to take ownership. Her knowledge and understandings grew beyond the school building. Sandy connected with the home environment and probably the most important person in David's life. And, for the first time, David understood that his mother and his teacher both cared about his learning. He could learn school subjects at home and could learn about home at school—*his* school!

Integrating the Subjects

Using categories to understand the world is so powerful and so habitual that we may not see the possibilities for integration. An example of this is the separation of math and language. This separation is essentially a habit we seldom question. We teach children (and adults) that quantitative and verbal skills are separate and different. Thus, many students and parents come to believe that they are good in one and bad in the other. To account for this, we keep them completely separate in education. The curriculum separates them, and on standardized tests they are considered almost the opposite of one another. We give separate tests and scores for them, and we expect that a highly verbal student might not be good in math, and vice versa. There are math skills and verbal skills, and it has become acceptable to have one but not the other.

Is it possible that this categorization is an impediment to learning? Does it fail to recognize that language and math have a great deal in common? Could more integration lead to more learning? For example, from the earliest grades, or even before "grade" school, we might ask students to write or speak about the relationships in arithmetic. And conversely, we might ask students to *calculate* the meaning of a sentence. We might say, "How do the words and the arrangement of the words add up?" Or "Does one part of the sentence subtract from another part?" Or "How does this sentence equal that sentence?"

We discuss these ideas more extensively in a later chapter on the role of symbols (such as letters and numbers) in cognition and their use in school. In the meantime, we can already see that integration gives us some provocative ideas about schooling and about the categories we create and then take for granted.

Categories can be walls of the mind. We should ask ourselves whether they are helpful or hurtful. Both can be true. Do they give us a lift in the journey toward mind, or are they blocking our progress?

Time Pressure

We are infatuated with speed and organization in school. This infatuation comes from our belief that learning can be produced by setting time limits and imposing structure (curriculum and classes). As stated earlier, it is not accidental that these features of school developed around the time when mass production emerged. We had become highly efficient in the production of machines, goods, and products. Why would we not strive to become highly efficient in the field of education as well?

But the concept of integration leads us to some ideas that are quite different from speed and efficiency. Many of our deepest insights take time to develop. There seems to be no specific recipe for integrating things, and certain structural features of the brain seem designed to slow down reflection. The slowness, however, is generally not a drawback. On the contrary, it is usually a good idea to take our time when we are trying to fit new experiences into some meaningful framework for our life.

Sleep in Education

An intriguing opportunity for integration occurs during sleep. Note that I did not say "dreaming." It is fascinating to consider that new ideas may occur to us in dreams, but some research now suggests that deeper sleep, beyond the dreaming stage, is a more effective mode for developing new ideas and insights.

My personal experience leads me to think that exploring the role of sleep in school might be a good idea. When I was a young man, I was quite impatient with sleep. It seemed like a waste of time. If I, like some of my friends, could only get along on less sleep, I would reach my life goals sooner. But I slept anyway. I needed a minimum of seven hours, it seemed, and sometimes I would sleep longer. Alarm clocks were remarkably ineffective. And if I did sleep less at night, I would fall asleep during the day. It was a losing battle.

Had I known then what we have learned about sleep in recent years, I probably would have behaved very differently. I would follow the model that I have developed for myself in recent years. This model begins with working very hard until I become aware that I am struggling. I might feel drowsy or have trouble paying attention, but the key point is that I am *conscious* of the feeling of inefficiency and ineffectiveness. When that happens, I don't fight it. I can just take a short nap. If that is not possible I change my attention to something else for a few minutes. I may go to the window and see what is going on outside. But as soon as I am aware that my break itself is distracting me, or I wake up, I immediately go back to the computer and plunge in again. The overall strategy is to work hard, allow for some subconscious reflection, then work hard *again*. I don't end things with the nap. I end them with work.

Could schools use this model? If so, would the day be structured differently? Would we go from class to class without some intervening time for a break, or even a nap? Would we interrupt our classes, take a nap, then go back to work on whatever we were doing? Would we encourage students to start hard problems before they went to sleep at night, and then finish them in the morning? Could we just slow down and wait for our integrative back brain to catch up a bit? Would we let sleep be integrated with learning?

Education and Front Cortex: First Priority

In the preceding sections we focused on back cortex integration and education. Now let's turn our attention away from experience and reflection and toward prediction and action. Let's focus more on getting involved and putting our own ideas to work, rather than worrying about getting more information, or waiting for new connections to reveal themselves. Let's consider what it might mean if we go beyond mimicry and focus on practicing the front cortex stage of integration.

Here is a proposal to begin this discussion: School actions should come from student thinking. They should be generated by the mind of the learner!

If I had the power to change schools, this is the first change I would try. I believe that ownership is the most significant and effective aspect of learning. If I want to learn something, I want to make it mine. And when that need is strong, I will find a way!

Practically speaking, I would search for ways to challenge students to develop and test their own theories, propositions, and explanations. I would try to discover and eliminate the practices that prevent students from doing this. I would put the learner at the center of front cortex integration.

As I argued in chapter 3, I would try to design ways that students experience the joy.

Working Memory: Consider the Limits

One of the best routes toward ownership is learner success in solving problems. This is most likely to happen when educators have a good understanding of working memory. Let's review a few key features of this kind of memory, to be sure we are on the same page.

Earlier in this chapter we saw that working memory is very limited but highly flexible. A good approach in using it is to identify a small number of key elements to "work" with. For example, we need to know the subject, object, and verb for a sentence (three things), or the cause and the effect for an explanation (two things). Success depends on defining small numbers of central elements in any experience, rather than extensive and complex explanations. Brevity and clarity are the virtues.

In school, this suggests that we should arrange students' experiences in direct and simple ways. This may be the most difficult part for the educator, since that individual must put himself or herself in the place of the learner. With complex situations, the first step would be to identify a small number of very basic elements. That might even be enough for a whole class period (if we even had classes). Taking working memory as our gauge, we might have shorter classes, or they might be of variable length rather than a set time. Deciding when to end a class would not be a matter of watching the clock, but of watching the ideas. The point would not be to have a lot of ideas, but exactly the opposite. I might judge success not by how much information was "covered," but by the significance and utility of the ideas, and by how much impact the ideas had on students.

We might have an "idea clock" rather than the time clock.

Dependency

If we were to implement suggestions like these, we would need to address the issue of dependency. In school, students learn to depend on teachers for instructions, assignments, behaviors, and information. In fact, we value this dependency and encourage it.

I have suggested that such dependency is an enemy of learning. The education exercise focuses more on the educator, less on the learner. Dependency does not exercise the front integrative cortex in the learner, and so it does not support either ownership or problem solving. It will be worth while if we can shake free of this habit by shifting more control from educator to learner.

I am not talking about chaos, and I am not suggesting that the educator would have no role. Instead, the educator would solicit ideas from students. His or her goal would be to lead students to awareness that the process depends on them. The students can generate their own ideas about *what* they would like to learn and *how* they might go about it. We can expect them to use their own integrative front cortex to address the challenge of their own learning.

In this model, teachers would provide opportunities for discovery by designing and organizing student experiences. They would also be guides and information sources, helping the students along, steering them away from pointless diversions, and suggesting to them where information can be found. Teachers would still give assignments, but they would be more open-ended, with an emphasis on process and idea rather than on facts.

Following are some examples.

A teacher might say, "See what you can find out about rats and how they live. Then write a story or an explanation of some part of what you discover that interests you." Or, to be even more general, he might ask, "Tonight I want you to think about our class and write a short story about what happened. If nothing interested you, write your story about something you wished had happened."

At the very least, assignments like these require students to use their working memory and organize their thoughts with regard to time (first this happened, then that happened). This requires manipulation of items in working memory and, in the act of writing the story, students develop ownership. The students might actually own their homework.

This approach is not limited to the school part of our journey toward mind. Parents might do the same things with preschool children and even babies. The action does not need to be writing. It could be telling, or acting, or even mimicking. Choosing what we mimic, and organizing the sequence of what we mimic, always engages the front integrative cortex.

Giving Up Control

I am aware of common objections to the approaches I have suggested. Those objections always surface when we consider giving freedom to learners, be they babies or retirees. One such objection is stated something like this: If people are just allowed to follow their interests or their own ideas, how can they learn the things they don't even know about? As a teacher or parent, it is my responsibility to tell them about the basics. For example, when you learn chemistry, you have to discuss atoms, bonds, reactions, and so on, but students may never pursue these topics unless I assign them—unless I am in control.

I used to worry about this, but the worry decreased as I gained more experience. In fact, I now feel downright optimistic; my faith in learning has been restored. I have found that when I allow students more choice in what they study, they ultimately end up discovering the things that I would have chosen. For example, in biochemistry, if I tell them to begin with a topic that has personal meaning to them (let's say a paragraph in the text on diabetes, which they notice because someone in their family is diabetic), they inevitably also begin to discover the things *I want* them to learn. They discover the content of biochemistry. They realize that they need to know about insulin, and that means they have to learn about peptides (take my word for it!). The pancreas must be discussed, as must the cells that make insulin. So they have to study cells and so on. These are exactly the things I would try to teach them.

This is probably true in any subject or discipline. The gains it can produce may far outweigh the challenges of a new approach. But it does take that faith!

Education Ideas: Formal and Personal

To a great extent, the capabilities of integrative cortex coincide with many objectives and goals we generally associate with education. But we may also conceive new ideas that are more challenging and adventuresome. Some of those ideas would represent significant change and might feel risky or even dangerous. Change often has that effect, and the ultimate effect of any specific change is hard to predict. But I have taken the risk in the following, closing pages of this chapter. These are my personal proposals, and they are presented mainly for your reflection and actions. Success is not guaranteed!

Below you will find some ideas of this sort. Some may seem reckless, and others may well already be accepted practice. In addition, the list is by no means inclusive, and you might want to insert your own ideas gained from reading this chapter. If these get your attention, I will have achieved one of my goals.

The choices are yours. Take ownership!

The List

In this spirit, consider the following:

1. Education should be integrated with daily life. It is all part of the journey from brain to mind.
2. We should experiment more with integration of subjects or domains of knowledge with each other. For example, language and math might be developed together in a way that the two support one another, and are considered as one.
3. Mathematical equations should not be studied in isolation, but rather where they have actual use. My belief is that all math should be "story problems." But they should be good stories, real stories about the real lives of real students!
4. Experiences should provide continual practice in thinking about categories and relationships, in both comprehending and problem solving (back and front cortices), with all subjects, at all ages.
5. The way time is used in education should be reconsidered. There should be more time for thought and remembering. Some of this time might well include napping. We should not think of education in time blocks but as a continuum.

6. If we use classes, they should not be run on a tight and immutable time schedule. Instead of watching the clock, we should watch the ideas.

7. Teachers and administrators should relinquish some control, while students and their families should be expected to make choices and decisions about their learning. Everyone in the system should have choices at appropriate points.

8. Education should always challenge students to solve real problems. Learners should develop and internalize the generic problem-solving method based on the capabilities of integrative cortex.

9. Educators should recognize and adapt to the possibility that we often overload working memory.

10. Ownership, ownership, ownership!

Journey Toward Mind

Looking back, we can see that we have made significant progress in our journey toward mind in this chapter. Including the back and front integrative cortices in our discussion has greatly extended our understanding of what we mean by "mind" and how mind-like capabilities develop. These capabilities include setting goals, identifying relationships and categories, breaking barriers, solving problems, creating ideas, and self-awareness. And we should own all of the above.

However, many if not all of these are highly abstract. It is difficult to define features of the mind, and their meaning will differ greatly with different individuals. It will help if we can be more concrete. That is our goal in the next chapter.

The topic of that chapter is the image. Integration leads to mental images. As we bring individual aspects of experience together, as we integrate them, we produce images. And, in one way, images are concrete. We picture a specific scene or event in very concrete terms. We see real individuals, real places, and real actions in our images.

I think we are ready to address the specific, concrete, question: *What are images?* And it may be that our answers to that question will lead to more concreteness in the questions we might ask about other aspects of the mind. What are categories? What are relationships? How do we manipulate the contents of working memory using images? Do our answers help us think about effective ways to educate?

How can we help people "get the picture" and "use the picture?"

Notes

1. The introduction of language (for example, labels such as words and scripts) into the networks of the integrative cortex occurs in a particular region found in the back half of the cerebrum. This is the region discovered by Wernicke over a century ago, the area for comprehension of language. I discuss this in more detail in chapter 6.

2. Sugrue, L. P., and colleagues (2004), *Science*, 304, p. 1782.

3. In *The Art of Changing the Brain*, I speculate on neurological reasons that may explain the slowness of integration (pp. 162–163).

4. Kenet, T., and colleagues (2003), *Nature*, 245, p. 954.

5. I have often thought this might be so. If I can doze off for 10 minutes in the middle of the day, or even several times in a day, it seems that I end up making better progress than if I stick doggedly at the computer. In fact, even when I find myself losing focus and my attention begins to wander, I now tend to just let it go. I may stroll down the hall and look out the window for a few minutes, just waiting. And although it may seem like wasted time, most often I end up wandering back to the problem I left behind, refreshed and unworried about any loss, forgetting my wandering.

6. Huber, R., and colleagues (2004), *Nature*, 430, p. 78; also see very readable commentary on this work by Laura Nelson on p. 962 of this same issue.

7. Note that this is not the phase of sleep when dreaming occurs—that is, not REM sleep, which has been most often associated with learning, but has produced variable results in experiments designed to demonstrate that connection.

8. Wagner, U., and colleagues (2004), *Nature*, 427, p. 352.

9. Notice how this construction of knowledge depends absolutely on the physical environment of the developing mind. As I stressed in *The Art of Changing the Brain*, we are all limited by our own personal experiences. This metaphor of enlightenment could not develop without its attendant physical environment, or some similar environment. Thus, in cultures that do not have stair steps, people may find themselves unable to interpret three-dimensional drawings of a stairway. Our metaphors come from our environment, and our language and culture derive from our metaphors. (See Lakoff and Johnson, *Metaphors We Live By*).

10. Forward regions of the human cortex are responsible for this powerful kind of integration. We use this area of integrative cortex when we solve problems, but also when we invent things, get a new idea, or make decisions—when we take conscious control of our actions to achieve a goal.

11. Fuster, J. M., (2003), *Cortex and Mind: Unifying Cognition*, Oxford Press, Oxford, UK—discovery of STM cells.

12. This consistency between upper and lower front and back integrative cortex appears to be explained either by the fasciculi described in chapter 3 of *The Art of Changing the Brain*, or similar signaling pathways carrying signals between back and front integrative cortex.

13. de Fockert, J. W., and colleagues (2001), *Science*, 291, p. 1803; also see comment by P. Bagla on p. 1684 of the same issue.

14. Ehrsson, H. H., and colleagues, (2004), *Science*, 305, p. 875; also see commentary on this work by M. Botvinick in the same issue of this journal.

15. This illusion can be produced if a person looks at a rubber hand while holding his or her own hand out of view while both the rubber hand and the real hand are brushed lightly to create a feeling of touch. Since this feeling comes as the person is looking at the false hand, the illusion sets in.

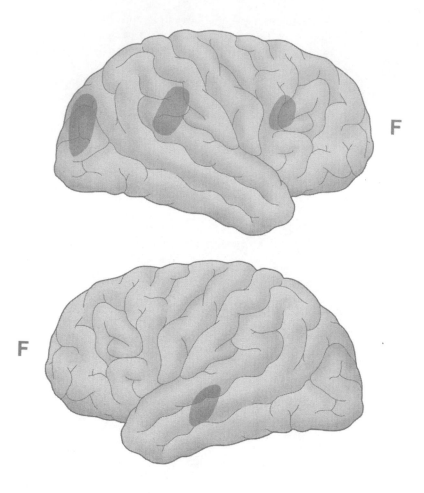

Multiple regions of cortex activated by perception of a single image (visual pattern). Top is right lateral view, and bottom is left lateral. Shaded areas indicate a firing pattern as described in the next chapter.

5

GETTING THE PICTURE

Images and Other Neuronal Patterns for Building Mind

The great mystery is . . . that we should draw,
from our own selves, images powerful enough to
deny our nothingness.

—André Malraux

I had just taken a seat in my doctor's reception area. The space was a bit cluttered with old magazines and, in some cases, parts of magazines. I picked up one of them and began to thumb through it. After a minute or two, a young woman and her preschool son came in and sat near me. The little boy looked around a bit, and then began to twist and turn in his chair, finally sliding to the floor and crawling under one of the other chairs. His mother spoke sharply to him, and he climbed back up into his own chair, but in another minute he was back on the floor crawling slowly toward me. I watched with curiosity, and as he approached, he reached up and grabbed one of the magazines. He opened it to an advertisement for a flashy red car. Soon he was shoving the magazine around on the floor, making sounds such as "vroom!" "roar!" and "eeeeeee" (the sound of squealing tires).

At this point, the boy's mother pulled a blank notebook and a box of crayons from her purse and gave them to her son. As if on cue, he put down the magazine, became totally quiet, and began to draw. He was very young, and his work impressed me. Clearly he was drawing a car. Then he colored it red. After a minute or two, he turned to a fresh page and drew another car, this time blue. Then, proud of his work, he showed them to his mother. She praised him and then said, "Now why don't you draw a black one?" She handed him a black crayon. He took the crayon, thought a minute, shook his head, turned the page, picked up another crayon, and began to draw another car.

It was yellow.

The first thing I noticed in this little event was how natural it is to make an image. This child obviously had done it often and wanted to do it. It just came naturally. Be it with a crayon and a piece of paper, a stick on a sandy beach, or a doodling with a pen in the notebook's margins during a lecture, the instinct to create images seems almost universal.

Recalling our earlier discussion of mirror neurons (chapter 2) may help us understand this naturalness. The brain has neurons that are wired so that they perceive things and then do them—mimicry. With images, this natural capability of the brain is extended to depiction. When mimicking becomes difficult, or is impossible, we may find ourselves making a copy. Creating images is a step beyond mimicry.

The story also suggests another reason why the copying instinct is so natural. It can satisfy our need to be in control, to make our own decisions, and to choose our own actions. When we make an image, we control things. We all make our own version. And if someone else tries to control our "image-ing," we may rebel.

It's a yellow car or no car!

Images and Mind

Images come from the integration process discussed in chapter 4. They are a mental picture assembled from individual bits of sensory information that are brought together in an integrated form. Images emerge from experience and convey the forms contained in experience—the physical structure of those forms. Among other things, they tell us the shape, size, and movements that define an experience.

Images are also an integral part of mental manipulations. Thought, memory, and attention all seem to operate via images. The connection between images and thought is so extensive that the verb "to see" is completely embedded in the vocabulary and scripts we use when writing and talking about cognition. When we say, "I see," we use this verb metaphorically rather than literally, but as we will discover in this chapter, the metaphor comes closer to the real thing than we might realize. We do, in fact, use the visual brain when we reach that sense of understanding. We picture things in our minds.

When we say we have an image of something, it is a claim that we understand it. We have the picture, and that claim is one we make with confidence. We "believe our own eyes" when we recall images of things we have seen in the physical world. Beyond that, we often believe images that we have *not* seen with our eyes, but have produced in our mind. If we can imagine, then we can believe. This is why I used the quotation from Malraux at the beginning of this chapter. The images we have about ourselves generate beliefs about ourselves, and one of the most powerful of these beliefs is that we are not "nothing." The reality of the image suggests a "somethingness."

Images are also highly memorable. I wrote about the research on images and memory earlier[1] so I will not go into detail here. Suffice it to say that when we are shown pictures, we are very likely to remember them. We may not absorb every detail, and we may not understand the images in a deep way, but research suggests that our ability to remember images may literally be unlimited. When shown an image, we almost always know whether we have seen it before.

Images also draw our attention. When we pick up a magazine, we often look first at the pictures. We are used to creating meaning through images, and we anticipate that they will be interesting and informative. In our mind, our life is a trail of images, one leading to another to another. The signposts along our journey from brain to mind consist of images. Our brain senses the world, but our mind comprehends it, and the vehicle that carries us along this journey is the image.

Seeing With the Eye, Seeing With the Mind

Images are visual. This sounds obvious, but when pressed we may not be absolutely sure what it means. We can get images through the sense of touch, which may actually happen in the womb, but when we imagine the form of something we touched, it does seem that we "see" it. One way to understand this is to realize that when we attend to images, visual regions of the cortex become engaged. This is true whether we literally see with our eyes or use our mind to visualize. There is no light in the brain, but still we see.

The difference between direct perception, actual *seeing*, and intentionally imagining helps us understand the journey from brain to mind. The *seeing* part is more appropriately attributed to brain. But visualizing with our mind is a different process, more related to memory. We remember form and features. We can replicate these by drawing them or talking about them, and such replication makes them more concrete and similar to physical seeing.

The Substance of Image

In earlier chapters I addressed the role of images in mimicry, setting purpose, data integration, manipulating ideas, and decisions to act. Now we can add more substance to these abstract ideas and make them more concrete. In short, I will try to explain what images are.

There are no photons bouncing around in our brain, but what does bounce around is electrical energy. When photons strike the cells of the retina of the eye, those cells generate electrical and chemical changes ultimately leading to electrical "action potentials," which are simply electrical changes on the neuron surface. There they trigger new action potentials in subsequent neurons that are part of the network. Electrical energy moves from eye to cortex, and from one region of cortex to others.

The image is the *pattern* this electrical energy makes. The pattern is different for every visual experience, but that difference arises from the experience itself, not from the retina or the brain. The substance of a mental image is a pattern of electrical activity.[2]

Images and the Senses

The sense of sight gives us information about shape, location, color, texture, and movement. We can also get some of this information through our sense of touch. However, there are limits to the amount of information obtainable by touch, since we can only get it when some part of our body physically encounters the object. Nevertheless, our sense of touch can be of great value. Helen Keller gained much of her factual knowledge of the world, and eventually of language, through her sense of touch.

The actual physical phenomenon touch detects is pressure. There are pressure sensors in our skin; thus, we can map the pressure changes generated when we press our hands or other parts of our body on objects. These sensory data also generate patterns of neuron firing in the brain. If I press my finger on a spot on my keyboard, it will generate a pattern of electrical firing in my sensory brain, just as vision does. And if I drag my finger across the keyboard, I will generate a series of electrical patterns similar to what takes place when I watch a video.

The other senses (hearing, smell, and taste) can also generate images in our mind, but this process is different from visual and tactile sensing. We cannot determine the shape of a rose by smelling, but the fragrance triggers our memory of an image. We can remember what roses look like and call up the image of one when we smell it. The same is true of sound and taste. The sound, taste, or smell of things trigger our memory of real objects in the world, but do not generate the image themselves. Rather, the memory actually consists of the same *pattern* of neuron firing that is activated when we look at the rose.

Vision and touch are not the only senses that directly generate an image. Another sense is called *proprioception*. This sense generates patterns of neuron firing that come from our body as we move, or as we hold our bodies in a particular posture. These images are not objects in the outside world, but rather of our body itself. We sense the position of our body and its parts through the pressures and tensions generated at the joints, tendons, and muscles. That information is integrated into our brain to create an image of our body in space. We can see our body and its position and posture in our "mind's eye."

This is an important part of our sense of self and our sense of ownership. It is also essential for purposeful actions such as those we discussed in chapters 3 and 4. For example, we can only kick a ball when we have an accurate image of where our foot is and how it is moving. And when we do kick it, it is our kick!

Patterns and Codes

In our efforts to understand the mind, we sometimes speak of "decoding" sensory information. This suggests the idea that the direct information from the experience must be translated into a form the brain understands. Such a translation would require a code, and, if it were true, discovering the code would be a mammoth accomplishment.

The reasons for our belief in a code are complex. Perhaps our success with the biological code in heredity (the genetic code) nudges our thoughts in that direction, but the idea of a brain code seems to precede that of the genetic code. There are other potential sources of the decoding concept, such as "breaking the code" of an enemy in wartime, the Morse code, and so on, but it may be that at the root of this idea is our natural love of patterns as well as the romance and power of coding things. Patterns imply structure and, by implication, a code. It is easy to think that a code would simplify, and without it everything would be too complex. And an explanation based on emotion also suggests itself. Discovering a code feels good. We love to think of ourselves as a very clever species, always able to break through mysteries with our intellectual powers. Maybe we invented the idea of a code just so we could break it.

However, in agreement with Hawkins[3], I believe it is very unlikely that such a code exists. In fact, the concept itself may be a detriment to our understanding. It is not a code that gives the brain its power. Codes are limited and limiting; they depend on rules and symbols. In contrast, only the actual numbers and character of individual experiences limit the number and character of electrical patterns in neuronal networks. As long as we can capture all the different patterns, we don't need a code.

In the next chapter I return to this idea and discuss what we call the "symbolic" brain. Our ability to create systems of symbols such as language or numbers, and to use those systems in problem solving, remembering, and predicting, is one of the most important aspects of the journey toward mind. In fact, in the history of our species, it was the *invention* of such symbols that led to the immense breakthrough that we identify today as language and mathematics.

But even so, these coding systems do not imply an inherent code system in the brain. We did not discover or break a code when we invented language and mathematics. We created them.

Patterns and the Cortex

If images are patterns of electrical activity, where are these patterns inscribed?

The answer to this question is simple, but may be difficult to grasp because of the complexity of brain structure. The answer is "on the cortex"; however, that answer does not always satisfy because it is difficult to get a good image of cortex. How can a pattern (a "regularity") reside on something as irregular and uneven as the cerebral cortex?

What image describes cortex? Here is one. Depending on your age, you have wrinkles on your skin. Some of these wrinkles are shallow folds in the skin, and some are deeper. In any case, you can see that your skin folds up and down, in and out, over parts of your body such as your face or hands. If you flatten out the skin by smoothing out the wrinkles, the area of skin seems greater. Actually, the area is the same. The skin (in all the ups and downs of the wrinkles) is always there, whether it is folded or flattened.

The cortex is like this. It is the skin of the brain, with deep wrinkles. Overall, it takes up an area equivalent to about six pages of this book. Like the book, information is recorded on those pages. It is recorded, however, not as language but like a drawing on a sheet of paper. And the drawing identifies the form of real objects in the real world.

Images are electrical patterns on the surface of our brain.

Qualia

As a biologist, I frequently take note of things that Francis Crick wrote. This is the Crick who, together with James Watson, discovered the structure of DNA. Later in his life, Crick changed fields; he began to study the brain and to develop theories about consciousness. I suspect every biologist followed Crick's life with interest and admiration.

In his writing about the brain, Crick often used the word "qualia," which is the plural form of the Latin noun "quale," meaning *what sort*, or *what kind*. It is often used in attempting to explain the qualitative or subjective aspects of objects and experiences. Crick didn't invent the term, but he found it useful to describe certain aspects of the mind. We can speak of the qualia of a rose, and by this we mean such things as the intensity of its redness, the magic of its fragrance, and the feelings generated by its beauty. Qualia are derived from real and physical aspects of the world, so we are conscious of them, but they are not images and they can't be measured. They are qualitative.[4]

The senses of smell, taste, and sound make us particularly aware of qualia. To access the knowledge provided by qualia, we rely on emotion and feelings. Smelling a rose generates pleasure, tasting vinegar generates discomfort, and hearing music can generate either, depending on what kind of music it is. The knowledge gained from these feelings is subjective and individual. Some like rock music and some don't. There is no right answer to the question, "Is rock music beautiful?"

Are qualia related to images in any way? The image itself is not a quale, because it has very specific size, shape, and form. We know whether an image represents a ball, but the way a ball makes us feel is subjective and qualitative. For me, if it is a baseball, it might make me fearful, since I was once hit by a baseball. So the qualia associated with a baseball, for me, are things such feelings as "tension" or "concern." But (as you well know) I also played a lot of basketball at one time, and once I scored nearly 20 points to help my team win a game. So, for me, the qualia associated with basketball are feelings of "beauty" or "sweet."

Images in themselves are not qualia, but they may generate body feelings that identify qualia and thus enrich our knowledge about images. Sound, smell, and taste modify our response to images. Thus, the electrical patterns generated by the image itself may be linked to other electrical patterns produced by emotion to produce feelings in the body. These links give personal meaning to images, meaning beyond the image.

Qualia are a major factor in the diversity of our images. They make experiences memorable, meaningful, and unique. Since the qualia are derived from our individual experiences, they contribute strongly to the feeling of recognition. We realize that certain images have been part of our real life at some time. When we "get the picture," we get more than the image. We get recognition. We get qualia.

Variance in Images

Everything we see produces a pattern of electrical activity on the visual cortex. In fact, each produces many patterns. Perhaps, if we could look at the same object from exactly the same perspective over and over, then the pattern would be the same every time. But that is impossible. Even slightly different perspectives generate a different pattern of light on the retina and thus a different electrical pattern in the visual cortex. For example, the electrical pattern generated from light bouncing off my key ring lying here on my desk will be different if I turn the ring over. It will also be different if I move my head or if the light changes slightly

When observing something visually, often we do not need very precise clues to guess what it is. We can get enough information to trigger a more careful look and focus on more details. Those details depend on the actual physical properties of what we see. My key ring has about 10 keys and my flash drive, which is gray. A couple of keys are much smaller than the others. These invariant properties will confirm that it is, indeed, my key ring. They are essential.

Conditions like those described in the paragraph above produce variance, but ultimately they do not prevent me from identifying the key ring. Images that have a few of the physical properties I expect are enough to trigger a more focused second look. Some variance in initial perceptions can be tolerated and produce good guesses about what we see, at a minimum. Another way variance is tolerated has also been discovered recently. In experiments with mice, it was found that images that are perceived close together in *time* can be accepted as part of the invariance.[5] In the natural world, objects or individuals are often moving, so the perceived form changes from instant to instant. The movement generates a sequence of images, like the frames in a movie, and each one gives a different perspective. In this case, the images may be greatly different physically, but their closeness in time suggests a shared identity.

Invariance and Reality

Invariance is key in our understanding of images. It is derived from the real features of real objects and experiences. Invariance confirms reality. The sensory brain has evolved to give us information about physical reality. If it did not, we would have found no use for sensory information and probably would have discarded it through natural selection.

Knowing what is real has been essential for survival of our species. It allows us to predict events and outcomes, invent tools and other objects, and have confidence in our perceptions. The invariance is part of the truth about the perceived world. It allows us to plan, manipulate, and design, because it is true.

At the same time, our individual personal experience leads to a somewhat different collection of invariant characteristics, and this collection becomes part of the uniqueness of each perceiver. This is one aspect of our diversity. Each of our minds develops differently, but we all still reach accurate and shared concepts of the nature of the real world. Those images are the same in their invariance, regardless of our individual differences in perception. To a great extent we all end up with categories and relationships on which we generally agree, but which we recognize are also somewhat different. Our journey from brain to mind includes this recognition of both invariance of objects (there are facts) and diversity of images (and there are interpretations.)

Leapfrogging Patterns

Imagine you are in a dark room and can see nothing. Suddenly a single image flashes on the room's white wall for a tenth of a second. Let's say the image is a checkerboard pattern. What happens in the cortex as you first sense the image, and then recognize and name it?

The development of a powerful brain-imaging method made it possible to do this experiment, tracing the activity of different regions of cortex in real time. Events that take only a few hundredths of a second can be detected, located, and separated from each other. This new method, referred to as MEG, is described at the end of this chapter.[6]

I bring it up now because this method has given us insights into the flow of images through the cortex. Specifically, the checkerboard experiment did not suggest a continuous flow of electrical energy along the cortex, but rather resembled leapfrogging. This is shown in the figure on page 121.

As you would predict, the electrical energy is localized in the visual cortex first, on both right and left hemispheres (1). This takes a bit over a tenth of a second. Then the electrical pattern "leaps" to the *where* region of cortex on the right side (2). This takes about another tenth of a second, and its location suggests that the cortex is analyzing the spatial location of the dark and light squares—the checkerboard pattern! Next, the signals leap to the right frontal cortex (3), near an area known to be important for spatial working memory and decision making. This takes about another tenth of a second, with the time apparently being dedicated to holding the image temporarily and working with it. The work is to analyze the image and decide what it is. Finally, the signals leap to the left/back cortex (the *what* region-region shown in light lines) (4). This final destination is the area where categories are named and identified in memory. The signals did not leap directly to this last region, but rather arrived there via a pathway through the front parts of the cortex on the opposite side. The leaps were not only from back to front, but also from side to side.

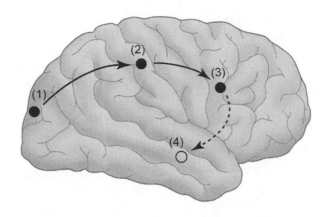

(1) Sense object   (2) Integrate spatial features   (3) Decide "what"   (4) Attach label

The figure above is my suggested interpretation of these results. The sequence of brain functions is: perception of an object, analysis of relationships in the object, deciding what the analysis means, labeling the object, and putting both the label and the image into memory.

It sounds a great deal like *mind*.

Overlap of Patterns

We can perceive an unlimited number of different images. At the same time, we can identify their similarities and thus what general category they fit into. For example, there is a region of the cortex that responds mainly to faces and distinguishes a particular face from another. With practice, this even applies to the faces of identical twins. The mind groups things together, but still distinguishes differences in those things.

There is much to be learned about how this happens, but one important generalization is the notion that we can identify and separately classify sub-patterns of larger ones. For example, a corner of a door and a corner of a window are sub-patterns of a door and a window. When this sub-pattern is found within a larger one, we look at the complete pattern to decide whether we are seeing a door or a window.

Images are composed of common patterns of firing that are integrated with other different patterns. The like and the unlike can be combined in a large number of ways, and this allows us to build new knowledge using old knowledge. The overlapping patterns are often the key to identifying things we have not seen before.

Images contain building blocks for comprehension. These blocks are the invariant physical aspects of the real world.

Rearranging Patterns

Images are also essential for problem solving, creative thought, and generating ideas. Particularly, patterns in the front integrative cortex can be held in working memory and rearranged, both intentionally and unintentionally. Ultimately the rearranged patterns can be reproduced through action, such as in mimicry, or used to make a plan for actions, as I described for grasping in chapter 2.

The ability to manipulate patterns in our minds is required for many aspects of thought. For example, a pattern may have a gap, such as in the following sequence: xxxxdxxx_xxdx. Our inclination to fill in the missing part (in this case, a "d") leads to what we call "interpolation." And if the gap is at an end—that is, if the sequence ends too soon—we may extrapolate. If we extrapolate in time, we call it prediction.

This manipulation of patterns of electrical activity in the front integrative cortex provides a potential explanation for thinking, creating, and solving problems. The explanation is as follows: we select bits of images; hold them in working memory; and move them around mentally on a timeline, or a space map, or both (in fact, they may be the same). We do this to get each of those images into a new relationship that is itself a new image, the image of our desired outcome. We imagine what we want to have happen, and then arrange the separate bits of the image in a sequence that ends with the image we want at the end. Ultimately, the images constructed internally in this way can be physically created in the real world in real space/time using our motor brain to drive muscle movements (motor programs). The motor brain is a central component in cognition. We use it when we mentally rearrange (manipulate and move) small bits of the world, or symbols of these bits, to imagine solutions to problems.

Doing all this rearranging triggers specific feelings. Qualia enter the process. We rearrange for a purpose, and if there is progress, we feel good. For example, if we are sorting apples according to size and we see that the smallest apple is in the middle, it feels good to move that one to the end where it belongs, getting closer to our goal. And in getting closer to the goal, we experience feelings of ownership both for the idea to move it and the action itself. After all, we imagined what we should do, and we actually did it ourselves.

We control both the idea and the action; they must be ours!

Primacy of the Image

Patterns of electrical firing on the sensory cortex are the first product of sensory experience. They can be used, alone or together, to construct meaning and ideas. They exist before language, before thought, before numbers, before any other mental capability or process. In our context, the journey from brain to mind, these patterns are a product of the brain, not yet in the category of mind.

As we have discussed, these patterns are generated by any sensory experience. In this chapter I have focused on the visual and the image, but it is also important to remember that patterns are generated by the other senses such as sound and touch. In humans, the visual sense is more powerful than the other senses, but it is the reproducibility of the patterns that makes them so valuable. Regardless of the sensory origin, all patterns can play a role in the journey toward mind. Many of them become central for cognition.

However, this centrality may not always be positive. Images may also interfere with development of the mind, and it may be difficult to overcome such barriers. We may come to believe that certain things are impossible or even choose to discard particular images. One image can block another. For example, we may have a certain image of a subject, such as calculus, that blocks our ability to perceive a different one. Often, our images become control points for further learning, either blocking or enhancing it.

Babies begin their life in the world with the patterns of electrical activity that have been generated by their experiences in the womb. Up to then, the womb has been their school. But once we leave the womb, there is a major change in our education. We now have experiences in an open and infinitely varied environment. We have *life* experience—life outside the womb. Our sense of vision improves dramatically, and our ability to create and perceive images explodes. Ultimately, those experiences begin to include school. We approach this learning with our earlier images and their attached qualia already in mind. The earliest and most powerful images are likely to be ones of home and family, but whatever patterns come from experience, those are the patterns that begin our education.

Education and Images

Recognizing the primacy of images can significantly influence our thoughts and ideas about education. Such recognition leads to fundamental questions about how education should begin, what the first experiences should be, what teachers should attend to, and how they themselves should be educated.

If the goal is to establish neuronal firing patterns that can serve as a foundation for comprehension of the outside world, the images that are of greatest value are those of real objects and people, rather than those produced by the symbols we use to represent them, such as the alphabet and numbers. I believe that babies build these "foundation images" from direct experience with the realities of the world when they see, touch, and hear physical objects and events without awareness of or reference to the academic subjects of language and mathematics. If vision is the most powerful "pattern generator," we should provide children with visual experience of "foundation images" as soon as their vision begins to sharpen (the first few months.)

What are "foundation images"? An illustration of the concept, which I mentioned earlier, is a right angle. In the world of buildings and other man-made structures, the neuron-firing patterns of right angles are continually triggered in the brain. They are the building blocks of more complex images. Another example might be the human face. The general pattern of mouth, nose, and eyes is a foundation image essential in the experiential world involving people. If this theory of perception and integration, also described in earlier chapters, is correct, then cognitive development might be enhanced by experience with these building blocks before encountering more complex images. If so, how would we prepare new teachers to take such an approach? Should we significantly modify the way we educate educators? Should teachers become "image experts"?

General Rules

In what follows, I try to address perspectives and approaches that may not have been emphasized in education, using our idea of the *primacy* of the image. These include both practical methods and conceptual arguments, ranging from topics such as use of videos and computers to concepts of "self-image." I do not try to be all-inclusive, but I do hope to be provocative and to stimulate you to develop your own ideas about images in education.

Let me propose a few rules about images. You already know one of them, the start early rule. Starting from birth, children's experiences should be rich with images. This should be a conscious objective. Be it in the crib or the classroom, educators should focus on preparing and designing relevant images. Educators should ask, "What is this child going to see?" "What do I want to show this child?" This rule applies with learners of any age, whether or not they are in school.

A second rule is that learners should see things in varied and flexible ways. One important variation is movement. As I explained earlier, perception of images close to one another in time, such as those generated in movement, generates recognition of the underlying invariance. An example of this would be physical objects or models of objects that can be held, played with, and explored visually from different perspectives. Included in this idea of movement are phenomena consisting of regular and predictable change, such as those implied by mathematics (adding things, dividing things, multiplying things), and others consisting of less predictable change such as play with a puppy or human behaviors.

A third rule is that experience with images should not be rushed. Learners should have time to perceive details. Time is needed if learners are to gather new images by exploration, form image collections that reflect their personal experiences, and compare them. Playing alone at their own pace will allow learners to develop new images and to enjoy their control.

A fourth rule is to think actively about whether the images educators use are likely to be are memorable. As I mentioned at the beginning of this chapter, memory may depend less on our inherent ability and more on experiencing memorable things. It is not easy to predict the images that will be remembered in any experience, but I suspect that educators could develop skills that help, just by paying more attention to the question, and by studying what has been observed about children at different ages. In the following section I try to give you an example from my own experience.

What Is Memorable?

This experience occurred when I was a child and was attending the one-room school I described in chapter 4. One particular day, a class of older students (older than I) was learning about different kinds of clouds (cirrus and cumulus) from the pictures the teacher held up. Since the class consisted of older students, it was natural for me to be interested. I was always curious about what the "big kids" did. So I learned something about clouds, as you must have noticed. But on this day I found myself more interested in observing the behavior of the students than in clouds. In particular, I was watching my friend Tom repeatedly try to put his arm around Sarah, who was sitting next to him. That memory remains firmly in my mind today. Even as I write about it, I am picturing those students and behaviors in my mind, 60 years later!

That may seem unpredictable, but looking back, I can see that it is natural and unsurprising. If our teacher had asked herself what memorable images could be found in that class, she might have predicted it. An image-aware teacher might even have used it as a tool for recall, a cue for images of clouds.

I did, of course, remember things other than those related to Tom and Sarah. In fact, looking back, I realize that this experience favored memory formation in general. For example, often when I see a boy putting his arm around a girl, I remember the types of clouds. Also, as an observer, I was free to interpret what I saw, even though much of the meaning remained below the level of language. I didn't try to explain anything to myself, but later simply remembered and reexperienced images of clouds. They became recognizable and I felt I understood them, without "teaching."[7]

Cut and Paste

You may be surprised at this heavy emphasis on images. It may even seem that there is nothing new. Much of what I have said already goes on in almost all elementary school classrooms. Almost inevitably, the walls are covered with images, both those from articles and books and others constructed by the students themselves. In some of these, students have cut out images from newspapers and magazines for illustrative purposes, and in others they have pasted different images together to construct new images using the cutouts in new and different contexts. Clearly, early education in schools already stresses the use of images, both as aids to comprehension and as components in assembling more complex new images—that is, both for back cortex and front cortex functions.

However, I am concerned that even with these standard practices we may have lost track of the reasons they have become standard. The brain perspective may help remind us of some of those reasons, and if we regain our awareness of the centrality of images in cognition, we may also recognize new ways to use them. How often does a teacher explain why images are important? How aware are learners of their value for learning? How often do we think about why children are making images, or comparing them, or cutting them out of magazines, or copying them off the Web?

This emphasis on image is frequently less apparent in higher education. The walls in those classrooms are nearly bare. Students spend most of their time copying things off the blackboard, or taking notes either on computers, or, sometimes still, with pen and paper. Cut and paste is for children!

I write more about this in chapter 6, where we discuss the use of symbols to describe images (language, mathematics, and music). Here, I will just remind you that serious thought about education leads us to realize the value of images for learning at any age, or background.

An Image Event

Without developing a specific recipe, let me plant the idea of a regular event designed to draw a learner's attention to the value of working with images. Such "image events" could become part of the curriculum. They might be organized by educators in any class, school, or even crib.

The regularity and repeated emphasis on images would emphasize their importance in comprehension and also provide practice in observing and analyzing images. In school it could center on a theme, a concept, an activity, a news story, and so forth. Students would be asked to choose and bring in their own images. They could work singly or in groups. They would develop good habits for examining images—good practice! They would have a lot of freedom, not only in the images they choose, but also in explaining their choices. Their individual contributions, thus, would become more personal and unique, focusing on images they see in their own daily experiences. This would result in integration with their life experience, as I discussed in chapter 3.

For different students, different images would stir different emotions. These images would differ in their qualia. They would go beyond form, shape, and color, bringing in emotional, qualitative content, such as serenity, beauty, anger, sadness, excitement, success, determination, and failure. In this way, learners will begin to pay attention to qualitative aspects of experiences, which they ultimately must learn to analyze and *judge*, because we cannot put a number on them or assign a geometry to them.

We may not be able to predict what images will engage the learners, and, I suggest, that should not even be a conscious goal. We should not be upset if students show more interest in images that are not particularly engaging for us as educators. Students will choose images that intrigue *them*.

As always, it is about the learner.

Extending the Action Connection

It may seem that this emphasis on images conflicts with my argument that schools should be about action. How can students be active if they are looking at pictures? But as we saw above, images naturally engage the action brain. The most obvious route for action is through mimicry, but when we cannot mimic something, we may try to draw it or color it.

There are other connections between images and action. When we study the images we make, we begin to use the integrative brain more, to see relationships, and to generate our own ideas about the image. This leads to actions directed at improving the images and, often, to the production of entirely new images. Images beget images.

The inclination to copy and manipulate images is natural, but it can also be frustrating. We may encounter barriers. For example, as children, we quickly learn whether we are good at making images. Many of us are dissatisfied with the images we try to make and just give up. "I am not an artist," we conclude.

But I suspect we never totally lose our interest in drawing. At least this has been true for me. I have not tried to draw anything for a long time, but even as I write, I am tempted at this moment to leave the computer and try again.

Or maybe we don't need to leave the computer. There are now many ways students can create and manipulate images on computers. Scanners are inexpensive and images can be cropped, repositioned, overlaid with each other. Colors can be modified. Drawing programs allow anyone to create new images, make them three-dimensional, and modify them extensively.

This seems to be a use for technology in education that has not been exploited as fully as it might be.

Movies, Videos, Etc.

In the history of recorded images, the invention of moving pictures has to be one of *the* central technical events, if not the most important one. It allowed storytelling through images and ultimately became a nearly completely separate science and art. Beyond their static appearance at a moment in time, behaviors could now be captured in all of their complexity. Ultimately, movies, videos, and television, became a major part of daily life and, inevitably, of education.

The moving image catches and holds our attention. Children are more likely to sit still when watching a movie or television program. That fact alone tempts educators to incorporate videos into their professional plans and practice. Movies and videos have become a routine part of our pedagogy in schools and in informal efforts to help people learn. We may even assume that they are equivalent to personally demonstrating ideas and skills.

However, moving pictures also have their drawbacks when it comes to learning. Ironically, these drawbacks arise from the fact that moving images increase the viewers' attention. When we look more carefully into the nature of movies and the human behaviors they produce, we may find ourselves wondering whether increased attention is always good. Might it actually be an enemy of learning?

Attention has come to imply quietude. But as we have seen, learning involves more than quiet and focused reception of information. It requires us to use not only the functions of our back regions of cortex, but also the creative and active front cortex functions. Attending will enhance the experience of watching, but if the experience is to generate learning, it must also engage the front cortex functions. Learning is enhanced when we develop explanations and predictions from what we perceive and initiate actions to test those explanations. We must transform the information we receive into ideas, plans, and actions, making something personal and new from what came through our senses. Taking ownership in this way is essential for learning, but the movie may seduce us into taking the easier route of just watching.

Other aspects of videos and movies may interfere with learning. Again, it is the movement, the action itself, that is the culprit. Things can move too much, leading to superficial perception. Mere recognition may replace careful and repeated study of images. We may lose depth and accuracy. Instead, we sit back, relax, and enjoy the film! It is fun to watch and see how the story goes, who wins the battle, or whose heart is broken, but there may be no sense of effort or purpose. A video is "just a video."

At such speed and superficiality, it is just entertainment.

A Moving Target

We are not going to get rid of movies and television in education. They are an integral part of pedagogy now, and although we may resist, ultimately it seems better to search for accommodation with this fact and look for its positive aspects. Can we do that? Can the modern educator keep the video, indeed, all technology that uses movement as I described above, but address its shortcomings—even turn it into an asset?

Two ideas present themselves. The first is simply to slow things down. If we are willing to take the time, we might well watch the video more than once. As we all know, watching a movie or video several times greatly deepens our understanding. Or we might "freeze frame" the video at key points, allowing viewers to inspect the images, discuss them, and map them out on the neocortex for future recall and study.

We also can separate the sound from the images to reduce the sensory content in any moment in time. This is highly brain-compatible. Despite all the hype about multitasking, our perception and comprehension are increased when we attend to either the visual or the auditory at any one time. Language research shows that we comprehend a great deal without actually hearing the exact words. Visual information such as that in gestures and facial expressions can be as valuable as spoken language. In addition, watching a video without the sound encourages the listener to postulate meanings and to actively test those postulates by replaying with the sound. Both of these processes, the postulating and the testing, are inherent aspects of the brain's cycle of learning, since they engage front cortical regions.

Videos can produce a passive frame of mind, rather than a creative one.

Images and Motivation

The power of images is their effect on the interest of the observer. Based on their experience and natural interests, students will want to arrive at their own interpretation of images. An image becomes personal as we interpret it and speculate about its origin and meaning. It can raise completely different questions and thoughts in different individuals. Encouraging students to describe what a particular image means to them will stimulate them to engage with it and begin to create new mental images. It will contribute new steps in the journey toward mind.

Another motivating aspect of images is that they can provoke the mind to "imagine" movement, origins, causes, and destinations. The image came from somewhere, and it suggests that there are now places to go. What happened to produce this image, and what will happen next? This sense of movement and goal-related thinking is pleasurable. It activates the motivation and pleasure centers of both the ancient structures of the brain and the dopamine pathways in frontal neocortex, which we discussed in chapter 3.

Even still images suggest movement. Specific aspects of one image may remind us of another one. We discover new possibilities and are motivated to explore them. We find ourselves expecting discoveries of this sort, predicting them, and looking for them. This discovery, expectation, and prediction are naturally rewarding and motivating.

Images can be an important tool for developing *intrinsic* motivation.

Movement as Completing the Image

An image is a pattern, and to be accurate, the entire pattern must fire in the cortex. However, patterns may often, perhaps most often, be incomplete. We may see or hear only a part of the whole. And when this happens, our predicting front cortex wants to know what is coming next. Will the pattern become complete? Will our predictions come true?

When recognized, an incomplete pattern is an annoyance to the mind. Almost always when a pattern seems disrupted or incomplete, we try to fix it. We may perceive part of an image, and immediately try to identify what the intact image might be—to complete it. Or we may hear a few notes of a tune, and then spend the next few minutes trying to assemble the whole tune, or at least the melody. This instinct seems to exist at all ages. A conceivable explanation is that we already have complete images that are derived from our experience, so we recognize incompleteness when it occurs. The incomplete is unsatisfying.

Incomplete images are not to be confused with ones that seem just plain wrong. Distinguishing the wrong from the incomplete is evidence of progress in the journey toward mind. Incompleteness suggests that there is more to do. We should act! We should complete the image. I suggest that the action of finishing the incomplete activates the reward system in the brain. We want to act because it gives us a sense of progress. That sense itself is strongly related to the brain's reward systems.[8]

On the other hand, a "wrong" image makes us want to start over, maybe even erase the wrong entirely. Often when writing, we will cross out, erase things, or throw away pages that end up sounding wrong. Perhaps the flaws are not large in number, but we still throw away the whole "wrong" thing. It disturbs us because it implies blocking progress and preventing movement. It is painful.

It has been recognized that teachers can make good use of this phenomenon. If we expose students to incomplete images, charts, or graphs where progressions are not finished, students become motivated to work on them. This suggests that rather than focusing on giving complete right answers, or detailed accurate images, educators might even invent ones that contain errors. The goal is not just to see the right image, but also to be able to know why it is right and to provoke interest in making it right.

In mathematics and science, completing images is a common method used to solve problems. We may need to interpolate data on a graph by filling in a blank spot or extrapolate data to obtain information about where a process is headed, or where it began, at the extremes. This is done by calculations in math, using equations that show relationships. Filling in the image, then, can occur when we use the equation to obtain the missing piece. This perspective may be of value to students if they can apply it to solve real problems, fill in the important parts.

Images and Creativity

Creativity is one of the most valued aspects of a mature mind, and images often are the stuff of creativity. We conceive a new image, and suddenly it leads in directions we have not imagined before. The conscious human mind can intentionally manipulate images by engaging the front cortical regions of the brain. The "work" of working memory often involves such manipulation. Here I attempt to illustrate two forms of this kind of creativity.

The first kind of manipulation is *rearranging* familiar images in new ways. The following quotation from Gabriel García Márquez's *Love in the Time of Cholera* is useful for illustrating rearrangement:

> She remembered when she would go walking . . . and clench her teeth so that her heart would not leap out of her mouth as they approached the telegraph office.

The familiar and complex images of teeth, heart, and mouth are presented in a way that leads our minds in totally new directions. We understand clenching teeth. Among other things, we see it as a sign of courage, determination, restraint, and tension. The leaping heart is a metaphor we recognize instantly. At some time in our lives we have all experienced that surge of feeling in the breast, brought about by sudden hope mixed with fear (could this be love?). But the image of literally clenching the teeth to keep the mouth closed and thus retain ownership of the heart is a new one. It brings all these emotions together and conveys the sense of danger that a leaping heart suggests. The heart might literally leap to its death because of joy and hope.

New ideas emerge from old ones.

A second type of creativity involves *replacement* of one image with another. A medical example may help us consider this. Generally, blood tests determine whether we have normal amounts of various substances in our blood. For example, there is an average (normal) level of sugar. If your level is higher or lower than normal, then a physician will suspect that you have some sort of metabolic disorder.

This way of thinking was initially used in interpreting a blood test for prostate cancer, the PSA test. This test was developed many years ago, but over time it became controversial. Like blood sugar, it was believed that a PSA value above normal meant trouble. However, it turned out that this belief was not useful. Frequently, an above-normal PSA did not prove the presence of cancer. A person could have a high PSA and be just fine. Eventually, some doctors decided not to do the test.

The image for this test might be a thermometer. When temperature registers above a specific level, things are bad, just like they are when the summer temperature goes above 100 degrees. But this was the wrong image. It was not useful, and a new one was needed. Creativity was needed!

Replacing the thermometer image with that of a barometer turned out to be helpful. With a barometer, it is *change* that matters the most, rather than the absolute reading. Rapid change in pressure leads to violent weather. And it turned out that this was often the case with the PSA test. Prediction of prostate cancer is more successful when PSA values increase significantly than when the level is consistently higher than normal.

Images can be vehicles of creativity. The image itself is a pattern on the brain, but manipulating images is a function of the mind.

Connecting Images and Qualia

Earlier I suggested that, although the physical form of an image is derived via the senses of vision and touch, the other senses (smell, taste, sound) strongly influence the impact of images. This influence is in the form of emotion. For example, if someone shows us a picture of a beautiful child, we may respond in an emotional way: "My, my!" The emotion is created by the image, but described by sound.

Sometimes the qualia in images are predictable, but often they are unique and surprising. I am reminded of the response of one of my relatives when she saw a blimp sailing quietly above us in the sky one sunny day. She literally covered her eyes to block out the image. I was astonished to hear her say that blimps made frightened her and made her feel deeply disturbed. She could not explain this response, and I had no explanation for it myself. Now I view it as an example of qualia associated with an image. But I still do not understand it.

We do know that this type of response to an image is the result of activating our fight-or-flight (adrenaline) and/or our reward (dopamine) systems. These systems directly modify synapses and play a role in brain plasticity, so it is not surprising that identifying the qualia in an image will have an impact on meaning and memory. Educators can take advantage of the emotion-cognition link if we challenge students to go beyond images and focus on qualia. Borrowing the script from our psychiatrist, we can ask, "How does that image make you feel?"

Self-Image: The Learner

One of the most compelling and confusing aspects of the human mind is the images we have of ourselves. Even in a single day we may imagine we are skillful, beautiful, heavy, weak, awkward, competent, happy, serious, silly, and so on. The worry about how we seem to others, the images they have of us, can be all-consuming. We understand the world with ourselves at the center. Our perception apparatus is our own brain, and it divides the world into parts that are to our left, our right, above us, below us, behind us, and even ahead of us. This is true both physically and metaphorically. Things to one side are less important than things in the center. Things above us are more important than things below us. Just as a photograph shows things in relationship to the camera, so our theories and explanations of the world start with our theories and explanations of ourselves and our place in our world.

Self-image is of great importance in education. It strongly influences both the learner and the educator. Educators (especially parents) tend to believe they can intentionally control or change the self-image of a learner: "We have to increase Jimmy's self confidence!" But for the most part, attempts to do so end up failing.

Understanding how images are formed in the brain can help us explain the futility of these attempts. Our images are inscribed on our own cerebral cortex. They originate in our own experience, and only new experience can change them. It is relatively futile to tell children that they can "do anything." Their self-image does not contain the idea of someone with super-powers. We overestimate the impact of our words on the image in others' minds. Those images belong only to the learner, so the most probable outcome of such a claim is distrust and confusion, both enemies of learning.

We cannot tell a learner, "Don't believe your own images." We might ask, "How is this new experience related to what you thought before? Do these new images remind you of anything? Can you see yourself doing that? Could you mimic what you saw?" The goal is not to see ourselves "doing anything," but rather doing one thing. And it does not matter *what* students can see themselves doing, but that their self-image allows them to imagine success in *something!* There will be times and experiences that challenge every student, but there *must* also be those that result in success. Finding those experiences is one of the most important goals for an educator.

There will be no journey toward mind if every path leads to a dead end.

Self-Image: The Educator

Educators may also be ineffective because their self-image is false. By its very nature, the responsibility to educate generates pressures of this sort. It is impossible to deliver the correct answer to every question, but to admit ignorance or resist the temptation to guess, or even just invent an answer, is a constant part of the profession. Educators cannot have both a true and a perfect self-image at the same time.

Failure is only bad when we view it as a personal flaw; when we see ourselves as deficient. We should recognize that the inability to perform well in some aspect of our life is not judgment on us; it is information for us. If our self-image says that we are able to deal with adversity without being destroyed, it will be a huge boost in our journey toward mind.

Being Mindful

As we think more about images and education, we find a seemingly endless list of new insights and applications. One picture is worth a thousand words! Literally.

However, this chapter cannot be endless, so to wind things up, I will try to touch on three additional points, the goal being to remind you of certain things, but not go into detail, to keep you mindful.

First, we should be mindful of the complexity to which I just referred. Even simple images trigger complex ideas and emotions. Entire books have been written about single works of art. A tiny stroke of the brush would change the Mona Lisa's smile. A single line drawn on a representation of a molecule would change all the chemistry that one could write about that molecule. Details are important.

Second, it takes time to discover such details—another thing to keep in mind. Reflection is central. Experts on a subject quickly recognize and integrate the details in images, but novices take longer. Even when a teacher states the important points, these are not instantly integrated into the student's mind. But educators are often reluctant to take such time. We are always in a hurry, even when we are not in school. Even when we are educating ourselves, it is a battle to find the time.

Third, images are personal. When left alone to create images, individual children (and adults) may favor a certain kind of image. The favored subjects of our images depend on our experiences and the associations we have in our minds. They give us information about "prior experiences." Spaceships, wars, family, animals, houses, mountains, race cars—the list grows! My own period of fascination with images focused on trying to draw horses. In grade school, I drew dozens of horses, not a single one of which pleased me. Although this led me to conclude that I was not skilled in drawing, that was not the main point. The reason I wanted to draw horses was a girl! No surprise! I thought she was very pretty and I knew she loved horses. I thought that if I could draw a good one, I would show it to her!

The images that interest us come from our experiences, and nothing engages our mind more powerfully than our own experiences. Our images are clues to our minds.

A New Pathway in the Journey

What you have read in this chapter is a theory of images. The theory derives from experimental observations, but still contains much that remains conjecture. It is based on the claim that images provide a direct route to physical reality. Different images are physically different. That difference comes from the physical fact that our real lives are a sequence of our real events mapped out in time and space. Images morph into other images as our experiences are recorded on the cortex of the brain. Every experience differs from another, and, in a way, our brain creates a continuous, ever-changing, integrated image of our life.

This theory, then, says that as long as we have experiences, we will be recording new images. They are limitless, in both number and content. If this is correct, it becomes obvious that some system of organizing and describing our images could be of great value. To make any generalizations or consistency out of this blur of images, it would help, in fact, it may even be essential, to have some system, or systems, for symbolizing the information contained in images. Any living organism in which such a system developed through natural selection would have an almost incomprehensible advantage for survival. Now we will focus on such symbolic systems possessed by the human mind. The road from the blur of images to discernable and flexible symbol systems that can be learned and remembered represents a unique and immensely significant new direction in the journey toward mind.

We head along that path in the next chapter.

Notes

1. See references 6 and 7 on pg, 157 in Zull, J. E., (2002), *The Art of Changing the Brain*, Stylus, Sterling, VA.

2. Actually, patterns of electrical energy are generated by all of the senses, but only with vision and touch do they give information about physical form. So electrical patterns are the substance not only of images but also of language and music. Sensory data are electrical signaling, regardless of the origin of the signal. Sound, light, and pressure are all converted into patterns of electrical signals in the sense organs. It is these patterns that enter the brain.

3. Hawkins, J. (2005), *On Intelligence*, St. Martins Press, New York, NY.

4. It has been suggested that the term "qualia" be discarded when speaking of brain functions. I won't abandon it here, but rather try to explain its usefulness. That explanation is based on the suggestion that qualia can be viewed simply as the sum of our feelings that are generated in the emotion centers through experience. The complex mix of the emotions produced by smelling and seeing a rose, the quale of a rose, is a combination of the body's feelings arising from the emotions.

5. Li, N., and DiCarlo, J. J. (2008), *Science*, 321, pp. 1502–1506.

6. Glanz, J., (1998), *Science*, 280, p. 37.

7. In fact, now I believe that conscious teaching through explaining is quite far down on the successful guidance of learners along the journey toward mind. Explanations can easily confuse or dominate the image experience. It may be better to develop "recognition" through direct experience and reflection, leaving explanations for later if necessary.

8. The neurological basis for this argument is developed in chapter 5 of *The Art of Changing the Brain*.

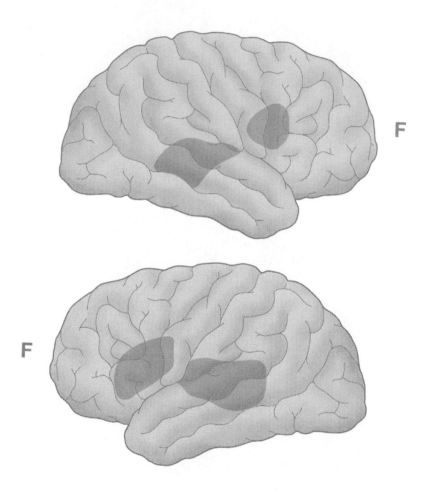

Regions of cortex activated by perception of language (back) and actual production of language (front). Top is right lateral view, and bottom is left
lateral.

6

BASICS

The Symbolic Brain and Education:
Language, Mathematics, and Music

Ex umbria et imaginibus in veritatem (From shadows and symbols into the truth!)

—John Henry Cardinal Newman's own epitaph

My department was trying an experiment in educating freshmen. Students were assigned to read books introducing biological ideas but written for the layperson: for example, Watson's The Double Helix, *or Sacks's* The Man who Mistook His Wife for a Hat. *The idea was that freshmen would be able to learn and discuss the science behind the stories.*

I was looking forward to our discussion of The Double Helix. *The freshmen had been taught the structure of DNA in high school, and they seemed very conversant with this subject. For example, even before reading the book, one student talked about DNA, explaining that it is, "a double helix made up of two strands going in opposite directions, and held together by hydrogen bonds between bases." I couldn't have said it better myself.*

However, as our conversation about The Double Helix *proceeded, I was surprised and then frustrated. It seemed that my students didn't understand DNA at all. They had no concept of the words they were using—no images. They could not talk about the meanings of things like a double helix, direction of a helix, hydrogen bonds, or bases. They could not draw even simple examples and could not see the errors or gaps in examples I gave them.*

As our discussions went on, I realized that their basic knowledge of chemistry was sorely deficient. But when I began to explain the chemistry they needed to know, they grew impatient with me. "We already know that," they argued. "We learned it in high school!"

They knew the words—the symbols—needed to describe DNA, but they did not know DNA itself. The fact that they knew the words deceived them into believing they knew the thing. Their symbolic brain had fooled itself.

Perhaps the most impressive aspect of the human brain is its ability to represent ourselves, our world, our images, our feelings, and our experiences with symbols and combinations of symbols. The two most apparent examples of this are language and mathematics. Language begins as we learn to use sounds for representing objects and experiences. The sounds are symbols. Language is a "symbolic system." Mathematics is a specialized symbolic system for exact expression of quantity or number, and for specific manipulations of quantities such as + or ÷.

Music is also a symbolic system.[1] In addition to possessing unique features of its own, music actually combines many of the essential aspects of language and mathematics such as sound and timing. In fact, some research indicates that extensive and repeated musical experience enhances development of language and mathematics skills, in addition to enriching the mental and psychological development of the whole child in unique ways.

Emergence of these symbolic systems was a defining step in the evolution of our species. Through natural selection, the human brain gained the unique ability to explain and describe both physical and mental experience. Individuals who developed expertise with these symbolic systems were more likely to survive and reproduce, as were their children. They were also more likely to remember how they survived and to tell others. They practiced these skills and learned how to express what was "on" or "in" their minds. And they were able to calculate and estimate, both of which increased their ability to solve the problem of survival.

Obviously, the development of such symbolic systems is central in the journey from brain to mind.[2] It is also a primary goal of education, so much so that we now refer to language and mathematics as "the basics." Mastering them greatly improves the likelihood of success in life.

Is There a Language Machine in the Brain?

When we begin a conversation about symbolic systems and the brain, we frequently encounter certain assumptions that can mislead us, at best, and may deceive us, at worst. One such assumption arises with language, and a second one with mathematics. Here I discuss both of them, starting with language.

The development of language is arguably the most important component in our journey toward mind. However, I want to distinguish that assertion from the common idea that the human brain contains a mysterious bit of special machinery for language. We tend to think of language as a unitary skill, unique among all other capabilities of the brain. It is usually the first "subject" in school, and we work continually over many years to improve and polish it. We speak of the inspiration needed to create compelling language, the "muse" that hovers over poets, and the sudden awareness of metaphor that expresses an emotion or a new idea. It is understandable how an aura of mystery came to envelop our ideas about language and the brain.

This aura has faded over the last few decades, but hasn't disappeared completely. Here I would like to describe what I believe is a more accurate and useful concept based on the fundamental brain functions we discussed in earlier chapters: sensory, integrative, and motor.

Let's begin with sensory cortex. Except for sign language, which I discuss briefly later, formal language is built on sound. This is not to say that meanings cannot be transmitted in other ways, for example, with gestures, but nonetheless the rule-based system of symbols used for different languages, and taught by educators, is nearly completely based on starting with sound. Sounds, then, are channeled from the ears to a sensory region of the brain called primary auditory cortex. Note that I did not say *"language* sounds." Auditory cortex is used to detect and sometimes identify all sounds, even those that have no particular role in language. For example, when we hear a bat hit a ball, we make meaning from the sound. When we scream in terror, we generate sound that has meaning. If we stick to the "machine" metaphor, it would be more accurate to say that our brain has a "sound machine" rather than a language machine.

How, then, do we make meaning from the sounds of language? Much as we discussed in chapter 4, sounds of the alphabet letters are integrated to form larger units that carry meaning: words, phrases, sentences, and so forth. The cortical region most heavily involved in this "meaning making" is not the auditory cortex itself, but rather an area of integrative cortex nearby. This region is commonly identified as Wernike's area for language comprehension. The patterns of neuronal firing produced in auditory cortex flow into this area and are integrated into images. If we are familiar with the images produced by the integrative process, we understand the language. Sensing and integrating language sounds produces meaning. We understand. We see what we hear.

However, just understanding is not enough. We also must learn to produce audible language. This production is action. Using the muscles of our diaphragm, we force air up through the "voice box," to make sounds that we modify and shape using muscles in the throat, tongue, and mouth. Generating speech is action, and it is controlled by the motor cortex. If we speak silently to ourselves, as we very often do, we are *preparing* to use the motor cortex. We can actually listen to our internal talk, organize and reorganize it, and store small amounts of it in memory. We might call this internal action.

In a way, this process of planning and organizing language is the reverse of what we called comprehension earlier. Instead of creating a mental image from the language, we create language from the image. We have these images in memories of our experience, and when we want to explain them with language, we have to get mentally organized. To do that we first use the front integrative cortex to mentally assemble the sound patterns we will use for speaking, and once our "language plan" is organized, we activate the region of motor cortex needed to create the sounds we want: integration first, then action. This kind of integration engages regions of front cortex that have been known to be central for language production for over a century: Broca's area.

As I noted previously, sign language isn't that different or special, either. Its primary distinctive feature is in the way it is sensed, with vision rather than sound. Otherwise, production of sign language depends on the motor systems in the brain, just like spoken language.[3] In fact, theories of the evolution of language often begin with gesture as the earliest means of communication. From there it is easy to see how auditory speech emerged. It had a special advantage for survival, since it freed the hands for other things, such as throwing a spear while shouting out instructions or warnings.

The biological point is that there is no particular reason to imagine that the parts of cortex involved in language are special, unique, or mysterious—more mysterious than any other part of cortex, that is. Auditory cortex is simply a region of cortex that gets information from the ears. Wernike's area integrates that information into image patterns. Broca's area converts image patterns into symbolic patterns (language). And motor cortex activates contraction of the muscles that produce the action of language—actually speaking words, phrases, sentences, and so forth.

It seems, then, that we can construct a logical theory of language using ideas and information that are already known. True, we do not actually know the details of "integration," but if we accept the concept (assembling parts into a larger whole) and its reverse (breaking the larger whole into parts) without knowing the mechanism, then at this level we can say that knowing the functions of auditory cortex, integrative back cortex, front integrative cortex, and motor cortex are, in themselves, significant steps toward understanding language.

They are steps that will bear some weight, rather than evaporating into a mysterious mist.

Brain as Calculator: Not!

It seems that nearly everyone thinks the brain is a *calculator*. Nearly! This idea is probably more firmly embedded that that of the language machine we discussed above. It seems that the mathematical calculator is waiting there in the brain, ready to perform all the marvelous mental feats that the science of mathematics has given us, even before the Egyptians were counting their assets and their debts. This calculator goes to work whenever we attempt to quantify something

However, although the meaning of "calculate" may seem clear at first, when we apply it to the brain, it becomes quite ambiguous. One meaning is simply the basic arithmetic, the "figuring" we do when solving numerical problems. Since we can sometimes do this in our head, we may imagine that the machinery in the brain, or perhaps in special parts of the brain, functions like little silicon chips like those in calculators.

We do know better. Calculating this way often requires us to use algorithms, a sequence of steps that is known to lead to correct answers, and that we memorize. The "calculating" is simply using these steps to solve a problem. However, as with language, we still rely on memory to access the correct algorithm and apply it in the correct sequence of steps. In some cases, we can also calculate this way by using images. We can picture four objects in our mind, and then take away two of them, now picturing only two remaining.

A second way we can think of the brain as a calculator (the one that seems most common) is to postulate that all mental activity involves firing of neurons in a specific quantitative way. This idea postulates that mental activity involves a specific, quantitative firing of synapses so that each neuron can send out a "calculated" output to another. The simplest version of this is that each neuron either triggers firing of a second one or does not. The output is either a 1 or a 0, again like a computer chip. This idea can get complicated quickly, but that is one of its virtues. Imagine that a neuron responds to a single signal by firing off five new ones. That neuron might then be said to do multiplication. Other neurons may not respond until several new signals are received, the equivalent of division. Millions of such calculations would accompany any firing patterns from a neuronal network, so the potential information content is huge. It might explain complex thought.[4]

However, this idea does not appear consistent with our knowledge of neuronal connections, especially with their plasticity. Neurons can have many synapses with other neurons—thousands of them—but the number and the organization of those connections are not fixed. They change through experience. A reliable mechanical or electronic calculator of the sort described above would have to remain constant, as does any mechanical device. Thus, it is difficult to imagine how the tangled and constantly changing networks of neurons in the biological brain could function in the precise and reproducible way implied by calculation.

A third, more philosophical meaning of "calculation" by the brain is illustrated by decision making. We say that we decide things by comparing the alternatives and "calculating" which is the more favorable, or predicting what the best outcome might be. However, as I discuss later in this chapter, the brain mechanisms involved in such comparisons turn out to be related more to the process of *estimation* than to calculation. As for prediction, as we will see in chapter 8, this phenomenon turns out to be satisfactorily explained by the use of memory.

Learning Language: A Model

Let's consider a model illustrating how the image patterns, such as those discussed in chapter 5, could combine with symbols, both auditory and visual, to create language. We will use an image to make meaning!

This model is illustrated in the figure below. It begins with visual perception of a specific object, a tree. This perception then is linked to a symbol for the image, a specific sound (the auditory expression of the word "tree"). Eventually, this symbol-image combination becomes associated with a new visual symbol, the written word, "tree." Start at the very right. There, I have illustrated the appearance of the tree image in the primary visual cortex (V). Of course, this image arises when we look at a tree. The pattern of neuron firing triggered by the tree then moves deeper into the cortex, arriving at the integrative cortex. There, or nearby, this image is at least partially stored in memory. We thus "have" the image.

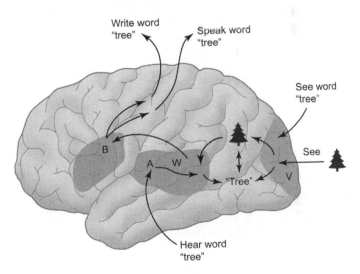

Now look at the bottom of the figure showing the sound signals, the spoken word "tree," entering the auditory cortex (A). This happens when we hear the word. From the auditory cortex, the neuronal patterns associated with the sound of the word also move into the back integrative cortex. Firing patterns for the image and the sound are physically close, in good position to become associated (integrated) with each other. This is shown by the double-headed arrow between the pattern of the image and the pattern of the word.

If the two patterns fire together frequently, the symbol (the word) always triggers the image. They form one pattern by integrating the two patterns.

Now look at the word "tree" on the right. This represents the written word. We become aware of it through vision, and the firing pattern generated by the image of the written word enters the visual cortex and then the integrative cortex. There it links up the actual image of the tree with both the spoken and written word. In the final form, the firing pattern consists of a combination of the actual image of the tree, the written word, and the spoken word: two visual patterns and a single auditory one. This integration process takes place in the area of cortex that has become known as Wernike's area, labeled W in the drawing.

Finally, Wernike's area is linked to the region in the front cortex labeled B, which stands for Broca's area. It is here that the sound and image encoded in the word "tree" is converted into the physical actions necessary for speech and writing. The function of this area is to convert the sensory experience of "tree" into the action experience of "tree." It sends instructions to the motor cortex for the actual muscular contractions that are needed to speak the word out loud or to write it.

Looking Deeper

The model makes a number of key points that may not be immediately apparent. Most of these points have been stressed in earlier chapters. But one that has not is the following: *The image either precedes the symbol or can be coincident with it.* The illustration depicts this principle, beginning with visual sensing of a tree, embedding the image in the integrative cortex (via patterns of electrical firing, as explained in chapter 4), and then, *subsequently or coincidentally*, associating a symbol (the spoken word "tree") with it. Here is the sequence: (1) see the thing, (2) store image of the thing, (3) hear the symbol (the word), (4) link the symbol to the image, and vice versa.

If by chance the symbol is experienced first, for example, hearing the word "tree" without actually experiencing a tree, there will be no image to link up with, and the sound of the word may lack meaning. Alternatively, the sound may resemble other sounds that are similar, and an alternative meaning emerges; say, "free" instead of "tree." In either case, meanings, right or wrong, must be based on prior knowledge.[5]

The processes involved in creating and storing images were discussed in chapters 4 and 5. Before developing symbolic systems to describe those images, the knowledge they contain may not be recognized. Understanding may lie hidden within our stored images. This is one reason why action is so important in learning. We discover the hidden images in our own brains when we begin to talk, write, practice, or test ideas through other actions, or experiments. I have been persuaded of this while writing this book. As I write, I find myself using new metaphors and analogies, ones I had not recognized before. I discover other associations that are inherent in the firing patterns I already possess. My images have been built through my daily experiences, and many of them remain waiting to be discovered. And, of course, the same is true of other neuronal patterns such as those generated by auditory experience or touch. I have spent a lifetime exploring the world through my senses and collecting the neuron firing patterns that go with those experiences. My mind is full of hidden knowledge that I am discovering as I use my symbolic brain.

I can hardly wait to discover it.

Symbols Without Images

The illustration above helps us understand how it is possible to speak the word "tree" *without* activating the actual image of the tree. It explains my students' problem with DNA in the story at the beginning of this chapter. The symbol, DNA, triggered the auditory sound of the word in memory, but not the image itself. In this model, language is a shortcut that, when it becomes very facile, may actually bypass the more complex image. We can read the symbol and say the symbol without using the image. In fact, it seems very likely that this happens routinely in our common speech. We do not recall every image when we are speaking rapidly, not consciously at least. If we have those images, we know it, and we also know that we can go back and recover any image at any time. No need to waste time and effort actually doing it all the time.

But if we only possess the image for the symbol, that is, the letters and/or the sound, we cannot describe a real tree; we only know the word!

Accelerating Learning? Hmmm . . .

It could be that one reason we like language is that it gives us shortcuts. We don't have to spend time remembering and examining the image. We are always interested in doing things faster. Those symbols sure help! They save energy.

In any case, language is very important. However, as I stressed above, the language symbols may get more attention than they should. We cannot depend totally on language. If we do, we may end up believing that we have the right image, when all we have are the symbols. We may find ourselves relying on memorized language as the primary way to define or explain things.

One reason I stress this point is because I wonder whether it is a danger to language development in children. It makes me question whether it is a good idea to use the "symbol-first" practices of teaching the alphabet to very young children, or exposing students to complex ideas like the structure of DNA when they do not understood fundamental ideas of chemistry. The purpose is to accelerate learning, but that hope is not well founded. The brain builds new knowledge based on prior knowledge. If our existing knowledge does not contain the foundations provided by the images them-selves, then the symbols become the foundation. Recent research reinforces this concern. For example, DeLoache warns that "children often conflate the symbol with the object itself," while pointing out the difficulties inherent in development of the symbolic mind.[6]

We examine more educational implications later in this chapter. At this point, however, let me stress that the challenges educators of children face may not have been adequately defined in the rush to learn the basics of lan-guage and math. While I am *not* denigrating teaching the "basics" in schools, I do suggest that we give serious thought to *preparing* students for learning them. Otherwise, in our urgency to get off to a good start, we may generate great difficulties for ourselves and our students throughout their schooling and, indeed, throughout life

Acceleration is a trap. Build the foundation first, no matter how long it takes.

Other Symbolic Traps

There are other symbolic traps that may lead us to overestimate our own or others' understanding. In language, for example, if we encounter someone who has a large vocabulary, we may believe that the individual is highly intel-ligent. Or, if a person can tell us a complex story or idea, we may be deceived into believing that he or she possesses deep insight. Or we may meet some-one who can carry out a complicated mathematical calculation, leading us to think that he or she must be a good problem solver in general.

We can fall into these traps throughout our lifetime, but with experience we become more aware of them. This awareness leads to a healthy skepticism of symbols and their influence over us. This apparently was the case with Cardinal Newman who, as quoted at the beginning of this chapter, under-stood that all our perceptions and symbols of perceptions are actually only shadows of the "true," and hoped to find the truth in an afterlife.

The more experience we have in using symbols to represent the real thing, the less we trust the symbols. As we mature, the struggle to explain what we "really mean" can become frustrating. The *inadequacy* of symbols, by themselves, for describing reality is a powerful and compelling discovery in our journey toward mind.

How to Fall Into the Trap

In my story at the beginning of this chapter, I stressed my experiences with students who did my assignments and remembered language descriptions of them, but still seemed to have inaccurate images or no images at all. It appeared that they had not pictured the descriptions, processes, objects, or stories in those assignments. They may have underlined almost every word on some pages of the book, but they were still studying without images. But I also want to stress that I do the same thing myself. I often realize that while reading several pages, I have retained very little recall or imagery for those pages. I have been reading words, but not creating images.

I suggest two explanations for this. First, symbols are less demanding of our energy and time than is the image itself. Drawing DNA is hard, time consuming, and full of potential error. Even imagining drawing it is hard. Creating or remembering an accurate visual image is much more difficult than simply resorting to remembered language.

A second reason is that our symbols themselves are images. The written word "tree" is perceived visually. So we have direct and strong brain connec-tions between the visual and auditory form of the *symbol*. The visual form is unambiguous. The letter sequence is always the same, two-dimensional, freestanding, and familiar. The symbol, then, is experienced through two different routes, one visual and one auditory. But the image itself comes only through the integrative areas of visual cortex. The *symbol* clamors for attention, and it is not hard to see how we might read the word "tree" using the direct visual-to-auditory connections, rather than looping off through the complex visual pathway that represents an actual tree.

Even though it is simpler to remember a string of words than to remember the details of an object or experience, we may often get by using the string of words. This "getting by" reinforces our success and causes us to develop strong emotional links to the symbolic route. We like to talk and can cover a lot of ground quickly that way. We can fall in love with our own voice or with the attention we get by using it.

Another Kind of Language

Earlier in this chapter, I said that the two most important symbolic systems for educators are language and mathematics. But up to now, I have not said much about mathematics. One reason for this is that the amount of cognitive neuroscience research on mathematics is generally less than that on language. A second reason is that language seems to get the most attention in education, or at least the earliest attention. One could argue that learning to read and write is more important in general than learning arithmetic and calculation, especially in this new era of universal access to calculators, but I will not.

I have no idea how one would decide the relative importance of language and mathematics. As I suggest later in this chapter, it undoubtedly depends on the individual. But regardless of that, the very question is based on the false premise that language and mathematics are categorically different. But, the more one examines the idea, the clearer it becomes that they are virtually identical. Mathematics is language, and vice versa.

I say this for many reasons. First, both are symbolic in nature. Both have specific rules that govern their use. Both can be phonological as well as visual. We learn numbers just as we learn letters—by saying them—and we think about both phonologically. When we see the price of apples, we say it in our minds or maybe even out loud. If bags of apples cost 50 cents, we multiply phonologically, saying to ourselves, "Three times 50 is 150—ah, $1.50!"

The fact that mathematical concepts, vocabulary, and rules are more rigid than those used in language contributes to our inclination to think differently about math. Language is less precise, word meanings can be ambiguous, and word choice is subjective when we are speaking or writing. On the other hand, number meanings are precise, and the rules for their use are unforgiving. When calculating, we don't "sort of add" or "kind of divide."

This rigidity, of course, does not mean that mathematics is not language. In fact, brain imaging studies show a strong overlap of arithmetic and language. Generally, both are left-lateralized and both engage specific regions of the cortex that have become known for their centrality in comprehending and producing language (Wernike's and Broca's areas). In addition, it has been found that brain damage in these areas not only generates *aphasia* (language problems) but also *acalculia,* which is characterized by impairment in rote arithmetic manipulations and calculations.

The language areas of cortex are also the arithmetic areas.

Abstraction

Generally, we think that mathematics is more abstract than language. This may be a reason for the common perception that math is "hard." Since abstractions, by definition, are not concrete, we struggle when we try to explain one. For example, the word "soul" refers to a non-physical entity, an abstraction. But we can only define it using physical examples. We might say, our soul is our essence. But that is not a great help since we must now define "essence." But we feel better if we say that our essence is what we are at the center, our core. We don't actually begin to feel satisfied until we get to the physical principle of a "core." And even then, we may feel the best when we think of an apple core. Abstract meanings grow in clarity as we get closer to the concrete.

An example of a mathematical abstraction might be the idea of multiplying by a fraction. I have read that children often begin to feel confused by mathematics when this concept is introduced. The idea of multiplication is concrete and unambiguous until then. If we multiply things we have more: $2 \times 6 = 12$. But suddenly we are told that multiplying by a *fraction* gives us less: $\frac{1}{2} \times 6 = 3$. I have heard that this is roughly the time in development when many children become afraid of math. And later they claim that math is abstract, so they cannot understand it.

However, in some ways mathematics seems more concrete than language. The aspects of mathematical rules and processes that seem to be abstract are still based on physical quantities with concrete meanings. Even the mathematical symbol for what is called an *imaginary unit* (an abstraction), "i," is invoked in some calculations because its use converts meaningless ideas into physically meaningful ones. We only use the imaginary number when it helps us create something concrete.

One can make the argument that if we can get to the root of it, nothing is actually abstract. When we track down the basis for things that are considered abstract, they turn out to be derived from or dependent on direct physical processes in our concrete, real-life experiences. Lakoff and Johnson make this point in their compelling book *Philosophy in the Flesh,* where they say "abstractions are metaphorical."[7]

For our purposes we should ask whether this view may influence education. For example, perhaps we can develop ways to better illustrate the concreteness of mathematics. Or, recognizing places where confusion arises, perhaps we can navigate the transition from concrete to abstract in a more deliberate and methodical ways that ultimately make the abstractness disappear. We revisit these suggestions later in this chapter.

Two Kinds of Mathematics[8]

Until now, I have used the terms "mathematics" and "calculation" essentially interchangeably. Now I will split off the numerical part and call it "arithmetic." What is left behind will retain its identity as "mathematics." At one time this would not be perceived as a new or even unusual approach, but some of my educator friends tell me that the term "arithmetic" is now used infrequently. So this is fair warning! For a few pages, I use it frequently.

My reason for resurrecting "arithmetic" is based on neuroscience. Research has shown us that the aspects of mathematics we identify as arithmetic engage a different region of the cortex from those aspects that appear abstract and most often engaged by professional mathematicians—beyond calculating.

First, we learn about arithmetic—exact arithmetic. We learn to count and to manipulate numbers by adding, subtracting, multiplying, and dividing. There is only one right answer for any exact arithmetic problem. Arithmetic is a very precise "number language."

The second skill that is of great importance in mathematical thinking is estimating, or approximating. This function activates regions of the human cortex different from those activated by arithmetic. Brain imaging studies indicate that when people are asked to identify numbers that are "about the same" or "closer in size to each other," they strongly engage what we have previously identified as the "where" region of cortex. In prior work and in chapter 4 of this book, I described this cortical area and its engagement in a wide range of judgments about relative importance, value, affection, size, speed, and other approximations. This region of cortex—the upper back integrative cortex of the right hemisphere—is the one most heavily engaged in analyzing spatial relationships.

These discoveries seem very important for educators, and I will address them more extensively shortly.

A Third Symbolic System: Could It Be the Most Educational?

An underlying assumption throughout this book is that when humans engage the brain in any particular learning experience, the parts of the brain used in that experience change physically; this is the physical nature of learning. Here, our example is music. Brain imaging experiments have shown that hearing piano music produces a significant increase in the amount of auditory cortex responsive to piano music. Experiencing and participating in music changes the brain.

I am bringing up this topic now, of course, because music is another symbolic system. In fact, participating in music engages regions of the cortex quite similar to those used in language and math. It engages and builds on the auditory brain and on the regions of integrative cortex that are central to language (Wernike's and Broca's) in both hemispheres. This is particularly true for children.[9]

The regions of cortex analogous to Wernike's area in the right hemisphere, the so-called prosody region (that is, the right auditory and surrounding areas) are more fully developed in musicians and in children who have listened to a great deal of music. Also, Broca's area (bilateral) responds when non-musicians hear chords with different degrees of dissonance, or a sense of unfulfilled resolution. We engage front cortical regions to predict patterns of sound and to anticipate where they will go. When the pattern doesn't proceed as anticipated, the prediction part of the language brain (Broca's area) becomes more active in both the right and left hemispheres.[10]

The Shape of Music

The regions of cortex used in approximation and in spatial analysis (described in earlier sections of this chapter) are also engaged in music. These regions are not strongly related to language, but they are central for the approximation and other spatial aspects of certain kinds of mathematics. They do not appear to be related to the symbolic nature of music but rather to what musicians sometimes call "contour."

Contour refers to the *pattern* of ups and downs in pitch plus variations in tempo that lend shape to a piece of music. In common usage, the "melody," or main theme, gives a piece of music contour. It is the part that is often most memorable and that we recall most frequently when thinking of a particular piece of music. It is what we whistle or hum to ourselves as we leave a concert. Recognizing and remembering this aspect of music is something we do naturally from childhood. In fact, research with young children revealed that they easily place different melodies in groups according to contour.[11] They have an image, or a picture, of the music.

You can perhaps understand this best by trying to sing a shape yourself. For example, hum the contour of a helix or a bookshelf. Or a neuron!

Brain and Symbols: Summary

Let's summarize the regions of cortex that are most engaged when our brain uses symbolic systems. For language, exact mathematics, and music, the major brain areas are very similar: the integrative cortex adjacent to auditory cortex, an area best known for its importance in comprehending language, and the integrative cortex in the frontal lobes that are most frequently engaged in the production of language. The latter area is adjacent to the parts of the motor cortex that produce movements associated with speech: movements of the mouth, tongue, face, arms and hands.

The brain areas engaged are also bilateral—both right and left. The left area is central for specific and precise details of the symbols, the exact meaning and correct sequence of each letter, phoneme, number, or note. The right areas are related to the context of the symbols. For example, punctuation often provides such context in language. A question mark is associated with the upward inflection in tone at the end of an utterance. In language, this is called prosody.

Since exact arithmetic is also a language, we often engage the prosody region of our cortex when we are counting. For example, we may count, 1, 2, 3 with a downward inflection, or reduced emphasis, on the "three," indicating that this is the end of the count. Music is also rich is these "prosodic" elements. We know whether a melody is just beginning or coming to an end based on inflection and emphasis on notes and chords. We feel it is incomplete when we are left hanging with an unresolved chord. These capabilities allow us to sense movement, anger, sorrow, joy, anticipation, and other emotions through music, perhaps more than through any other way.

Finally, location, shape, approximate position, relative value, and contour all engage the area of the brain used in seeing and analyzing spatial relationships in visual perception: upper right back integrative cortex—the "where" region.

The Auditory and the Symbol

Earlier in this book I paid a great deal of attention to the visual sensory systems and images that often seem to be the root of thought. But in this chapter we have seen that the *auditory* sensory brain is often the linchpin. In people with normal hearing, language, arithmetic, and music all make extensive use of the auditory systems. We sense letters and words visually, but we read by use of auditory cortex. We count the numbers we see in our minds, and we hear ourselves counting them, internally. We also remember symbols by sound. To remember them, we speak addresses or phone numbers to ourselves, internally, in what some have called a "phonological loop."[12] Music is possibly the most memorable kind of auditory input. Tunes stay in our heads for a lifetime. We can remember an entire song once cued by two or three notes played with the correct beat.

One reason, perhaps the main one, for this dependence on the auditory system is simply that it frees the other sensory systems to carry out tasks and to explore and analyze the environment, while we communicate through sound. As I mentioned earlier in this chapter, survival was greatly enhanced by this.

Another advantage of the auditory system is that the symbolic elements and structure are easy to learn, primarily by mimicry. We hear a sound, and we make that sound—exactly. The nearly infinite nuance in the phonology of language (the accent) is essential to determine meaning. In addition, sound is very effective in communicating emotion; we can tell how people feel by the way they sound.

Education

Recognizing the overlap in the cortical areas engaged by the different symbolic systems leads to questions about how we educate. First, consider our tendency to separate math and language in education. We almost always teach reading completely separately from arithmetic. We also have the habit of separating language intelligence from math intelligence. We have the verbal and the quantitative scores in our "scholastic aptitude tests."

Is it possible that this separation is misguided? Does the cortical overlap suggest that there should also be overlap in how children are introduced to these basic subjects? These questions sound a bit radical, and some of the answers I considered were radical as well. For example, when I realized that arithmetic and language engage similar regions of cortex, I began to experiment with the idea that they might actually be completely blended in education. Maybe such blending would enhance early learning of both.

I haven't discarded this idea. Maybe radical is necessary. But as I explored it, I became aware that, despite the similarities in these two symbolic systems, there are also significant differences. The similarities are that both begin with images, followed by auditory symbols, and, eventually, written ones. The major difference is that one (number system) builds on the other (language). To demonstrate that, imagine the following scenario:

> A child sees more than one object, for example, three spoons. He forms an image (pattern) of the object and then learns the auditory symbol, the word "spoon." If he does not yet have numbers, perhaps he fires the "spoon pattern" three times, and each time experiences the word "spoon, spoon, spoon." This is language without numbers. But now he can add the word "three" to his language vocabulary. Subsequently, he can put this new layer of auditory and written symbols (the numbers) in their own category and recognize them and their meaning.

This scenario illustrates a similarity between learning language and learning numbers. Numbers are a language shortcut. But numbers, and the concept of "number," build on language. Cognitively, language precedes arithmetic. It may be impossible to comprehend number systems without a language basis.

Mathematics is a language. Actually, it may be the only language shared by the entire world and independent of culture or geography. This is one reason it is so important and powerful. If we know the language of mathematics, we can communicate mathematically with anyone, anywhere. Becoming familiar with use of symbols in representing functions or manipulations is a key part of being able to comprehend and build mathematical skills. In fact, it is hard to imagine how one can carry out mathematical operations without engaging language.

Perhaps this is the most important message we can get from neuroscience in regard to mathematics. *When doing arithmetic, the brain engages the language centers.* This happens for two reasons: first, mathematics is itself a language; second, we explain math to ourselves with internal language. In the journey toward mind, it might seem that mathematics is a step beyond language. Or, put another way, mathematics is more demanding than language, and thus we feel it should be taught later.

An Alternative: Math Through Experience

The conclusion stated above is based on pedagogical and logical reasoning. I must admit, though, that I am still skeptical about it. I can't dismiss the possibility that math might develop naturally through the experience of a beginner even at a very early age, even while language is also developing. Nature does not always follow our linear and logical paths.

My skepticism arises from the fact that experiential learning in general is unpredictable. This is one reason that education is so challenging. We can't predict the nature of our experiences, their timing, or the personal meaning they will have to each individual. Educators must be continually alert as to how new experiences become integrated with older ones. It doesn't matter exactly when experiences happen, as much as what they are and how they mesh with prior experiences. The most effective education comes from the natural interests and instincts of each learner, developed through his or her own experiences.

This takes us back to the emotional aspects of learning—the joy. When faced with questions or uncertainties of the sort we are discussing, we may be better off turning away from pedagogical theories and toward the emotional aspects of learning. It seems to me that we should let the child lead us. Whatever the child seems to prefer may be best. If the child likes numbers and manipulations, let him or her have new experiences that involve mathematics. Don't worry whether the child is ready for it; motivation and interest are always more powerful than adult theories about learning.

Don't lose the joy!

Integration of Symbolic Systems

There are other arguments supporting the idea of integrating language learning and math learning. In agreement with programs for "writing across the curriculum" the integrative approach mentioned in chapter 4, can be extended to integrate experience with symbols. For example, we can explain algebra in word symbols rather than special math symbols: "If two people have candy bars, then things are equal. If we divide one candy bar into two pieces to feed two people, then to feed another two equally well, we will have to divide the other half of the candy bar in two; it's fair that way."

Of course, it is much quicker and easier to simply write,

$$\text{First bar} = \text{Second bar}$$
$$\text{so}$$
$$\text{First bar}/2 = \text{Second bar}/2$$

where the slash generates an image of cutting into two parts, combining symbols with images. More integration!

Algebra is about keeping things equal—keeping them fair!

Singing

We have discussed music as a symbolic system. Before we get too far in our thinking about education, I would like to bring music, particularly singing, back into our thinking.

I grew up singing a lot. We went to church several times a week, and every church service involved singing. I knew the words and tunes for literally dozens of hymns before I ever started school, and I am convinced that this childhood experience improved my brain.

The benefits of singing are obvious and numerous. Perhaps most important for me, I liked singing and I was always motivated to sing. There was the joy! I also learned many of the rules of the English language effortlessly by singing. The words in the hymns usually followed those rules, although sometimes with poetic license. I also naturally came to understand prosody, and I developed an instinct for recognizing and using correct grammar: "It just sounds right."

I believe singing should be part of childhood experience, from as early an age as possible and continuing through college age and into adulthood. For the skeptics—those of you that claim you cannot "carry a tune" or just don't like to sing—it may also help to realize that, early on, virtually all children enjoy singing.[13] We may deny that we like singing, or assert that we can't, but these beliefs may originate from negative social experience: someone told us we can't sing. We are afraid of the social judgment, not of the singing.

Barriers like this are not insurmountable. We should work to overcome them. It can be worth the effort.

Visualizing Spoken Symbols: Something New

In earlier chapters we were reminded of the centrality of vision in human cognition. Recently, this idea has been used to develop a new method for helping children learn the sounds of the letters in the alphabet by visualizing how the mouth looks when we pronounce them.

An Australian educator, Anna Gill, describes this method in a little book called *Look At My Mouth.* The book has a small mirror in the center of each page, so as children speak the letter, or a word that begins with the letter, they can see what their mouth actually does. How does their mouth look when they say "a," or "apple?" This method seems to be growing in acceptance. It has been recommended for preschool and kindergarten children, but more research is required to determine the age range for which it is most effective. Gill also claims that once children learn how it feels to make the sounds, the physical feeling in their mouth, they can focus on and remember the sounds more easily in a noisy classroom. The approach uses several "cognitive senses"—sight, sound, and proprioception (feel of mouth position)—and meshes well with our neurological view of learning that stresses the extensive connections between the senses.

Revisiting Approximating

As discussed earlier, educators often encounter a surprising lack of the instinct to approximate in learners. One explanation for this is the extensive use of calculators and computers, which give precise results to many decimal places. I believe that one "unintended" consequence of extensive use of calculators and computers is the habitual use of algorithms to get "answers" without any associated image. In chemistry, an example would be the calculation of the diameter of an atom generating an answer of 1.2346389 meters. The very precise nature of such an answer lends credibility, and the student may never notice that this atom is about the length of my arm!

This is another example of the danger of separating school from "real life." My students might routinely estimate things in their "real life" outside school, but once they take on a school assignment, they blindly calculate. As I suggested, many factors contribute to this behavior, including a lack of relevance in the student mind, extensive emphasis on algorithms as methods for solving problems, and ready availability of computers and calculators. At the root of the issue, we are likely to find a missing or incomplete image.

We might find symbols, but the symbols have no foundation.

Symbols and Beauty

In the final sections of this chapter, I discuss four aspects of symbolic systems that enrich our experiences and enhance the development of our mind: beauty, memory, power, and truth. They all influence teaching and learning, and they are of particular significance in student motivation.

First, we find symbols themselves beautiful and even exciting. Beautiful handwriting ("penmanship") is a lost art. It is, infrequently taught in school these days. Still we appreciate seeing it. Even the writing generated by a keyboard can be appealing to look at, with the regularity and rhythm apparent in the flow of the printed text. For example, a child I know loves to write stories. One of the reasons she enjoys this is that the printed story looks so nice when it is finished; she finds it beautiful.

Of course, she uses a computer, so the stories are always printed.

Even though we might never have mastered the skill of beautiful handwriting, at some time in our lives most of us have tried. That is how we came to believe we can't do it. But we still try, instinctively. This instinct takes us back to mimicry and copying. Our human instinct to copy shows up from early childhood. As I pointed out in chapter 5, give a child a blank piece of paper and a crayon, and that child will begin to make marks, symbols, and pictures. We naturally try to draw. In fact, in the history of writing, at least some of the earliest symbols developed were shorthand versions of objects themselves. Over time the symbols became simpler and easier to reproduce. Ultimately, we developed alphabets and the strings of letters had their own beauty. Beautifully written—literally!

Beautiful writing seemed to convey more than the meanings of the words. We can begin to feel an emotional pull along the page as the writing flows. Through use of punctuation we can play with the flow. The writing itself may imply breaks, rhythm, and "melody." Smoothing out rough-looking places may increase the impact of our sentences and paragraphs.

Language symbols began with art and returned to art. The human brain evolved to see beauty in symbols and experience joy in making symbols.[14]

This idea applies equally to arithmetic and other areas of mathematics. When I set up a derivation of a math relationship in my former life as a biochemist, I consciously tried to make it appear symmetrical and physically beautiful. Likewise, I enjoyed writing out the biochemical structures and pathways in a physically beautiful way. There was more to it than the abstract meaning; there was the physical impact of the symbols. Likewise, a bookkeeper friend of mine enjoys the appearance of columns of numbers. The pleasure goes beyond the bottom line. There is beauty in getting to the bottom line.

The beauty of the symbols produces joy.

Symbols and Memory

Symbols are at the core of memory. There are chapters on memory later in this book, but it is appropriate to point out here this connection between the symbolic brain and the process of remembering. All we need is a symbolic cue to trigger reconstruction of a long and complicated memory. For example, the word symbol "camp" may trigger detailed memories of childhood summers. Symbolic cues are our entry to poems, stories, songs, equations, calculations, designs, and many other creative activities. Symbols evoke images of our experience. Those images are related not only to concrete experiences, but also to the process and nature of the symbolic experience itself. For example, as we recall the song, we may also recall an image of someone at the piano, or a mother singing, or our high school team's "fight song" sung with great enthusiasm when riding home after a game—a win that is!

Another aspect of memory recall triggered by symbolic cues is found in the rules of the symbolic system itself. I remember how to speak correctly when I begin to use English grammar, and can even adapt to my audience, sometimes using different rules for different audience. Use of the symbols triggers memory of the entire symbol system. I hear the words and sentences in my head as I type them, and I correct them through memory of other examples. Every time I write a sentence, I strengthen my memory of how to write a sentence. In fact, I believe my use of language is based almost entirely on memory of specific examples and exceptions to those examples.

These comments apply to mathematics as well as language and music. For example, I remember the rules of long division, or the rules of algebra, when I begin to solve a problem. All I need is the symbol, $\div$, to recall, initiate, and complete the division process, entirely in symbols!

Symbols and Power

A third important aspect of symbolic systems is that they give us power, power of persuasion and power of transmission.

I have always been struck by the first words in the Book of John found in the King James Bible: "In the beginning was the word, and the word was with God, and the word was God." Although my conservative Christian upbringing gave me a very literal interpretation of this quotation as a child, later in life I came to think of it as a claim for the power of symbols. The symbol for God was "the word," and the symbol was so powerful that it actually became God. This claim was a sort of prophesy, foretelling the inclination of some Christians to revere the Bible almost as though it were God himself.

The power of symbols, particularly the symbols in language, is great because of our tendency to substitute the symbol for what it symbolizes. The power of language must be at least partially due to the actual images it calls up in our mind. The concrete world is located right in our head. Our best route to that world is through symbols.

Language and mathematics are powerful because they can initiate change, first in our minds, and then in the world. Wars and religious movements are first conceived and then initiated by language. Through mathematics we write out the formulas and make the designs for skyscrapers, the Golden Gate Bridge, and the atomic bomb.

Symbols are power. Children who learn this are more likely to become our leaders, for better or worse.

Symbols, Truth, and Error

Matching the meanings of symbols with the images of real objects and experiences is essential if symbols are to work. Such matching is a test of truth. We learn to distrust experiences where the symbols do not match the image. The image rules. Still, we all have experiences in which claims based on the language symbolic system disagree with our remembered images, or we believe they disagree. The symbolic systems, then, are a rigorous test of memory. It behooves us to actively and consciously ask ourselves whether claims made through language actually match the images we remember, or have created in our own mind.

A mismatch may occur more often than we think. We can discover them in the dynamic interchange of images between educator and learner, or between one learner and another, using symbolic systems. If we cannot describe our images, they probably are incorrect or incomplete. On the other hand, accurate description of them is convincing evidence of comprehension, both for ourselves and for others.

Often a great deal of our conversation involves using symbols to explain and discover our individual, but *different*, images for the same object or experience. We are trying to discover the truth by envisioning the perceptions of others, through use of a shared symbolic system. We are discussing!

Another aspect of gaining insight through use of language symbolic systems shows itself when the symbols are used grammatically incorrectly. For example, someone might say "the bridge are long." In this instance, the mismatch derives from the fact that the symbols actually generate two images simultaneously, one with a single bridge and one with more than one bridge. The symbolic representation is incoherent grammatically. It is not true. Often educators point out this type of error by making rules, rather than asking about image and symbols. In my example above, we would inform learners that subject and object must agree *in number*; both must be singular, or both must be plural. But unless we simply memorize the rule, the best route to the truth is through the image. Do we see one bridge or more? We have a symbol for both possibilities.

Above, I pointed out two kinds of error in use of language symbolic systems. One kind is error-in-fact, when images and language disagree. The second is error in usage, when language does not generate a coherent image. Research indicates that the brain seems to identify both kinds of "truth" simultaneously. Correct *use* of symbols is evaluated in parallel with the factual correctness of the image the symbols generate.[15] This is consistent with our proposal that the image is a test of the language. To the brain, there is matching or not-matching; image either conforms to symbol or it does not.

Does this suggest anything about education? Should students learn to ask, "Is it true?" when using symbol systems? Could they recognize false or flawed images more easily than they could false symbols? Would the ability to identify grammatical error increase if, instead of rules, we used an evaluation of image to determine correct grammar? Does our language produce clear, unambiguous images?

Education and Symbolic Systems

A great challenge facing educators is the pressure to improve use of the symbolic systems by children (and adults!). Language and math are the keys. We must master them! The importance of this cannot be disputed, but the methods being used are highly problematic. Fundamentally, those methods are all constructed on the belief that learning can be forced. This is based on a belief that success will come when we institute severe penalties for failure. Not only can you "lead a horse to water," but you can also "make him drink!"

Standardized testing and closing "failed schools," are the main tools used in this approach, and many educators question their value. There is a high level of frustration in the ranks. Many believe that threats and force lead to shallow learning that is soon partially or totally forgotten. Thus, when educators are forced to use methods they believe are inherently inferior, they are literally *forced to become poor teachers.*

I have written about this earlier; it is an example of a lack of integration. It is putting the symbols before the image. When learners focus on reading or mathematics as isolated skills, rather than integrating these skills into situations and problems they encounter in their daily experiences, they are deprived of images. It is quite possible to learn the symbols and the rules temporarily without fitting them into a meaningful picture, but this deprives them of memories. The basics are experienced out on an island separate from the mainland of their real life, and they have little motivation to use them again and few cues for meaningful memories.

Another factor that makes standardized testing problematic is that it often ignores approximation. Students may not be asked to estimate relationships, thus ignoring the spatial capabilities of the "where" region in the integrative cortices. They also may not be asked to make decisions about what they must *do* (actions), neglecting other front integrative cortex functions described in chapter 4. This neglect of the estimation and approximation regions of their brain is potentially highly damaging, since approximate answers often reveal deep understanding, or the lack of it.

Finally, standardized tests most often focus on the agreed-upon "correct" answer, rather than allowing for student flexibility and creativity. Otherwise, the test cannot be "standardized." Students may create unexpected yet ultimately correct answers, but the less imaginative tester does not recognize or accept these.

Creativity is hard to standardize.

Another List

Below I summarize this chapter's message by listing 10 points we discussed. Each point contains a "do" and a "don't," but I stress that these are suggestions, not instructions. They are to be tested, not memorized.

1. Music for everyone! Not only listening, but participating.
2. Images before symbols. The symbol itself is not the image.
3. The child will lead. Don't teach symbols when you want, but when the child wants.
4. Provide time for reflection during learning symbols. Do not rush the process.
5. Encourage approximation. Do not demand an exact answer unless it matters.
6. Attend to the joy. Do not ignore the intrinsic beauty of symbols.

7. Attend to memory. Don't ignore the use of symbols in memory recall.
8. Stress the power. Don't ignore the practical value of symbolic systems.
9. Stress *choice* for learners. Educator control is not the point.
10. Use symbolic systems for creating the new. Do not focus on what is known (or believed to be known).

Continuing the Journey

Mastery of the symbolic systems provides us with new and powerful vehicles to facilitate our journey from brain to mind. We can master them in the mindless way discussed in chapter 2, but once we begin to integrate their use into our experience, the journey toward mind will accelerate. On the other hand, if we do not develop symbolic systems, we may become aware that our brain has a huge reservoir of images, but struggle to access and use them.

What we want, and what we can all have, is a synergism between knowledge and symbols of that knowledge. Each helps us access and develop the other. As we develop our skills in language, mathematics, and music, we begin to recognize that they help us solve problems and create ideas. Our experiences are richer and more memorable. We remember not only images, but how to work with them; not only *what* and *where*, but why. Those memories of success will begin to drive us in new rewarding directions along our journey. We will remember the joy.

Forming new memories that have deep personal meaning is the natural part of our journey. As awareness of our experiences and our memories of these experiences increase, we find ourselves making good use of them. They tend to become what we turn to when we encounter new challenges. We use the older "mindless" and borrowed (mimicked) memories less as we stamp our personal label on experiences. Our memories become truly "ours." We keep the useful ones because they will help us in the future.

We remember where we have been, so we know where to go next.

Notes

1. Our focus is primarily on language and mathematics, but it should be noted that there are other symbol systems used by humans. Premack (*Science*, 303, p. 318, 2004) identified six such symbolic systems: the genetic code, spoken language, numbers, music notation, written language, and labanotation (code for choreography).

Of course, the genetic code is qualitatively distinct from the others and is not limited to humans. But we can go beyond Premack's list and include things like a second language or chemistry. In fact, any subject or area of endeavor may develop its own symbolic system.

2. Deacon, (1997), argues in *The Symbolic Species*, Norton, New York, NY, that the use of symbols is a central activity in the human mind, one that may literally be *the* factor that distinguishes *Homo sapiens* from all other species.

3. Recently it has been found that infants respond to sign language earlier in development than they do to spoken language. Further, children who used sign language as their first language experience learn spoken language more easily later. This is a widely accepted practice, and a Google search reveals numerous references.

4. An example of this concept is explained by Karl H. Pribram as follows: It is "a complex mathematical operation similar to Fourier analysis . . . in which the cells carry out their processing by summation and inhibition and other physiological processes . . ." See: Pribram, K. H. (2004), "Brain and Mathematics," www.paricenter.com/library/papers/pribram01.php.

5. Zull, J. E. (2002), *The Art of Changing the Brain*, Stylus, Sterling, VA, chapter 6.

6. Beginning to think symbolically is a major transition, and substitution of the symbol for the real object is a common barrier to development of language skills. See: DeLoache, J. S. (2005, August), *Scientific American*, pp 73–77.

7. The arguments supporting this basic idea are presented in Lakoff, G., and Nunez, R.E. (2000), *Where Mathematics Comes From: How the Embodied Mind Brings Mathematics into Being*, Basic Books, New York, NY.

8. Much of the specific research described in the following sections on mathematics is described in Dehaene, S., et al. (1999), *Science*, 284, pp. 970–974; also see Dehaene, S. (1997), *The Number Sense*, Oxford University Press, New York, NY.

9. Pantev, C., et al. (1998), *Nature*, 392, pp. 811–814.

10. This work by B. Maess and colleagues is discussed by Holden, C. (2001), *Science*, 292, p. 623.

11. A Web search of music contour brings up many credible sites. For the Wikipedia link, use http://en.wikipedia.org/wiki/Pitch_contour.

12. For a recent perspective on the phonological loop, see Baddeley, A. D., and Della Sala, S. (1996), Working Memory and Executive Control, *Philosophical Transactions of the Royal Society of London*, 351, pp. 1397–1404.

13. The Shepherd School of Music at Rice University has developed an excellent website on the use of music and singing in child development. The site includes references to brain research as well as developmental studies with children: http://www.ruf.rice.edu/~musi/preparatory/singing02.html.

14. Archaeological research now suggests that fascination with and use of symbols in the form of body paint and jewelry may have originated as long ago as 100,000–200,000 years ago; see: Wong, K. (2005, June), The Morning of the Modern Mind, *Scientific American*, pp. 86–95.

15. Hagoort, P., et al. (2004), *Science*, 304, pp. 438–441.

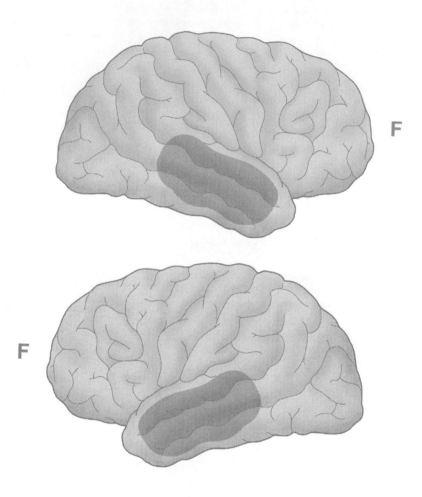

Cortical location of regions heavily involved in declarative memory formation and consolidation. Top is right lateral view, and bottom is left lateral.

7

CREATING MEMORY
Foundations for Building the Mind

. . . and nine she-camel hairs aid memory.
—Marianne Moore

I was at a crisis moment in my life. For three years I had been studying and doing research in biochemistry. Now it was finally time to take my qualifying exam. This exam was the key hurdle between me and pursuing a Ph.D.

The oral exam, given by a committee of internationally known biochemists, allowed questions about almost any topic. This was only my second oral exam, and I had not done very well on the first one. I wasn't exactly a model of confidence!

However, there was one subject I thought they might bring up and actually hoped they would: enzyme kinetics. I had loved learning about enzymes and had even been asked to teach this material to the other graduate students. I felt ready for any question on this topic.

I was very happy when the first question was on this very topic. It focused on a key relationship, called the Michealis-Menton equation, which describes the action of the simplest enzymes. I was sure I knew all about it.

My confidence was misplaced. Suddenly, I couldn't remember the equation; I completely forgot it. I remembered a lot, including how to use it and the variables in it, but I couldn't actually write it down. I even volunteered to derive the equation, but my committee in its wisdom didn't take me up on it.

As always happens in oral exams, new topics came up. I began to remember things, and I gradually calmed down. The rest of the exam went quite well. But as we were winding down, my advisor gently said, "So now, Jim, why don't you write down the Michealis-Menton equation?"

To everyone's dismay, I went absolutely blank all over again! (to be continued in chapter 8).

Of all the fascinating things about the brain, memory is at the top of the list. People always seem to think of memory when they refer to learning or "being smart." We also tend to think that each person has a certain quality of memory that is beyond his or her control; we may believe that our fate is decided. We have been given good or poor memory machinery at birth, and that determines how smart we will be.

This chapter begins by questioning these assumptions. We explore the possibility that the effectiveness of our memory machinery depends a great deal on our experiences. In that case, the task for an educator is to discover the nature of experiences that are memorable for individuals. Finding the right kinds of experience for each person is our challenge.

Formation and Recall

It is important to recognize that memory is not a unitary brain function. We break it into two fundamental elements: forming memories and recalling them. The challenge is to record the things that will make up our memories, and then, to recall them when needed. As implied previously, we are all given the machinery needed to form memories—the neurons that grow branches and form networks—but establishing the networks is one thing and putting them to use is another.

This chapter is about establishing them. I stress three aspects of this process. First, we examine the idea that the very earliest experiences of the newborn child are also the beginnings of memories. These memories are not conscious or expressed in language, but they are a foundation for future development of the mind. They are subconscious prior knowledge. I provide specific examples from the sciences.

Second, I discuss some more general aspects of the neuronal processes of memory formation, and what conditions either enhance or inhibit these processes. This includes discussion of long- and short-term memory and the value of each.

Finally, I explore ways some formal educational experiences may actually work against formation of useful and meaningful memories. This can happen when we become more concerned about efficiency and organizing the large number of learners commonly attending school. We can break the biological rules for memory formation by the very way we organize the school day or other aspect of a learning environment that we take for granted.

Memory and the Journey

Memory is based on the most fundamental function of the neuron: the ability to form connections with other neurons. This capability begins to express itself even before birth.[1] It is what neurons do. As I have claimed in earlier chapters, the brain may not be a language machine or a calculator, but it *is* a memory machine.

We do not discuss prenatal development, but, instead, begin with the newborn child who already has most (but not all) of the neurons he or she will need. Starting this way facilitates discussion of the role experience plays in development of mind, since it is primarily after birth that educators (that is, teachers, parents, siblings, and other influential people that are part of the baby's experience) can both observe and modify. Even at this very early time in development, we can give thought and planning to make experiences memorable.

Expression of these early memories does not use formal language, but the behavior of the baby, including some sounds, makes us aware of his or her existence. These also make us aware of the dynamic nature of the networks on which those memories rely. Behaviors change, becoming less random. With sounds, we notice that some disappear, some are used in new ways, and new ones appear. Those sounds and the changes are evidence of change in neuronal networks. Such change is part of the dynamic of life and is retained through development and into adulthood. As long as we have new experiences, our neuronal networks change.

We could say that these dynamic connections are "soft-wired." They build on each other, adding new networks with new experience, and weakening or even eliminating portions that are not activated consistently or that are not associated with emotion—that are not memorable.

All this change and plasticity, this "mental development," is part of the journey toward mind. Fundamental networks in the brain evolve into complex and almost unending ones that we need for the functions we associate with the mind. New capacities appear, built on the very earliest experiences. And, because of their newness, their novelty, these capacities are inherently emotional. If they are repeated consistently, these new and continually growing memories can become part of implicit knowledge, serving as a foundation for future understandings.

This profound intermingling of early childhood experiences and development of instinctive understandings of the world was expressed by Walt Whitman in *Leaves of Grass*:

> There was a child went forth every day;
> And the first object he look'd upon, that object he became;
> And that object became part of him for the day, or a certain part of the
> day, or for many years, or stretching cycles of years.

Richness

Experiences are memorable when they trigger emotions and when they are repeated. These requirements explain why Whitman says, "that object he became." Such early experiences, the actual "becoming," totally engage the attention and the emotion of the child. They are "part of him," and they remain, whether consciously or not. They are consistent and repeated without thought, possibly for as long as a lifetime. They are memories!

One key to experiences of this nature is expressed in Whitman's "going forth." It is the *discovery* stressed in chapter 2. Whitman implies that this can happen any time, even all the time! And, although he writes about a child, this "going forth" can apply throughout a lifetime. Any time and at any age, if we go out and immerse ourselves in our experiences in this deep but instinctive way, we are continuing our personal journey toward mind.

Experiences of this sort are deep and rich. They are important for development of the mind, and educators should attend to this richness for every learner at any point in life, starting with the newborn baby. I discuss specific examples below, but there is a way to think in broad neuroscience terms about this suggestion. We can define "rich" experiences as those that engage many different areas of the brain. A short list of such experiences would include those that use all the senses, produce new outcomes, require problem solving, build on diverse cultures and environments, use physical movement, include new shapes and spaces, sometimes change unexpectedly, and may produce surprise.

This is quite an order, but many if not all of these qualities are naturally associated with one another and, thus, engage the developing mind. Even a simple experience such as playing in the backyard can do much of this. And, importantly, although the nature of these experiences, and the "repeating" I mentioned above, may be designed by the educator, the ultimate goal should be to provide freedom for the child. Eventually the experiences reflect the choices of the children, themselves.[2] That freedom of choice enhances the richness.

Examples of Spatial Enrichment

On the Web, we can find many excellent suggestions for enriching the experiences of babies and children. Just Google "enriching experience for children [babies]." So, here, let me mention two ideas that occur to me from my personal experience as a scientist. These are meant as examples taken from my field of expertise, and I am sure many readers will be able to identify other examples based on their own specialized area of knowledge.

Earlier, I suggested that babies might be exposed to objects of different shapes. By "different" I mean those that are infrequently encountered in baby toys, but are very commonly found in nature and, thus, in science. As a biochemist, I thought first of a tetrahedron (the most common structure found in carbon compounds—that is, chemistry,) and a helix (a repeating structure found in DNA and enzymes—that is, biology). We can think of many other examples of "scientific" shapes, but these illustrate my point.

My suggestion is that simply providing objects with these shapes for children to hold in their hands (and probably their mouths) can become an experience that leads to implicit memory. Although he will not be aware of it, the child may become familiar and comfortable with the different shapes. The neuron patterns associated with objects of such shapes will be stabilized by repeated firing. And in this example, for contrast, we might also provide objects with other shapes, say a cube or a pyramid. Experiencing shapes and their differences will be a part of children's earliest experience.

Notice that colors or sounds are not necessarily part of this idea. They may even be distractions.[3] The point is not to entertain children, nor to instruct them, but to have them experience solid shapes and their differences. And, as I stressed in chapter 6, the point is not to learn the names of objects. That will come in time; there is no rush. The symbols are easy; it's the shapes that are important for understanding.

Videos for Baby? Not!

In the suggestions above I focused on the sense of touch and understanding shapes.[4] Unlike vision, which is not well developed at birth and does not sharpen for months, the sense of touch develops very early, possibly even in the womb. Three-week-old babies can respond to the shape of objects placed in their hands. For example, they can tell a prism from a cylinder.[5]

I also want to distinguish my proposals from watching videos, which can often be confused with *experiencing* the topic shown in the video. That confusion has led to the growth of an education industry for babies based on videos that are purported to enhance cognitive development. The distinction is essential, since those products have lost credibility in many cases. Their cognitive benefit has been seriously challenged.[6]

I find myself unsurprised by this. There is a fundamental difference between watching a video of something and actually experiencing that thing. More than that, any exposure of infants to moving images on TV or computer screens for long times and at a very young age may actually be cognitively damaging. Jane Healy has written about this for over two decades, and we should not be surprised if we ultimately discover that our current attention deficit epidemic is traced to overdosing on visual media, even while in the crib.[7]

In contrast to the videos, the exploration of and reflection on shapes described above seems relatively benign. Whether or not it enhances spatial cognition, it is not dangerous. We need not fear that stationary objects in the hand will damage the mind of the child.

Memory of Physics: More Enrichment

Physics is a special creature in science education. Some students find it very difficult, while others seem to pick it up naturally. In my classes I often encounter students in the former category. I suffered from this "fear of physics" for some time, myself. For me, one of the more difficult aspects dealt with waves. I first experienced this when my teachers began to talk about alternating current and electricity. I could understand direct current (DC); it was just like water coming through a pipe. It went in one direction and, just like the plumbing in our house, the "electricity" came out one end of the wire. But I struggled with the idea of alternating current (AC). That kind of electricity didn't really go anywhere. It just vibrated up and down but stood still. What was that?

Over the years I came to better understand energy in waves, but there has always been a little worry associated with that "understanding." This is still true in some ways. I'm not yet comfortable with this idea, but even now I am slowly becoming more so.

I suspect that this difficulty is traceable to limited exposure to waves. I knew about the waves on the beach, but those waves were going somewhere—toward the beach. I had no experience with this new kind of wave that didn't go anywhere.

Waves having this property, I learned later, are called "standing waves." An example is what happened when I got in the bathtub. Sometimes I noticed that when I sat down, the waves would go back and forth for a while before calming down. The wave I made reversed direction when it reached the end of the tub, so it was going back and forth, but never really getting anywhere. Perhaps if I had had more experience with that kind of wave, if my parents (educators) had told me to watch the waves, I might have begun to form the neuronal patterns that represent them.

In any case, I wonder about this. Maybe babies should simply have more experience with waves. Maybe dropping some pebbles in a dish. Not to explain waves, or to represent them with symbols, or make them too complex, but to create the neuronal firing patterns that represent a standing wave in the brain—to be recovered later in physics class.

Culture and Neuroscience: Memory Foundation

The suggestions I have just made are based on the idea that we form memories based on our experience, and those experiences are derived from the culture in which we find ourselves. My chemistry and physics proposals above can be said to be aspects of a "science culture." We can observe this brain impact of inherent cultural factors in many ways, ranging from optical illusions, to language, to attitudes, to emotions.[8]

It seems likely that these memories, formed very early in life, are an example of "implicit memory." This term is used in the sense that we are unaware of some of our memories, but our actions and behaviors imply they exist. When we become aware of them and can express in language, they become "explicit." The topic of implicit memory has been studied extensively, but my objective here is primarily to stress the physical nature of memories, and to remind you that our memory networks can exist, even when we are unaware of them. If we think in such physical terms, it is easy to comprehend the *foundation* metaphor, and to realize that prior knowledge is not necessarily something we are aware of, or can access on demand. Part of the foundation may be explicit and part implicit.

It is also interesting to ask what triggers the appearance of explicit memories around the general age of three to five years. Although there is some evidence that implicit and explicit memories reflect different brain processes, fundamentally they are the same: that is, they are based on networks of neurons. In that sense, they are more alike than they are different. And we still possess implicit memories throughout our life, not just in childhood. In fact, the primary way we differentiate implicit and explicit is through language. It could be that the difference comes from our ability to describe, rather than an inherent difference in the nature of the memory. When we can say, "I remember," we can create explicit memory; that is, when we develop language.

This suggestion could influence how we educate. If there is a developmental link between explicit memory and language, then just *using* the language may, by itself, enhance explicit memory.

She-Camels?

This ends our discussion of early memories in the journey toward mind. The point has been made: early memories are the foundation for later ones. Now we can direct our thoughts to the actual processes that take place in neurons during memory formation. This will help us understand the difference between memories that last a long time and those that are gone almost immediately, and what kinds of environments and experience are memorable or not.

It is remarkable that we are even in a position to discuss these topics. Memory has puzzled us for millennia. Even in an advanced technological age, we all struggle with memory and often invent "tricks" to help us remember things. My students sometimes write chemical reactions on different-color cards to remember them. A friend once told me that she remembers sequences of things by imagining them placed on different pieces of furniture in her house. But sometimes there seems to be no help. So we turn to exotic or magical recipes for remembering, such as Marianne Moore's "nine she-camel hairs."

A great deal of this concern arises from what we perceive to be a lack of memory formation. We remember things for a little while, but later find that the memory is gone. Or so it seems. So we work harder on trying to *create* longer-lasting memories. We spend a lot of time and energy devising ways to trap the memory. And when those efforts fail, we conclude that our memory-creating machinery must be defective or deteriorating.

We just can't make them anymore.

Reflex as Memory

I hope to discuss memory formation in direct, physical, and non-technical terms, to leave the she-camel hairs behind. To do that, I will start with a simple but very real neurological phenomenon, the reflex.

Although they are arguably the simplest networks of neurons in our body, reflexes are excellent models for memories. In fact, we can argue that they are memories. When we sense a specific event such as touching something hot, our body remembers what to do and does it; it jerks our hand away. Of course, this is not a conscious memory. And it really doesn't qualify as an implicit memory either. It would be too slow if we had to think what to do.

At this fundamental level, the reflex process is the same as that involved in more complex cognitive activities, such as reading aloud. When we read (sense) words, our neurons represent a memory of what to do (action). We remember to speak the words we see.

Reflexes are actually prenatal. The right synapses exist before birth. We could quibble and say they are not really memories since they are not "learned." But my argument is that knowledge of learning is not part of our definition for a memory. I am asking whether memories actually require learning. And my reply is that the memory *is* the network. How we got it is irrelevant.

Whether or not you buy into this argument, the reflex is still a useful model for memory. Its virtue is its simplicity. It requires only three kinds of neurons. We need a sensory neuron in the hand, a connecting neuron in the spine, and a motor neuron in the arm. The electrical impulse goes from hand (sense), up the arm to a small connecting neuron in the spine (connect), and back out a long neuron from the spine to the muscle in the arm, which then contracts (act). Sense-connect-act. In fact, these kinds of networks are what we find throughout our nervous system. They are the foundation for all functions of the nervous system from a three-neuron-reflex to a many-neuron cognitive action such as reading aloud.

A memory is simply a stable network, relatively speaking. It may not be so stable that it lasts forever, and as we will see later, it changes a lot with new experience. But still, when the network changes, so does the memory. Every mental function depends on such networks. They are at the heart of cognition and behavior.

Two Biological Ideas

Let's continue to look for generalizations that provide deeper insights into memory. In addition to the reflex example, there are two other simple ideas that will help. The first is the realization that living things must deal with the present, using existing cellular machinery. Whether they are single-cell organisms like bacteria, or the cells in our own body, living things carry out the chemical reactions necessary to support life on a moment-to-moment basis. These reactions include things like metabolizing our food, or responding to different chemicals right outside the cells, such as the salt in our blood. A living cell has the machinery in place for thousands of such reactions, ready to kick into action any time they are needed. Even isolated cells remember how to deal with what they confront in the moment.

The machines are enzymes. Each kind of enzyme is responsible for catalyzing a particular chemical reaction that occurs in the cell. Enzymes speed up these reactions, making them go thousands of times faster than they otherwise would. They are ideal for quick responses. Sometimes we call them "housekeeping" enzymes. The dustpan and broom are always there, ready to clean up the floor—right away!

The second idea is that cells also have the ability to change their structure and their existing machinery. The instructions for such changes are in the genes. When the instructions are read, they enable the cell to respond to new, "non-housekeeping" challenges. Maybe we need to put a small addition on the house, in addition to keeping things up. That change can be initiated by activating some new, previously quiescent genes.

Neurons and the Two Ways

The "housekeeping" metaphors are not perfect, but they help us understand neuronal processes in formation of both short- and long-term memory. Short-term memory requires enzymes that are like the housekeeping enzymes. These are present in regions of neurons where connections to other neurons can be found. These regions are the famous "synapses" that we use to discuss neurons and "connections." The housekeeping enzymes are in the synapse region of neurons all the time and can quickly stimulate the actions needed to send signals to connecting neurons. However, if they are not repeated very often, these transient signals die out rapidly, and the networks begin to weaken. So do the memories.

With long-term memories, neurons modify and improve the tools at hand. These changes can be relatively stable, and can actually involve production of new synapses or more stable versions of the synapse machinery. It is similar to the analogy of making an addition to the house. These additions are synapses that are new, stronger, and longer-lasting. They are the source of long-term memory, and the addition is long lasting.

The dramatic changes needed to generate long-term memory also take longer to carry out. Adding a room to the house takes time. For one thing, the instructions for assembly (genes in the nucleus of the neuron) are often quite far removed from the synapses. Also, the instructions must be copied down in a message to be sent out into the cell, since the genes themselves always stay in the nucleus. Just copying the instructions and sending them out to the necessary places in the cell is time-consuming. And once the copied instructions have arrived at the right place, actually building the more stable synapses takes additional time. They are complicated and cannot be thrown together instantly.

Why different memories last longer than others turns out to be straightforward and not at all mysterious. Short-term memories are the result of rapid changes in the activity of enzymes already present at the synapse. Those enzymes are activated quickly and remain active for a short time. The synapse changes they produce also come quickly but last only a short time. However, long-term memory requires the second, slower process of assembly and cell change. Such memories alter the actual structure of the cell, and the alteration can last a long time.

An Image of Memory

The ideas I have described are shown in the figure below, which illustrates a single sensory neuron with one synapse to a motor neuron. The normal "housekeeping" enzymes in the sensory neuron produce glutamate (a special chemical represented by the small, black dots). When the sensory neuron fires, glutamate is secreted onto the motor neuron surface, which has receptors for it.[9]

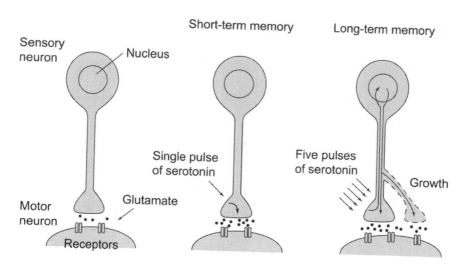

Recall that emotion is a major factor triggering synapse change in neuronal networks. Thus, as shown in the figure above,[10] when a small amount of an emotion chemical (serotonin) is sprayed on the synapse, the synapse becomes more active; in particular, it secretes more glutamate onto the motor receptors. This leads to increased activity of the synapse (motor cell firing), which lasts for a bit, but then fades out (short-term). The nuclear processes and structural changes are not engaged.

But with intense serotonin exposure, as shown on the right, the signal is transported all the way to the sensory neuron nucleus, where the genes needed for growth are turned on. Development of new branches that can form new synapses then occurs and generates stronger signals for a long time (long-term memory).

This is intriguing, but not really mysterious. No she-camel hairs!

Consolidation

The cellular story of memory is a dynamic one. At first, specific synapses are involved in very rapid responses to stimuli, creating a relatively unstable network that may last a while or weaken quickly. But, under certain conditions, the network firing begins to activate the slower nuclear responses, above, leading to the assembly of new sensory neuron branches, new synapses, and, ultimately, to very long-lasting ones. The memories become consolidated.

There does not seem to be any specific borderline between short-term and long-term memory. Rather than a specific "consolidation point," there are degrees of consolidation. For example, a mild stimulus may produce a low amount of nuclear involvement, perhaps leading to a small increase in synapses and intensity of signaling. This dynamic process is regulated by the presence or absence of what we call "modulating" factors, such as serotonin (shown above). These factors are involved in emotion responses of nervous systems and in consolidation. When emotional experiences produce changes in serotonin in the brain, synapse changes occur and memory is deepened and lengthened—consolidated.

Memory is also consolidated by *repetition*. Biologists have been able to study the impact of repetitive stimuli on synapse strength directly, and this research has led to discovery of a major neurological phenomenon directly related to memory. This phenomenon is called "long-term potentiation" (LTP). It has been examined for decades and now is known to be at least part of the essential processes that explain memory.[11]

The idea behind LTP is that if synapse change is the heart of memory formation, then we should be able to see some change in response to a stimulus that is "memorable." For example, maybe if we sent an intense, repetitive electrical stimulus to a neuron, it would be remembered. Neuroscientists began to play that game many years ago and discovered that neurons given a large burst of current do remember the large burst and respond with their own large burst for hours, days, or even weeks. The fascinating part of this is not that neuron response is greater, but that neurons seem to *remember* it is greater for a very long time after the initial event; hence, the name "long-term potentiation."

More work of this sort led to more subtle but highly important additional findings. It turns out that duration of the LTP response depended based on the strength of the stimulus. If the initial event is smaller, the memory is shorter. And, strikingly, if the stimulus is very small, in the absence of competing strong stimuli, the response is weaker, but it is actually remembered better! The weakness is remembered. This later phenomenon is called long-term depression (LTD). The cell remembers that the signal was weak—possibly even inconsequential![12]

Repetition, Emotion, and Plasticity

Let's look more carefully at LTP and LTD. First, LTP. You may have noticed that this process is strikingly similar to the responses produced by spraying serotonin on neurons. LTP comes from repeated experience, that is, bursts of intense electrical stimuli, while the serotonin effects are the result of strong application of emotion chemicals. But there is little doubt that both approaches are measuring the same biological processes. For example, the quicker but short-lived responses are analogous to the weak firing burst produced by a single application of serotonin—short-term memory. Furthermore, the process of LTP requires the synthesis of new enzymes and proceeds by the slower, serotonin-activated pathway involving new gene expression and molecular traffic between the nucleus and the synapses of the neuron.

These longer, slower processes are of great interest since they are the best candidates for a model of long-term memory. However, the short-term processes and long-term depression (LTD) are also very interesting. They probably play a role in thinking and problem solving where we form memories that are useful and necessary at the moment, but are not needed for the long term ("working memory"). Flexibility and variability in the length of memories enable us to keep what is most important, but eventually forget the unimportant.

Statistical Remembering

LTP and LTD are the extremes in a continuum. Synapse strength can range from very strong to very weak, and from short- to long-lasting. This reinforces the idea that learning is as much about discovering and remembering when networks should *not* fire as it is about when they should. In the total picture, reducing neuron signaling is as important as stimulating it.[13]

There is also an important conceptual inference in this research. The behavior of existing synapses in the moment depends on their past behavior. This suggests that neuronal networks function as statistical systems. Evolution has given us biochemical processes for keeping strong networks strong and weak ones weak. When it is very likely that a neuron will fire, the networks containing that particular neuron are stabilized. On the other hand, when it is unlikely that a neuron will fire, the networks where it is found remain weak. The statistical record of the past is the basis for adapting to the future.

This way of thinking should be familiar: it is biology's way—nature's way. Just like evolution, memory is not driven by need or by design, but rather by probability and selection. What looks like instruction is just selection. Many possibilities exist in the immense collection of networks in a brain, but only the useful ones, those that fire a lot, are statistically most likely to fire again. Memory provides the data that influence firing decisions when conditions change.

It is the experience of each neuron in a pattern that guides memory formation.

Jean's Dance

LTP and LTD are both important. One is triggered by intense and repeated neuron firing, and the other by weak and infrequent neuron firing. But that is not all. These two processes share other features and influence each other in an additional way.[14] Both involve gene expression.

Two different nuclear enzymes are key elements in this regulation of gene expression; one enzyme produces LTP, and the other produces LTD.[15] One turns expression of a specific gene on, and one turns it off. The "turn-on" enzyme is responsible for LTP, and the "turn-off" enzyme for LTD.

It is like a dance. Two dancers compete for the same partner—let's call her *Jean*. One would-be partner lets Jean express herself freely, and the other dominates her and expresses himself. But she likes both. It is fun to express herself, but it takes effort and entails some risks. It is also exciting to be dominated and let her partner make all the decisions.

Jean's partners represent the two enzymes I described above. Both want to dance with Jean, but their effects on her are very different. With one she expresses herself, and with the other she cannot. In the first case, the result is LTP, and in the latter it is LTD. Exact opposites!

In mundane biochemistry terminology, one of the two enzymes stimulates production of new synapse enzymes by activating a gene, and the other biochemical stimulus prevents such synthesis by inhibiting expression of that gene. There is no mystery or instruction; it is simply probabilities. Whichever enzyme is most likely to be associated with the gene at any particular time determines whether LTD or LTP will occur. And the reason one or the other is most likely is that experience has generated more of one or the other enzyme.

But there are some complications: there are issues of timing.

If our neuron is involved in an experience that generates LTD (that is, prior experience with low-frequency signals), the cell cannot induce LTP for some time. During this time, it looks like would-be number two wins out. But if too much time passes between LTD's apparent victory and the new signals that normally generate LTP, then the neuron is ready to develop LTP again.

There is a dynamic back and forth between enhancing long-term memory and reducing it. Where we are at any moment depends on where we were before. This is a simple and beautiful example of the mind adapting to the world through experience.[16]

An Image of Memory

This discussion about LTP (long-term potentiation) and LTD (long-term depression) began earlier in this chapter when we first encountered the term "consolidation." My goal was to explain some ideas about how memory seems to be stabilized, and to see whether those ideas give us new thoughts about education.

From what we have seen so far, it is clear that memory is dynamic and flexible. Rather than a file cabinet model, or a hard drive, or even a RAM model of memory, it seems more accurate to view it as a process that is continuing and constantly changing. The terminology we find most often in our discussions of memory does not suggest images like "bits" or "hard-wired," but rather stresses "assembly," "reconstruction," or "weakening." For example, in the previous section, I created an image of "dance" or "flow." It is an image not only of recording facts and events, but also of the emotion of the learner, and the feelings that influence the mind during consolidation. To the extent that it involves this process of memory, the journey from brain to mind is flexible, emotional, dynamic, peaceful, restless, and gentle all at once.

Losing Memories: A Story

To introduce our next topic, here is another story.

> Recently, my wife and I took a trip to New York City to visit some museums. We always stay in the Murray Hill area, and one nearby museum is the Pierpont Morgan. Morgan collected a wide variety of beautiful things, including an amazing assortment of old books and manuscripts. For example, we saw one of the five remaining copies of the Gutenberg Bible, and in the same room there was a collection of the complete works of Goethe (which was huge!). If you have ever visited the relatively new part of the British Museum for books and manuscripts, you will have some picture of the Morgan. In fact, during my visit to the Morgan, I found myself remembering the British Museum often.
>
> We spent the entire morning at the Morgan and ate lunch in its cafeteria. I had an awful lunch, not because the food was awful, but because I chose weird things. I had what they called a "brie fondue" and a plate of mushroom deviled eggs.
>
> I am telling you all this because I want you to appreciate what happened later when I talked about my trip with a friend. It was a truly memorable experience, and I was quite confident that I would remember almost everything. But when I began to talk about it, I suddenly discovered a huge hole in my memory. I could remember the eggs, but I could not remember the name of the Morgan Museum!
>
> When I say hole, I mean a deep, black hole! In fact, I had the sensation of looking down into a black well every time I tried to remember the name. And it didn't come back to me! It seemed to be literally extinguished! Eventually, I had to ask my wife (something I really didn't want to do, for reasons some of you may understand).

This went on for several days. Every time I tried to think of the name Morgan, I came up blank. I could remember "British Museum" but not Morgan!

Extinction? Reconsolidation?

Before I turn to my theory of the Morgan Museum experience, let me mention a few additional terms that are frequently useful in describing memory experiences.

Extinction is one such term. When memories are recalled, they can become very fragile. And the fresher the memory, the more fragile it is. In some cases, connections seem to disappear completely; like ill-suited species in natural selection, they become extinct. Actually, Pavlov discovered memory extinction nearly a century ago, in his work with dogs. That work has been repeated in more recent times using rats or mice, and the following paragraphs describe an example of this research.

First, rats are placed in a cage that has an electrically wired floor. A few seconds later, the rat is given a small shock. It doesn't take long for the rat to remember that the cage means a shock is coming. If the experience is consistent—that is, every time the rat is put in the cage, it gets a shock after a few seconds—very soon the rat will begin to react to the cage by exhibiting the common fear behavior of tensing and freezing, even when there is no shock! The memory is clear and strong: cage = shock.

However, if the shock is taken out of the procedure, and the rat is placed in the cage multiple times without a shock, the fear behavior disappears. The association of the cage with the shock is not evident. It seems to be extinct. But, again, the dynamic nature of memory shows itself. After apparently being extinguished, the memory returns over time. And even more remarkable, the extinction itself becomes a memory. Research with humans shows that we can remember forgetting.

But back to rats. If the shock memory is reinforced consistently, the memory can become more stable. It can be *reconsolidated*. When memories are recalled, they are checked out. If they turn out to be right, they become stronger, but if they consistently turn out to be wrong, they can weaken and even seem to disappear.[17]

Finally, each of these three phenomena (consolidation, reconsolidation, extinction) has a biological story. Each requires the synthesis of new enzymes, engaging the slower cellular processes involving the expression of genes in the neuron nucleus. They are associated with changes in LTM (long-term memory), but at the same time, each one is linked with some separate and distinct biochemical processes. Each involves expression of different genes.[18]

Memory is dynamic and can be modified at any time, which could be the most complex and important (to us) example of the interaction of genes and experience.

My Extinction Experience

Here is my theory about the Morgan Museum experience:

I had just turned 65 (that is why we went to NYC), and am a bit of a hypochondriac, so this dramatic gap in my memory bothered me a lot for a few days. Ah! Early Alzheimer's! But I found an answer, which I now believe to be a viable explanation, rather than just a result of my state of denial. I believe that I experienced memory extinction.

The whole time I was visiting the Morgan, the British Museum was on my mind. In fact, I am not sure if I even explicitly or implicitly actively recalled the name Morgan. I probably did, but I was more aware of recalling British Museum. Of course, in planning our New York visit, my wife and I discussed the Morgan, the fact that it was near our B&B, and our interest in it. So the association of Murray Hill with Morgan was in my memory, but not the association between Morgan and manuscripts.

My guess is that my cues were inconsistent, a condition known to lead to memory extinction. My memory of books/manuscripts museum was cued most strongly and most frequently by "British Museum." But now it was also cued by Morgan Museum. The two cues could not exist in the same place in my networks. Just as in physics, two objects (cues) cannot exist at the same time in the same place. If the memory is a pattern of firing produced by a network of neurons, then the "cue position" in the networks cannot be occupied by two different things at once.

Remembering is physical.

Reconsolidation and a Heresy

Reconsolidation depends on activation of specific genes that regulate differentiation and mitogenesis. And those genes are different from the ones regulated in the original consolidation of LTP we discussed above.

What does this mean? What is differentiation? What is mitogenesis?

Differentiation is the development of differences between different cell types. For example, the processes that lead from an embryonic cell to a brain cell are different from those that would lead from the same embryonic cell if it were to differentiate into a kidney. Mitogenesis is simply the activation of cell division. The division of one cell into two requires a process of gene reproduction, called "mitosis." For a single human cell to divide into two *new* cells, mitogenesis must occur. Reconsolidation might actually require growth and development of *new cells* in some parts of the brain.

When it was first realized, this was surprising, almost heretical. For decades, neurologists believed that once a baby is born, no new cells develop in the brain. Rather, the process of learning begins and continues by development of connections between the *existing* neurons.

Early on, this belief was partially based on a lack of methods for actually detecting new cells even if they were there; it was primarily a technical barrier. However, this "no new neurons" belief was also a compelling idea because it seemed to provide an explanation for how memories and learning could be retained over a lifetime. If new neurons were actually being produced, wouldn't they invade the networks of existing neurons and, at the least, interfere with them or, at the worst, destroy them? It seemed, then, that learning must occur through new connections to neurons that have been present from the beginning of a lifetime.

Now it is generally accepted that over time new neurons do, indeed, develop in certain regions of the brain, in both the human brain and the brains of other animals. Of great interest, one of the primary regions where the new neurons appear is in the hippocampus, which is the structure in the brain most directly associated with memory formation.

Reconsolidation of memories is probably related to generation of new neurons. And, if so, this may open up new ideas and insights about the most important capability of the human brain: memory![19]

Where We Are

The topic of LTP is a difficult one, and it may be helpful to generalize and summarize before moving on to a discussion of "education for natural memory."

	Nature of Signal	Result	Key biochemical changes
1	Consistently very weak	Memory weakens	Synapse weakening
2	Intermediate	Short-term memory forms	Short-term synapse-strengthening-no nuclear change
3	Single intense burst	Long-term memory forms	Synapse growth and strengthening-nuclear events
4	Weak, then multiple intense	**Failure** of long-term memory formation	Inactivation of nuclear events
5	Weak, delay, multiple intense	Long-term memory forms	Same as 3 above for LTP

The table above is an attempt at such a summary. It shows the neuronal effect and biochemical events associated with different strength and timing of stimulating signals. Remember that the table would not change much if we used an emotion-chemical (for example, serotonin) as the signal, rather than electrical pulses.

Let's briefly review this table. Rows 1–3 show the effects we have just discussed, leading to weakening of synapses for a long time, strengthening of synapses for a short time, and strengthening of synapses for a long time. Rows 4 and 5 show an interesting outcome. When neurons are weakly stimulated and then given multiple intense stimuli, the weak signal seems to dominate the response, if it is followed immediately by strong ones. But if the weak stimulus is followed by a "rest period," normal LTP will result in response to multiple intense signals.

You might ask yourself whether rows 4 and 5 suggest anything about curriculum and timing in formal education settings. I will come back to this question later in the chapter.

Remembering Flow

I have said that memory is a dynamic process, but that concept may not be apparent in the table above. Dynamic and adaptive processes aren't necessarily represented well by tables, with their sharp boundaries that imply that a thing in one compartment is really separate from a thing in another compartment. There is not much room for change and process. Let's take a different perspective and try to imagine memory as process, a much more realistic image.

A dynamic representation of memory can be obtained if we imagine a continuous flow of cellular biochemical reactions. Each reaction has the potential to overlap with, interfere with, or enhance others in some way, and thus make a contribution to short-term memory, long-term memory, consolidation, extinction, and reconsolidation. Experiences are recorded and monitored moment-to-moment by billions of neurons. Some of the experiences are intense, some are weak and barely recognized, and some are actually below our consciousness. Some are repeated, and some happen only once. Some are very important to us, and others are not.

Neurons, then, experience a mix of all the processes I have described, and probably others as well that we do not yet know about. At any moment, short-term memory systems are active, both developing and fading out. At this same moment, long-term memory systems are being activated at many different levels of intensity. These long-term processes may lead to a lasting increase in strength of memory, or to a lasting weakening of memory. In the nucleus of some neurons, the frequency and timing of intense signaling favors consolidation, while in others, reconsolidation or extinction may be favored. In many cases these processes may be working together or competing with each other.

Memory is about flow, not file!

Education and Memory Formation

Following the research on LTP and LTD, it is obvious that timing of experiences plays a major role in memory. We may not quite know what the best timing is, but we may be getting the feeling that the way time is organized in a normal school day, or school year, may not be the most favorable for creating strong memories. It may well be worthwhile to experiment with different timing of classes, subject experiences, and even grading periods or semesters.

In addition to timing, it is obvious that intensity of experiences plays a key role. It seems natural that high-intensity stimulation, repeated frequently, favors establishment of long-term memory. However, the impact of low-intensity stimulation may be a bit of a surprise. And what surprises us is not the reduced signal (the D part of LTD,) but the "long-term" part. If neurons are accustomed to being quiet, then it may not be a surprise that their response to normal stimuli would be small. But that is not the main point. It is the idea that they *remember* to be quieter that catches our attention. As I have stressed, neurons remember both activity and inactivity.

The LTD/LTP research also points out a third factor important in memory: consistency. If stimulation does not have a pattern, the brain cannot develop a memory. Whether signals are strong or weak, they must be consistent to be remembered.

Neuron networks are a continuing project, dynamically strengthening and weakening as a function of experience. Consistent intense experience creates a dependable strong response, and consistent weak experiences create consistently small response. But both lead to long-term memory.

Timing and School

The three ideas I just described seem obvious, but it is surprising how often they are forgotten. However, if we want to apply them, there is one caution. Even if our assumptions that LTP and LTD are the neurological equivalents of memory, and electrical stimulation of neurons is the same as intense experience, it is important to realize that the details, such as the exact timing of LTM in a single neuron, may not transfer directly to memory in living organisms, such as people. For example, if research reveals that LTP takes an hour to develop in a single rat hippocampal cell, we should be careful in interpreting that result. We should not assume that establishing LTM in a human being will also take an hour.

I do think, however, that the neuroscience data may suggest some useful "ballpark" ideas or some possible starting points. For example, if it takes a few minutes to see development of LTP in a single neuron, we might use this information as a starting point for examining the timing of intermediate-term memories in people. We probably would not want to design such experiments over time spans of seconds, days, or weeks.

In some cases, the neuroscience results actually coincide reasonably well with our intuitions about the time factor for memory formation in people. For example, the nuclear processes for creation of LTP in mouse neurons last about 30 minutes, which is consistent with the practice times needed for humans to learn new skills.[20]

Here are a few more suggestions of this sort:

1. Since LTP requires *repeated* strong stimulation, schedules and curriculum should be arranged so that key ideas, skills, and facts are repeated in our courses. One-time exposures such as those produced by a "linear" syllabus are not the ideal.
2. In our experimenting with repetition, we can make some general suggestions. For example, we might repeat specific ideas or facts three or four times, and the time interval between repetition events might be on the order of hours, rather than minutes or days.
3. Since development of LTP is inhibited when very strong pulses have been immediately preceded by very weak ones, classes might be arranged so that students who have been daydreaming do not have to jump promptly and intensely into new material.
4. Very intense experiences should not follow other intense ones immediately, as suggested by the results of a series of multiple strong bursts in the table above. This can happen in schools at all levels; for example, a Mon/Wed/Fri schedule in college with three science classes in a row separated by 10-minute intervals. Curricular planning could take the neuroscience research into consideration.

I offer these suggestions as examples, but I believe that all of them deserve experimentation and rethinking of our decades-old educational schedules and curricula.

Certainly, these have never been guided by neuroscience!

Revisiting Errorless Learning

Other interesting ideas emerge from the discovery of LTD. For example, this neuronal phenomenon seems to support the idea of "errorless learning" that I described in *The Art of Changing the Brain*. When signals are weak, and the background level even, synapses may be weakened through LTD. But the intensity of signaling is determined by the *nature* of the experiences and environment, not by the intent of the educator. In education, if we stress what is wrong, we may not find a reduced level of error. Error may even be enhanced because we stress it so much. Better to be quiet about the wrong and stress what is right. Don't repeatedly engage networks that demonstrate errors or remind learners of error.

In education, the brain perspective helps us realize once again that learning is not something directly transferred by instruction. Rather it is the brain's natural response to changes in signaling produced by experience. Educators who understand that firing of specific individual neurons is changed simply and directly by the firing of other neurons in a network, will realize that it is the experiences themselves that generate change. Lesson plans and their inherent philosophy that learning can be "planned," or controlled, do not always fit this biological picture.

Remembering Emotion

The images we remember most easily are the ones we associate with emotion. They are images of friends, nature, cars, graves, skeletons, friendly faces, angry faces, frightened faces, and so forth. The images that are harder to remember just don't trigger much in us. As I stressed at the beginning of this chapter, almost all of a baby's experiences have the potential for emotional engagement. An example of this is found in research on recognizing faces of chimpanzees. If exposed to such faces during the first year of life, human babies can recognize different chimps later in life. But if the exposure begins during later years, this ability does not develop in the child. They remain more like you and me who shrug and say, "All chimps look alike." Things that look neutral and bland are that way because they do not trigger strong memories.

The experience of remembering is, in itself, emotional. This is wonderful because it can become a central tool for educators. Success in recall creates emotion links that enhance the chance of remembering better. And intrinsic motivation develops from success!

This topic of recall is for the next chapter, but here it seems worthwhile to point out a logical reason why recall is emotional and motivating. This explanation takes us back to evolution. The survival brain remembered the things that might change our life: danger, opportunity, attraction, and repulsion. For survival, it was essential to remember these, and, by definition, importance triggers emotion. It *is* emotion.

Salience generates memory because emotion chemicals change synapses.

Environment, Attention, and Memory

We have not yet mentioned a very obvious ideas about memory formation: the impact of the environment and the importance of paying attention to it.

This aspect is directly related to a question about memory that has mystified neuroscientists for many decades: Where is the memory stored? Many experiments have been done trying to find a physical place in the brain where memories are located.

To see the relationship between this question of brain location for a memory and the environment, it is helpful to discuss briefly why the search for a brain location was so frustrating. This search was based on the "filing cabinet" metaphor for memory, and, for a long time, no one questioned this model. The search for memory files continued, with little or no consideration of the possibility that they don't exist. Now, however, we have a more dynamic model of memory. This model envisions memory as a continuing *process* of synapse changes in networks of neurons. This process includes the original short-term changes, followed by consolidation into longer-lasting ones. It also includes recall, in which the networks become more labile. The memory itself seems to be a moving target. In fact, in experiments with simple organisms like fruit flies, research suggests that memories do shift physical locations with time.[21]

In this model, the process, then, begins with activation of cortical regions that were part of the original experience or event. For example, visual experiences are initially formed in visual cortex, auditory ones in auditory cortex. The strongest elements of the memory are those that are part of the original experience, of the environment, and the sensory nature of the experience.

This, then, is where the question of environment resurfaces. If we pay attention to the process of forming memory, including the brain sensory systems that were activated, and the environment associated with the central elements, the memory will contain information about those aspects, so the networks that represent it will be more extensive. For educators, this suggests that memory formation may be aided by paying attention to the setting, timing, and particular sensory nature of the original experience and information. Trying to create a memory of the full experience, rather than just parts of it, may be more likely to generate LTP.

Advice for learners: remember that memory is a process and attend to the brain systems where the process began and the environment in which it proceeded.

Revisiting

To help remember important parts of this chapter, here are 10 key points. They don't cover everything, but they may give us cues for future recall.

- Timing, intensity, and consistency all play important roles in memory formation.
- Memories are distributed throughout the cortex; they are not "filed."
- Memories do not last for a specific length of time; they are dynamic.
- Memory is a tool for learning, not a goal.
- Memories are remodeled with time and recall.
- Memories can be extinguished.
- Emotion strengthens memory, and vice versa.
- Strength of memories can be increased or decreased by attached "baggage."
- Cues are often "baggage," contextual and/or extraneous, but still part of the scene.
- Attending to the context, as well as the main point, will form stronger memories.

Transition

This chapter has focused on formation of memories. My goal has been to provide an overview of the dynamic and complex nature of the process. Now it is time to turn to the phenomenon of recalling memories. Recall is essential in making memories useful, and it depends on many brain functions that are centered in areas of cortex found toward the front of the cerebrum. This is in contrast to the location of the memory-*forming* regions of the brain discussed in this chapter, which are located more toward the back.

The total memory package involves major regions of both front and back cortex. Both of them represent major components in the development of mind. Once useful memories have begun to build, we can use them as material for thought and the other processes we associate with mind, such as problem solving, choice, and intent. In fact, we could argue that recall of memories is the only way they can be useful. Reaching a point where we can use our memories to achieve our life objectives. and overcome barriers that prevent us from reaching them, is the ultimate goal in the journey toward mind.[22]

This can happen with recall.

Notes

1. Prenatal memory and learning is now a widely accepted concept. This topic is beyond what we discuss here, but for a concise and authoritative description of this assertion, see David Chamberlain's essay at http://www.birthpsychology.com/lifebefore/earlymem.html.

2. Mindless repeating can be the enemy of enrichment, so that is another challenge for education. More on this later, in chapter 9.

3. In this example, I am influenced by my impression that toys for children can be overkill. In the desire to elicit a laugh or some other behavior, there can be too much sensory experience. I am thinking of simple, primal observation and reflection over time—rich reflection.

4. Reiner, M. (2008), Visualization: Theory and Practice in Science Education, *Models and Modeling in Science Education*, 3, section A, pp. 73–84.

5. http://ww1.babyzone.com/baby/nurturing/baby_week_by_week/article/week-3-baby

6. http://www.loweringthebar.net/2010/02/baby-einstein-will-not-make-your-baby-einstein-lawsuit-claims.html

7. http://www.janehealy.com/

8. http://en.wikipedia.org/wiki/Cultural_neuroscience

9. This drawing shows the changes as occurring in the sensory neuron. Other models show them in the motor neuron, where the changes are primarily in the receptor molecules. change in both sensory and motor neuron probably can occur.

10. This figure is reprinted with permission from Kandel, E. R. (2006), *In Search of Memory*, W. W. Norton, New York, NY, p. 256.

11. Whitlock, J. R., and colleagues (2006), *Science*, 313, 1093–1097; Gruart, A., et al. (2007), *Learning and Memory*, 14, pp. 54–62; also see review of the Gruart paper by Claudia Wiedemann (2007), *Nature Reviews Neuroscience*, 8, p. 84.

12. This may be highly confusing, but I urge you not to give up. Rather, look at Eric Kandel's new book, *In Search of Memory*, which places these biochemical ideas in the context of his day-to-day life and experiences. The story is engaging and will help you understand and remember more of the specifics. And, in particular, you will frequently find the term CREB when reading about memory. This is a key molecule that is involved in the nuclear expression of new memory enzymes, and its central role has been demonstrated in sea slugs, fruit flies, mice, apes, and humans.

13. We revisit this idea in later chapters when we discuss the creative functions of the frontal regions of cortex and recognize that many of the synapses in this region of cortex are *inhibitory* in nature.

14. A useful reference that provides the specific timing and relationships between LTP and LTD is Klann, E., (2002), Commentary, *Learning and Memory*, 9, pp. 153–155.

15. These are not the only enzymes involved, but they are key ones. There undoubtedly are many others with roles that we do not yet understand or do not know about.

16. It helps our understanding of these timing data to realize that the background firing (not related to particular stimuli, but just spontaneous activity) of neurons can actually be higher than the 5 per second. Every spike takes a few milliseconds (thousandth of a second), so there is time for up to, perhaps, a few hundred each second. Thus, at 5 per second, the neuron is experiencing about 1 percent of its capabilities. A train of 5 per second is actually relatively quiet. This is also discussed in chapter 3.

17. It must be said that these ideas are based primarily on stimulus-response learning, where the evidence of memory is a behavior. There is still much to be done to test their validity for the deeper learning we discussed in earlier chapters.

18. Lee, J., Everitt, B., and Thomas, K. (2004), *Science*, 304, pp. 830–843; also see Izquierdo, I., and Cammarota, M., on p. 829 of the same issue for commentary; Suzuki, A., et al. (2004), *Journal of Neuroscience*, 24, pp. 4787–4795.

19. I will not go into the factors that may stimulate production of new neurons in the brain. But so far, those things are the most obvious you could think of. Consistent with everything we have learned about neurons and their response to experience, two of the most obvious ways to stimulate new neuron generation are new learning and exercise. With all of the research we have discussed, we are reminded once again that the human mind is biological. If we want the mind to develop, we first must care for its biological needs; needs as basic as food, oxygen, and activity. Learning is, indeed, about biology!

20. Important work on the biochemical nature of cell signaling processes and the timing of stimuli for memory formation has been done by R. Douglas Fields and his colleagues at the NIH: Fields, R. D. (2005, February), Making Memories Stick, *Scientific American*, pp. 75–81.

21. This research is described in SoRelle, R. (2005), Memories Reside in Different Brain Cells at Different Times, *From the Laboratories at Baylor*, 4:10, which explains the work of Dr. R. L. Davis at the Baylor College of Medicine.

22. This back/front separation was the central theme of the *Art of Changing the Brain*. Readers can find its rationale there.

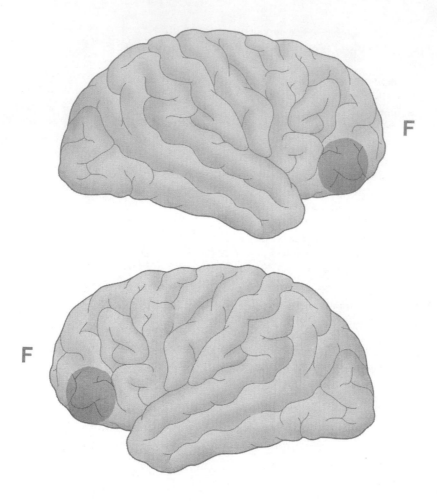

Areas of cortex heavily involved in memory recall. Top is right lateral view (episodic memory), and bottom is left lateral (declarative memory).

8

USING MEMORY
Destination and the Journey Toward Mind

It is a poor sort of memory that only works
backward.

—The Queen of Hearts, speaking to Alice

*(Continuing the story from chapter 7 about my oral exam and major
failure of recall.) Fortunately, there was a good outcome. I was not left
to wallow in utter dejection for very long. I did pass the examination;
my committee gave me a break. But still, I was embarrassed and frustrated. That exam was in the back of my mind every minute!*

*My mental salvation appeared unexpectedly. The next day in the
lab, one of my fellow students asked me about enzymes. She wanted to
analyze her own data and wasn't sure how to do that. She did not know
what had happened in my exam—that I had been exposed as an enzyme
ignoramus—so she still thought I might be able to help.*

*After she talked to me for a few minutes, I got very interested and
began to think about her problem. I momentarily forgot my exam angst,
grabbed a piece of chalk, and drew a graph on the board. I explained
how to use the graph and the value of that information. Effortlessly, I
found myself using the equation that I could not even recall the day
before.*

*We talked a bit more, and she thanked me and went back to her
lab bench. And as I stood there in my lab, looking at the blackboard, I
suddenly realized what had happened.*

*My heart soared! When I needed to use that equation to solve a real
problem, I remembered everything. Not only did I remember it, but I
explained it and used it. Once the challenge became real—more than a*

test question out of the blue or a stand-alone memory—my knowledge became accessible and almost automatic.

I was almost (but not quite) excited enough to demand another exam!

This chapter is about the capabilities of nature's mind that we assigned to the front integrative cortex in chapter 4. In general, these capabilities tend to be linked to what we call intelligence. Thus, we begin by referencing a provocative and intriguing book by Jeff Hawkins, entitled *On Intelligence.*[1]

In this book, among others, two proposals struck me. The first is that "calculation" is not an appropriate term to describe the capabilities of the brain. Any functions that might appear to depend on calculation can be explained by memory. The second is that a good definition of intelligence requires reference to "prediction," and prediction also depends on memory.

Mind is all about memory.

A Giant Leap

Hawkins's proposals are a huge leap. If correct, they help us over hurdles that have hindered understanding of the most interesting functions of the human brain: (1) the capability of idea generation (producing new patterns), and (2) the action response to ideas evidenced by capabilities such as creative work or making choices. If these most intriguing aspects of thought and intelligence can be linked to memory, then we are much closer than we may have imagined to explaining the concept of mind. There is more research on the details of memory than on any other cognitive topic about the brain. If, indeed, cognition can be explained by memory, then we may realize one day soon that we already have explanations for questions about mind with which we have struggled ever since we became aware of them.

The Two-Way Highway

When I say that intelligence is based on memory, I don't mean that it's about *memorizing.* By itself, knowing things does not define intelligence. As I have argued from the beginning of this book, intelligence is what we can do with what we know; it is about action.

We talked about forming memories in chapter 7. But, as this chapter title implies, and the Queen of Hearts asserts, memory is much more than a trail to the past. It is also the vehicle that takes us to the future; it is a two-way street. We travel one way when we create memories and come back the other way when we use them. In chapter 7 we discussed the first direction, the creation of memories; now we examine the other direction, the recall and use of memory.

This separation between forming memories and recalling them may not occur to us when we find ourselves wishing we had a better memory. We just complain that we forget things. But usually it is failure of recall that sets off the alarm. We may have a strong feeling that we do have a memory somewhere, but we just can't access it.

Memories Come With Attachments: A Reminder

As the two stories about my doctoral examination illustrate, we frequently try to remember things in isolation. Exhibit number one is my failure to remember the enzyme equation. I was asked to recall the intact memory without any of the connections that come with it—a memory in a vacuum. But, by itself, a memory may be of little use. We want access to the memory so we can do something with it. Memory served me well when I needed to solve a problem; it failed me in a vacuum.

This point is certainly worth emphasizing. Stand-alone memories may help you become a millionaire on a TV quiz show or even pass a chemistry test in college, but for real work with real problems, memory cannot stand alone. Everything we remember is associated with something else, something unique. Recalling a specific memory or part of a memory can be just the first step in a continuing process of following a "trail." Any specific aspect of a memory is part of solving a problem, making a prediction, making a decision, or creating something new.

It leads us to the future.

Memory as a Tool

To develop this idea further, here is a word-processing analogy.

When we open a document, we bring back something that we have stored on the hard drive. It was created in the past, and we can bring it into the present. There can be many reasons for doing this. For example, we may want to confirm a fact, or give the memory to another person (send it or print it), or make an exact copy to be sure we do not lose it in the future.

Possibly the most important reason to call up a document is so we can use it to make something new. When I bring up a chapter of this book from my hard drive, my purpose is almost always to build on or change it. As I begin to read the chapter, my fingers go to the keyboard, and I begin immediately to improve it (or so I think at the time). I edit sentences, move topics around, and so on. Eventually, I have something that may be vastly different from the file I first opened. I have been thinking forward.

The original file is only a tool for creating a new one, and creating the new one destroys the original. The original was most important when it stimulated new ideas.

If we are going to *use* the memory, we need more than just recall. We need to use the "action programs" in our word processor to work on the memory—to manipulate, supplement, and invent new parts. Otherwise, the memories just sit there on the screen.

We need more than storage and, indeed, more than recall.

Driving Recall

Despite memory failures, we need to recognize how well and how frequently recall works for us. Most often, whatever we need is right there when we need it. For example, in writing or speaking, we continually recall the right words as we need them, the images that are part of the story we are telling, and the way our language requires us to weave the two together in effective and essential ways.

Any failures of recall remind us of another important fact: recall is intimately connected to emotion. We have our intentions—things we want—so it is frustrating when memory fails, but it is satisfying and rewarding when it succeeds. Recalling memories is a key to creating new ones. This takes energy, but we are willing to invest that energy to get what we need to satisfy ourselves. As we discussed earlier, recall is driven by the emotional brain, by our wants and ambitions.

Recall and Place

In chapter 7 we discussed the idea that memories are formed in context. The focal point is important, but so are the peripheral ones. Both are part of sensory experience. Sometimes memories of the central aspects can be triggered by working on the peripheral ones, the environment in which things happened.

When I find myself striding purposefully out of my home office and toward the kitchen, but suddenly cannot remember why, I may regain my recall of my purpose by going back to the room where the idea for my kitchen trip originated. Returning to the place where I realized my need to head to the kitchen may remind me what that need was/is. The sensory networks that fire when I am back in the study are linked (although perhaps weakly) to other networks that fired the last time I was there, and the image of my keys may suddenly come along with them. Aha! I need those keys! They're in the kitchen.

The spatial environment can be a strong cue for recall (remembering back). However, it can also be a catalyst for remembering ahead. Our predictions of the future are strongly based on what happened in the past. This can be a good thing or a bad thing. It is good when I can remember my keys, but it may be bad if I try to predict where they are later. Strong links with the past tend to bias us when we want to predict. We may fail to recognize subtle but distinct differences between past and present.

Here is a neuroscience example: In research with rats, it was found that "place cells" in the hippocampus remain linked to specific environments, but also may be mistakenly used when the environment is ambiguous. A rat might learn that a piece of cheese is always found in a circular space and never in a square space. But if the rat finds itself in an octagonal space, the hippocampal "place cells" that identify the circular environment still fire, albeit more weakly, and the rat looks for the cheese in the wrong place.[2]

Another example is the difference between home court and visitor in basketball. The "home court advantage" has always puzzled me. Players often shoot the ball better on the home court. The basket is the same height and size at home or away, the ball is the same, the three-point line is the same distance from the basket, the "key" is the same size, and the free throw line is the same distance from the basket. Why would the visiting team have more difficulty?

One popular explanation is the support of the fans' home team, but that cuts both ways. You may play better with support, or you may play worse. The pressure may get to you when others are hoping you do well. An explanation I prefer has to do with "place cells." The environmental cues are a little bit different. The home building is larger or smaller, the home crowd is closer or farther away, the visiting and home benches may be in slightly different places, the scoreboard may be larger or smaller. The place cells of the visiting players may send some confusing or uncertain signals. The physical surroundings are a bit unfamiliar, and memory recall may lack certainty. The emotional link to memory may be slightly different, generating mild anxiety, loss of confidence, or even fear.

It could be that our team would shoot better when away from home if they visualize their home space. Hmmm . . . I'll have to speak to our coach about that!

Sequence and Memory

In general, we recall things that happened in a sequence. But the sequence an expert (educator) uses may not be the same one a novice uses. Educators' inclination to logical thought tends to focus their memory on cause and effect. In time, this means that we pay attention first to the things that happen first. One thing happened, and that caused the second thing to happen: first cause, then effect.

We educate that way. We design curricula to build logically from first causes, we teach a class starting with what came first (which may be one of the most significant reasons why children and young people dislike history so much), and we build ideas in science and math starting with abstract, thus distant or faint (or invisible), causes. For example, in chemistry, we start with atoms. To a novice the atom is an abstraction, but to the expert chemist it is the first and most essential aspect for understanding chemistry.

However, another memory experiment leads to a different idea with regard to students. Rats were allowed to run through a maze that had a piece of cheese at the end. As the animals progressed through the maze, different place cells fired in the rat hippocampus. The cells for the first parts of the maze fired first, those for the middle fired second, and those at the end fired last. This was the predicted result.

However, as the rat nibbled away, the place cells for the previous locations also fired; the rat was remembering the way through the maze. Most important, the *sequence* of firing as the rat remembered was not in the sequence of discovery, but the reverse. The place visited most recently was remembered first, then the earlier ones. The last set of place cells to fire were the ones that came earliest in the experience of the rat.[3]

There are at least two possible explanations for this result. One is that events closest in time are remembered better than those more distant in time. For a novice, that would seem likely. It may be the way we *all* recall first experiences. Alternatively, the sequence of firing may be specific for reward pathways, with the strongest neuron firing associated with the most likely locus for reward (that is, the closest one).

Whatever the explanation, the observed sequence in the rat experiment is different from that of the expert where recall of first *causes* is first. This is the way deep understanding is achieved. The expert reconstructs memories of the whole experience, since first events may cause second ones. This deeper understanding also allows for the possibility of prediction. When one knows the cause, an expert can predict the outcome, and thus he or she does not have to remember it.

This research provokes serious questions for education. For example: What are the consequences if we ask learners to learn things in an unnatural sequence, beginning the process with the parts that are least recent?

Are we expecting education to run backward?

Category and Recall

These experiments were done with rats, so, although the results give us interesting ideas for human beings, we can't be sure those ideas are correct until more research is done. Let's move ahead and look at some research with humans.

Analysis of recall in real time has been conducted using brain imaging (fMRI) techniques. People were asked to randomly recall 30 pictures they had already studied for several minutes. Each picture was a face, an object, or a location, and the recall assignment was to speak the word at the top of each picture—for example, "Tom Jones," "Hawaii," "Buick," etc. During the experiment, fMRI scans of the three regions of temporal cortex associated with these categories (face, object, and location) were obtained.

The results were striking. During the studying time, as the images were shown, the region of cortex consistent with the category became most active. For example, as they studied a face, the face area of temporal cortex was most active. During the time the participants were asked to remember the pictures, successful recall was most often preceded by activation of these same regions of cortex: the category regions.

Such a linkage of recall to the category does not necessarily surprise us. However, the time factors in these experiments may. Reactivation of the category regions of cortex preceded successful recall of specific labels by *seconds*. That is, the process of recall moved through two stages: first, activation of category regions of cortex, followed one or more seconds later by actual verbal recall of the specific label. The category was remembered first, and then—after a delay—the exact label (for example, first identify *face* category, then identify the specific person, *Tom Jones.*)

Two education generalizations seem apparent from this study. First, it may help learners to consciously identify the category of things they want to remember before attempting specific declarative recall. Second, the time lag of seconds is longer than teachers usually allow when students are asked to recall specifics.

Memory Extinction: A Role for School

In chapter 7 I stated that memories seem to become fragile when recalled. Once we bring a memory back into our consciousness, it is in danger of being damaged or even destroyed. We are not sure why this happens, but it is probably related to the fact that memories brought into the conscious state are also exposed to all the other high-intensity neurological patterns that are firing as we attend to our other conscious experiences and the environment. In the conscious state, perhaps there are just too many competing networks firing at the same time. Bits and pieces of unreinforced memory may be lost in all the chatter.

This extinction of memories draws our attention back to the idea that the purpose of recall is to use the memory. Recalled memories are only partway along their journey—a dangerous part! But dangerous only if the parts that are lost are critical. Losing aspects of a memory that have changed with time or that are more distracting than helpful is not a bad thing; it may actually be helpful. It appears that we have the machinery needed to continually remodel memories, especially to forget things that aren't useful or are not part of something that must be used in its totality. In that view, recall becomes a moment of opportunity. It is a chance to discard aspects that are not relevant or useful—not reinforced—while at the same time reconsolidating and strengthening those aspects that are essential.

It is only through the *use* of memory that this becomes apparent. In my story at the beginning of this chapter, my recall was complete when I used it to solve a real problem. The parts fell into place when they were used. But the isolated memory of the equation itself had disappeared; it was useless.

Extinction can be a part of repair.

Choosing

Recall often requires choice. We must choose what memories we need at any particular time. Often it is this first step that goes off target. We make the wrong choice and recall memories that are irrelevant or only partly relevant. Thus, although our understanding of choice is fuzzy at best, it is still worthwhile to examine existing theories and models for the phenomenon of choosing.

A common feature in such models is the idea that choosing between two network patterns formed in the integrative back cortex (chapter 4) depends on processes that engage the front integrative cortex. For example, one recent proposal suggests that we create images of the possible choices (there may be several possibilities) that we then hold in back integrative cortex while each one is analyzed by comparing it to an "ideal" image created and held in front cortex.[4] When one back cortex image (a pattern of firing neurons) comes closest to matching the front cortex image, the other back cortex images are "quenched." The remaining back cortex image then serves as the template for action, initiated and controlled by motor cortex.

This theory uses vague terms, and we do not know much about those terms, how they work, or even if they are appropriate. I mention them because the forward remembering that leads to plans and actions depends totally on what memories we "choose" to recall. Those memories contain the back cortex images I mentioned above. If we make the wrong choices, recalling the wrong things, we will make the wrong predictions.

It is important for educators to know how different students, or different groups of students, may make their choices. Good choices are ones that are useful for predictions. When faced with a problem to solve, or the need for an idea, it helps to focus on neuron-firing patterns (memories) that overlap with those that make up the new problem (the prediction).

Attention to overlapping patterns may be essential for correct recall.

The Foundation of Choice

Sometimes I wonder whether the term "cognitive" raises the wrong images in our minds. Primarily out of habit, we may find ourselves thinking that cognition is mechanical, and our goal is to discover the mechanics. Those mechanics are such things as patterns, representations, networks of neurons, and so on. In searching for explanations or mechanisms of cognition, we naturally turn to the mechanics. We believe they provide us with the basis for cognition. This idea is at least partially true, and I have just used it in the paragraphs above.

But "partially" is the key word, and the missing part is significant. That "missing part" consists of emotional or affective processes also linked to cognition. Understandings depend on more than the physical structure of neuron networks. One important reason that we may ignore the role of emotion in cognition is that we do not yet have good physical explanations for emotion and feeling. We know that certain parts of the brain and certain chemicals are involved, and we also know that awareness of affective processes comes through the body. But we cannot yet write out a series of steps that actually explains what emotion is. What is joy? What is grief? What are the molecular processes that explain them?

I also sense a bias among researchers that comes from an attraction to the precise and analytical, and an aversion to the "softer" ideas of feelings. As cognitive science has left the fields of philosophy and psychology, and moved toward the molecular and physical disciplines, there is an attendant inclination to prefer ideas of "calculations," and even complex mathematics. When we say that the brain "calculates" or makes "calculations," the images of mathematics come up. With those images may come other images of precise and invariant answers—true answers!

However, as noted in earlier chapters, if we accept the statistical nature of biological phenomena, the term "calculation" may seem inadequate, even misleading. Statistical models force us to ask, "What is most likely?" rather than "What is the right answer?" Furthermore, when we think of the irregular, immensely complex, and totally unpredictable networks of neurons, we are forced to seriously question the idea that they can identify or direct any precise process originating from intent, and following a specific set of "operations." Rather, it appears that there are a large number (perhaps even an unlimited number) of complex connections, and that nature's mind involves trial and error more than the exact "wiring" we imagine is needed for "calculation."

In this book, the argument is that choices are not calculated but, rather, estimated. This involves the emotion systems. We may use the factual data from patterns of images to make estimates, but the act of choice is an emotional one. Even when we use reason to arrive at a choice, we still make the rational choice because it produces the best feelings; we have the most confidence in reason, and confidence is a feeling.

Opportunistic Mind: Choosing on the Run

Our efforts to commit to our choices are a bit humorous. We analyze things carefully, try to see logical outcomes, and keep our eye on the ball. But despite our intentions, this is really not our nature. Often we drift off topic; we are easily distracted. The excitement of the moment and the movement of our thoughts and conversations often lead us to nearly subconscious decisions to go off-target. We begin to make choices on the run. Our interests drift, depending on the stimulus of the moment. Suddenly a new memory pops into mind, and we begin thinking and talking about it. It feels too important to ignore, and before we know it we are responding to this emotional impulse to go off on a tangent. The imprecise and statistical nature of our choices leads to this behavior.

We don't drift intentionally, and it is not a character flaw. I observe it every day in my colleagues, the great majority of whom are dependable and respectable people. In my experience, the best opportunity to watch people go off-target is a faculty meeting. It seems that the more active the collection of minds, the more likely it is to encounter endless and unique diversions. They provide us with opportunities for a joke or for telling a story, and few of us can resist.

Wandering

This opportunistic behavior suggests a dynamic and active image of mind, responding to external stimuli with emotion and energy, shifting attention, and continually inclined to go off on personal tangents.

But there is another aspect of the opportunistic mind, one less characterized by effort and more by drifting. We might call this wandering, or daydreaming. This phenomenon has been called "stimulus–independent activity."[5] Rather than responding to stimuli in the environment, the mind wanders. It reverts to a more passive state, taking a break and even ignoring challenges or stimuli. Often we enter this wandering state of mind soon after we have been working hard, paying careful attention, and expending a lot of mental energy. Then our mind just takes a rest.

Experiments have been done to define regions of cortex that are more active when the mind enters such a resting stage, and that become less active when the mind is challenged to focus or learn new skills. The findings suggest the existence of a "default network" that characterizes wandering. Of considerable interest, this network consists primarily of deeper regions of cortex commonly considered part of the limbic system. These deep middle parts of the frontal cortex have frequently been associated with flexibility and social cooperation. In addition, these networks include the insula, a region of cortex that monitors body feelings such as pain. The cognitive regions of cortex that we have focused on (sensory, integrative, motor) are noticeably inactive in this "default network."

These observations suggest that the wandering mode is primarily associated with emotions, feelings, and behavior instincts. It is as if the brain is monitoring the internal frame of mind and body, staying flexible, while ignoring external events and processes.

Staying easy!

Emotion and Recall

Earlier in this chapter I discussed choice and how it is involved in recall. I argued that choice is based on emotion and how we feel about our experiences. We recall the ones with the greatest emotional impact, and we find it difficult to separate cognition, or thought, from feelings.

More recent research tends to strengthen this entanglement of memory with emotion. Experiments with monkeys have shown that dense amnesia can be induced by cutting axons that carry signals from the brain stem and emotion centers (regions rich in chemicals such as dopamine or serotonin) *without* disturbing at all the hippocampus or the cortical regions around it. Presumably, in these animals with intact hippocampus and the surrounding regions of cortex that are so heavily engaged in memory *formation*, this amnesia arises through failure of recall. This finding strengthens the concept of intense and ancient association between memory recall and emotion, since it depends so strongly on the evolutionarily most primitive regions of primate brain.[6]

Paying attention to the emotional context in recalled memories may, in fact, provide the most powerful cues to the central aspect of the memory. Remembering how something "felt" may open the way to extensive and detailed recall.

Working Memory and Prediction

To use memory for predicting, our theory is that the images and symbols generated in the back parts of the cerebral cortex are dynamically "moved" to the frontal regions, where they can be processed by working memory. This transfer of patterns from back to front cortex can be either a conscious process or a subconscious one, if it is habitual. Once the neuronal network representing a memory has been placed in working memory, we can do the "work." This involves manipulation and rearrangement of patterns derived from or related to images. It provides us with new images from which we select those that are predicted to be most beneficial and most likely to lead to our goals. It is from these new combinations of bits of memory that new firing patterns are produced, and thus may lead to prediction. The images of the future are assembled from memories of the past.

The following story is an attempt to give you a concrete example.

On a mild October Saturday, you decide to take a drive out into farm country to see the autumn colors. As you drive along one of the scenic back roads, you come upon an apple orchard. You know that it is an apple orchard because the trees are in rows, and you can see red objects hanging from the branches. In brain terminology, it is likely that the form and color of the trees and the apples is assembled by integration into one image, ultimately to arrive at single cells that respond only to apple trees. These "apple tree cells" fire most strongly when the visual system "sees" apple trees, and less strongly or not at all when we see other fruit trees. This first part of the example uses the capabilities of back cortex in gathering sensory data and integrating it (see chapter 4).

You then notice that one tree has a ladder lying on the ground beneath it. Our memory system allows us to identify the ladder in exactly the same way we identified the apples and the trees. We remember what ladders look like, and we have a language symbol system that allows us to label them. It's a "ladder" or, perhaps, a "stepladder."

Memory kicks in again. Our mind brings up remembered images of ladders leaning against tree branches with people picking the apples. Now, we predict: someone is going to pick apples.

But the prediction is not a certainty; it is a guess based on probability. Maybe the ladder was left there by accident or by intent, and someone plans to pick it up later. Still, it is the time of year to pick apples, so that prediction seems most probable. There can be additions to a list of possibilities, but in every case the prediction is a new image, assembled with parts of old memories taking the form of a probability.

This is a highly simplified illustration, but we can quickly imagine more complex and more impressive predictions. For example, we can sometimes finish the sentences of a person who is speaking to us. We predict what the person is going to say based on memories of what he or she has already said and other remembered clues.

Interestingly, predictions often lead to inventions. Before we all had them, computer engineers predicted cell phones. By remembering what computers do and that we all have phones, this prediction seemed obvious. To intentionally create a new object or process, we must first imagine it. We must remember forward.

Attending and Memory Recall

To become aware of our ideas, we must attend to them. In fact, one of the more important aspects of learning is our ability to attend to our own thought processes. This ability is sometimes called *metacognition*, and is defined as consciousness of our own thinking. It is the central topic of the last chapter in this book.

It would be a great step forward if we developed an understanding of the brain processes involved in attention. It would bring us deeper insight into consciousness itself. The most commonly mentioned idea is that neurons that make up a pattern seem to begin firing in phase with each other, thus strengthening the sensory patterns of interest. Of great interest, this process actually leads to *weaker* firing of neurons that are not part of the stimulus, because they are not in phase. That fact makes them irrelevant.[7]

This idea is of major importance in any situation where we try to pay attention to specific aspects of our experience. This is illustrated in the figure below. The main point of the figure is that when two neurons fire to produce a quick change in voltage (firing up)[8] at the same time (in phase), the net signal is increased. But if one fires up at the same time that another fires down (out of phase), the total signal is smaller and can even disappear if the two signals completely cancel each other out.

The brain waves that are increased in attention are quite high in frequency (roughly between 40 and 70 per second) and are characteristic of awake, alert, and conscious behaviors. Those that are weakened are of significantly lower frequency, taking them nearly into the range that characterizes drowsiness.

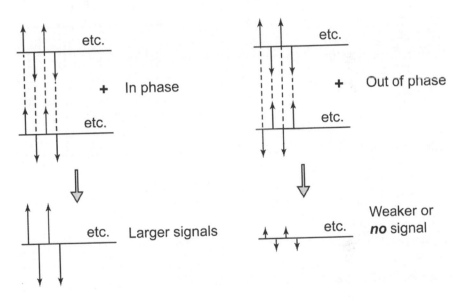

Possibly the most interesting aspect of attention is the *reduced* attention to the irrelevant. This phenomenon is not widely known, but it may be helpful when thinking about schooling and education. Often, when we focus intensely on a particular thing, we may miss something else that is physically right next to it. I had this experience once in a college class when I sat next to a girl with whom I was in love. I expressed all the typical male behaviors designed to get attention from a potential mate. I made jokes, talked too much, smiled a lot, and complimented her in every way I could think of. I paid a lot of attention to her! At the same time, another interesting girl sat down right in front of me, and I did not notice her at all. I was astonished to see her there at the end of class.

A particularly compelling example of this can be found at the website given as reference[9] at the end of this chapter. If you watch the movie, pay careful attention to the two teams (white shirts and black shirts) and how many successful throws they make. Who is winning? But don't watch it just once!

Inattention and Memory Recall

In certain clinical conditions people can be totally unaware of objects in specific parts or regions of the outside world. This difficulty most often arises as a result of damage to the upper right part of the brain (particularly the back part) due to a stroke or an accident. Most often people with this problem show no awareness of objects, events, or actions that are part of the left visual field. So when asked to draw the face of a clock, they will draw the right side (numbers 1, 2, 3, . . . etc.) but neglect the left side. Basically, they are only aware of half a clock.

This condition, called the "neglect syndrome," has been of great interest to neuroscientists. Neglect implies that the issue is attention: "If only they would quit neglecting parts of the world and pay attention to them!" But more recent work also links neglect to memory recall. People with this condition fail to recall representations of parts of the world, or even fail to remember that there is both a left and a right region of space. This is suggested by experiments in which people with the neglect syndrome are asked to describe a scene from memory. In these experiments the descriptions derived from memory also omitted the left regions of space. It seems that neglect is not a failure to perceive parts of the world, but rather the inability to remember things related to that space. In neglect syndrome, people remember only half of the visual space.[10]

Neglect and Remembering Forward

Neglect usually results from damage to the right hemisphere, and it has been presumed to involve destruction or degradation of the function of cortical cells in the "where" region of back integrative cortex (see chapter 4). This is a sensory area of cortex, so it was natural to think that neglect might be a sensory deficit.

Recently it has been discovered that neglect is probably not related to cortex damage at all. Rather, it seems to arise from damage to the axon cables that directly link back integrative cortex and front integrative cortex.[11] These cables (called fasciculi) play an important role in the back-and-forth signaling between cortical regions that must occur in mental activity (such as that I described in my example of the apple orchard). We now know that this is exactly the explanation for the neglect syndrome. Neglect is caused by a failure in *connection* between the sensory areas of cortex (back) and the working memory and action areas of cortex (front).

Thus, as I said earlier, neglect is not a perceptual problem. It is an inability to send perceptions back and forth between front and back cortex, and the loss of this capability is related to memory loss. Attention requires that perceptual information be sent forward to be recognized or brought into consciousness. Failure of this process means that representations of memories cannot be used to make predictions. In the apple orchard example, if we cannot retrieve the representation of a ladder (remember that retrieval is a front cortex function), we cannot predict apple-picking.

We may neglect both the past and the future!

Preparing as Remembering Forward

The integrative ability of the front cortex means that we create hypotheses about the future and make plans to get ready. We prepare!

But our conscious preparations may not be the whole story. Our brain may be at work preparing in a way that we are unaware of—and fast! A neuroscience experiment provides an example of this.

People were shown four-letter words on a screen. The words looked normal except that one letter was red rather than black. There were two simple tasks assigned. One was to determine whether the word contained a particular letter (does it have a T?), and the second was to determine whether the red letter was to the right or left of center in the word (in the word BATH written with a red T, the answer would be "right"). The regions of the brain that were active during each task were monitored by fMRI.

As is often the case in research, the results of this experiment surprised the investigators. They expected that since both tasks involved words and letters (language), the brain regions involved would be in the left hemisphere[12] for both questions. This was true for the first question; however, the second question primarily activated regions in the right hemisphere. There were no changes in activity in the left hemisphere when looking for specific letters in words!

Other details of these experiments are described in the research, but what struck me was the efficiency of the brain. Although the tasks were based on language, the real task was a spatial one. Where is the letter? That is the question. The brain responded by ignoring the language aspect and immediately engaged the spatial regions of cortex in the right hemisphere. It went to work on the central question as soon as the word came into view. Without any time for thought or preparation, when the task showed up, the brain was ready. Subconsciously, it had prepared itself.[13]

Expectation: More Remembering Forward

The experiment described above demonstrates the importance of expectation. If the mind expects a certain experience or challenge, it gets ready right away. If the mind misunderstands the expectations, it will work on the wrong problem. This will be important later in this chapter, when we turn our attention back to the journey from brain to mind.

Here, however, I want to point out that the connection between expectation and observation is a key part of the blending of past and future that I have stressed throughout this chapter. One of the most recent studies that seems to strongly demonstrate this blending examined the connection between amnesia (inability to remember the past) and imagination (ability to create an image of the future, to predict). It was found that *both* functions are affected when the hippocampus is damaged. We have known for years that this brain structure is involved in forming new memories. So this new result suggests that imagining the future depends on creating memories of the past.[14] Remembering backward and forward both use the same brain structure.

The idea that thinking about the past and thinking about the future are part of the same process is not new. In fact, it was actually proposed by the Greeks. In our era, these old ideas are inviting new thoughts about cognition and development. For example, in aging, we should not be surprised if we observe changes both in memory recall and in imagination. In addition, we should not necessarily think of memory and imagination as antagonists. In education, we might give memorization more respect and find more uses for it in prediction.

Recall of Episodic Memory

As you know, cognitive scientists have defined different categories of memory. One of the most interesting is episodic memory—the memory of stories, events, or episodes—and one of the key elements of this kind of memory is time. Events take place in sequence, and the time relationship is absolutely essential to getting the memory right. Changing the time relationship changes the memory. If the memory is of a baseball game, then the pitch must precede the hit in time. Episodic memory is in contrast to what is called "semantic" memory, memory of isolated objects, words, people, and so forth, that have no time component.

I mention episodic memory because the connection between past and future, between memory and imagination, is very clear in this kind of memory. Recalling an episodic memory sometimes requires us to imagine and recall things. The invention aspect can be a great help in recall. If we can't remember an exact sequence, we can deduce it. Indeed, often we end up inventing episodes; we remember their content, but the sequence itself is the product of reasoning. We do not have to depend on isolated memories (like the enzyme equation). Rather, we can work with the content and place the various elements in a sequence demanded by reason.

This contributes to the fact that stories are often easy to remember, while remembering exact dates may be hard. We can reassemble the story using our reason. For example, we can realize that our trip to the grocery store came before we went to the drug store by the fact that the gallon of milk was in the car when we arrived at the drugstore. But it is more difficult to reason out an exact date unless we put it in an episodic memory.

Semantic Memory: Language and Remembering Forward

It seems easy to see how episodic memory requires remembering forward, but this is also true for semantic memory. Semantic memory, by its very name, is language-based. If we recall the name of something, the language symbol for it, we are using semantic memory. In fact, only when we speak or write the symbols—only when we use language (including the language of mathematics)—do we become aware that we possess semantic memory. Clearly, semantic memory is a tool for demonstrating memory of the past.

Semantic memory is also a tool for remembering forward. We explain our predictions, our imaginings, and our expectations through language. And as we use our semantic tools, we generate new images, ones that are predictions. You may have noticed that putting your ideas into language, either speech or writing, always seems to generate new ideas. A single word can bring up multiple images, some of which we had not consciously considered, which then can lead to new combinations of neuron firing representing new ideas.

When I was a child, my parents often warned me to "think before you speak." Of course, this was good advice, and I still tend to follow it as well as I can. However, with more experience in life, I began to notice that when I failed to follow this advice, things didn't always go badly. Sometimes speaking before analyzing and planning my thoughts would lead me to a new idea, and sometimes that idea was useful. The very act of creating speech brings in new lines of thought, and working to describe my thoughts in logical and effective language not only produces a trail of my past thinking, but also generates new thinking.

Creating language leads us forward.

Umbrellas

The next sections of this chapter focus more specifically on education. We revisit the topics I have discussed from the perspective of the educator. Parts of this discussion may sound redundant, and they may be! But in many cases they are so important that it is better to err by repetition than to risk missing some key idea. These topics are very important in our imagined journey from brain to mind and suggest practical applications for education.

There are a number of such key ideas, so to keep things as clear as possible, I have organized this section by creating three umbrellas, each of which covers a small number of major categories related to remembering forward and its role in education. The three umbrellas are: *recall, attention,* and *predicting*.

Under "recall" we find the following: *episodic, category,* and *extinction*. Under "attention," *opportunistic, neglect,* and *wandering*. And finally, under "predicting," we focus on *symbolic systems* and *concreteness.* Each of these eight topics is revisited in the context of education.

Umbrella I: Recall

Episodic memory. Aspects of episodic memory are often cues to recall of specific memories. Two such aspects are place and sequence. Both are key parts of episodes in our life: Where did things happen, and in what sequence did they happen? These "where" and "when" aspects may be as important as the factual declarative content of the memory. Also, since the idea of episodic memory itself rests on the individual experiences in our lives, the emotional element is strong. Our choices of what we try to remember are determined by the role those things play in our life. We try hard to remember some things and ignore others. Those choices are highly individual.

The places, event sequences, and emotional content inherent in experiences all contribute to episodic recall. Accuracy and speed of recall are enhanced by focusing the attention of each learner on place, time, and feeling. For example, when reading history, learners might be asked to consciously address these *three* things (place, time, feelings) rather than just one or two of them (for example, date). It is an advantage to focus on the whole experience, rather than trying to remember just the parts that may be asked on a test (such as a date). Ignoring the place, timing, or feelings that go along with the experience of doing an assignment can reduce recall of the entire memory.

Category. Another factor in recall of memories is the recognition of category. If we identify the wrong category, recall probably will fail; at best, it will be slowed down. An example of this is a research project on how medical school students solve problems. Most students approach the problem by first defining the nature, or category, of the question. For example, was the problem a genetics problem or an immunology problem? Once the category was identified, the students began to work on the problem using methods and approaches that are characteristic in that category. On average, the students who initially picked the right category solved the problems better. Those who didn't might eventually solve the problem, but by a less efficient route.[15]

Extinction. Finally, under this recall umbrella I have placed the phenomenon of extinction. As mentioned earlier in this chapter, recall can lead to extinction, but that may not always be a bad thing. In fact, it is a way of eliminating connections that are not correct, have changed with time, or should never have been there. When recalled, aspects of a memory that are not *consistently* reinforced can be extinguished, as they should be!

In some situations, extinction may actually become a goal for educators. Extinguishing inconsistent and inaccurate aspects of recalled memories is desirable, so repeated recall suggests itself as a pedagogical tool for learning. Revisiting can have greater value than just reinforcing things. It can become a sieve by which we filter out errors.

Umbrella II: Attention

Attention is a big word for educators. In fact, any experience where learners actually seem to be paying attention can be considered a success on that merit alone. At least they were quiet! And they didn't fall asleep![16]

Opportunistic. An important and unexpected aspect of attention is that the behaviors that suggest someone is paying attention aren't necessarily sending the right message. Our ideas about those behaviors are often such things as sitting still, being quiet, and focusing on one thing with eyes and ears. And, often, the most common way for educators to encourage those behaviors is to simply to demand them: "Pay attention!"

As I discussed in *The Art of Changing the Brain*, attention is less characterized by these traditional behaviors, and more by scanning and revisiting. In the terminology we are using here, scanning and revisiting is more a natural brain function—a property of the vision system—and less associated with mind. The brain has evolved to drive this scanning and revisiting as a means of survival in natural selection. This "natural attending" involves subconscious and spontaneous visual scanning of the environment, noticing aspects that are of greatest interest, and revisiting them. It occurs naturally in all of us and is the basis for my use of the term "opportunistic" to describe the process of attending.

Converting this brain behavior to one more mind-like involves a conscious manipulation of the natural scanning and revisiting. This can be achieved by both the educator and the student. If students are aware of this natural process, they may be able to identify specific aspects of their experience that they find naturally interesting, or perhaps surprising; those they just naturally want to find and revisit. This is in contrast to the common approach of a learner, which is to begin at the beginning and focus on proceeding in an experience or learning new information according to instructions. It is better to put the "search and revisit" process under the learner's control.

This initial engagement can occur anywhere or anytime. In my own experience teaching a course in biochemistry, I have asked students to thumb through the book and find something related to their prior experience, or that engages them emotionally for some reason. The purpose of this assignment is to activate and directly influence the "search and revisit" response of the brain. I believe this approach is more mind-like and may well become habitual. It does not rely on chance, but on conscious actions and conscious choice—functions of mind.

An effective educator may be able to understand a student's natural interests, his or her prior knowledge and experience. But either through volition of the learner or effectiveness of the educator, adapting to the brain's natural processes is preferable to simply demanding change in the "MO" of the human brain or, even worse, drugging people so their behavior will match our image of attention.

Neglect. In addition to opportunistic behavior of the brain, earlier in this chapter I pointed out the phenomena of "neglect" and "wandering" as elements of attention. Both are related to memory recall, and educators can be helped by recognizing how they affect learning. What about neglect? In addition to the pathological "neglect syndrome," it actually turns out that the normal brain can use neglect as an aid to attention. We often neglect to pay attention to things that we already expect. We are likely to pay attention to novel events, and to ignore aspects of our experience that are *not* a surprise, things that always happen.

There is pathological neglect, due to brain damage or faulty development, but educators must also be aware of the normal type of neglect mentioned above. The traditional processes of "telling" and "explaining" things are highly susceptible to neglect. Learners do not, cannot, consciously sense every word we say. In fact, I suspect that neglect occurs in every conversation we have. But it is not necessarily a negative. If we already know what to expect, it may help us attend to the unexpected. It may help us refine, improve, and enrich memories. Recognizing that learners may be neglecting some sensory experience, finding out what is being neglected, deciding whether such neglect is helpful or harmful, and devising approaches that change the "expected" into the "unexpected" may all be useful as a guide to how we approach our practice. And awareness of neglect may well be a goal for facilitating our progress from brain to mind.

Wandering. Finally, in this discussion of attending, it helps to revisit the notion of mental "wandering." The default network discovered in studies of the wandering mind discussed earlier in this chapter suggests that when we are released from problems or challenges in the outside world, we revisit our internal connections having to do with body comfort, receptiveness, and cooperation. This "frame of mind" is more reminiscent of acceptance and drifting; it may well be what we call *reflection*. During such internal discovery we are more likely to find new meanings and connections that have deeper significance in our life. Those discoveries emerge as we recall certain experiences or places ourselves, no matter what instructions others give us. We learn when our individual lives give us the opportunity, when we can neglect the irrelevant, and when our minds can stroll back through our experiences without impediments. When that happens, all the structure, planning, and logical curricula we have invented can become unimportant.

Umbrella III: Predicting

Remember that the purpose of recall is to *use* memory. And the most powerful way to use memory is prediction. Although we may not realize it at first, predicting actually is the basis for nearly all the mind-like things we do, or try to do. I try to illustrate this in the following paragraphs.

Symbolic systems. When we construct a sentence, we are trying to communicate an image, and we predict that our language will produce the same image in another person. Language is conceivably the most common act of prediction. We speak and write because we expect others will understand, and we anticipate that our explanations will clarify our thoughts and ideas. We predict that the words we use will generate images and feelings in others. We hope (predict?) that we can solve a problem by talking about it. We predict that our reasoning will convince others. Many (most?) acts of language production are about the future.

Likewise, mathematics is prediction. In fact, it is precise prediction. When we add two numbers, we predict that we will get a true answer. Any equation is a prediction. For example, $F = ma$ (force equals mass times acceleration) is a prediction. It tells us that if we want to know the force of something, we will discover it (in the future) by multiplying the mass of an object by how rapidly its speed is increasing.

Logic and reasoning are also based on prediction. They often are expressed with symbols of one sort or another, so we briefly mention them here. If we try to put two objects in the same location at the same time, we can predict the result: failure. If sugar causes pleasure, when we want pleasure we can taste some sugar: cause and effect. If a, and if b, then c: c is a prediction.

I wrote about these basic subjects in chapter 6, and it is not necessary to discuss their importance in education again. However, I do want to mention one idea in that chapter with regard to prediction. That idea is that learning and using those symbolic systems gives us power. The power comes via prediction. It is, in fact, the most powerful tool that language, mathematics, and logic give us. Growth of mind is growth of power.

Concreteness. Prediction is central in education through experience, and as we discussed earlier, the power of experience lies in its concreteness. We learn by experiencing the actual, real outcomes of actions; the outcome is a necessary part of experience. Struggling to learn makes us aware of this, primarily because we are not making correct predictions.

In discussions with colleagues, I have become aware that many of us are concerned about this failure to remember and apply lessons learned through experience. A friend of mine recently said, "Our students are experience-poor." By this he meant that children who develop in a passive environment, or whose choices and actions are made for them by a well-meaning parent, miss out on the real-world experiences that build a repertoire of prediction abilities. Prediction ability comes from real-world experience; it derives from the concrete. Our abstract or theoretical predictions seem smart, but are often wrong. It seems likely that successful predictions are more often based on fact and memory of fact than on abstractions or theories.

These ideas take us back to our earlier discussion of the concrete and the abstract (chapter 6). Education is most effective when it relies on concrete events and personal experiences, rather than on abstractions, theories, and ideas. A very practical example is the "scope on a rope" that educators at Louisiana State University are using to help children see the real physical structure of matter, rather than telling them with words or with drawings on a blackboard.[17] This tool for learning science has been found to engage children as young as three, and to lead to the natural cycle of learning I described earlier.[18] Let people see the real thing in detail, or touch it, or experience it in other concrete ways, and the well-developed mind will automatically begin to generate predictions.

Proceeding, but on a Firm Foundation

Our journey has now taken us through many major regions of cortex, ending with the front integrative capability of prediction as the ultimate achievement of the mind. But it is not really an end. In fact, we have traveled full circle, back to where we started, back to *action*. Our predictions will have no use if we cannot test and use them. That requires us to do things, to act! The journey has turned out to be a cycle.

And we are not quite finished. There still remains the task of designing and organizing education that uses what we have discovered. This challenge exists both for organized education systems and for the individual experiential learning that happens in us all as we move along in the journey from brain to mind. We address the first in chapter 9, and the second in chapter 10.

Notes

1. Hawkins, J., (2005), *On Intelligence*. St. Martin's Griffin, New York, NY.
2. Willis, T. G., and colleagues (2005), Attractor Dynamics in the Hippocampal Representation of the Local Environment, *Science*, 308, p. 873; also see comments on this work by Poucet and Save on p. 799 of the same issue.
3. Foster, D. J., and Wilson, M. A. (2006), *Nature*, 440, pp. 680–683; also see comment by Colgin and Moser in the same issue, p. 615.
4. See Bestman's analysis of this decision-making model proposed by Cisek, P. (2006), *Journal of Neuroscience*,. 26, p. 9761.
5. This term is used by M. F. Mason and colleagues in a 1985 research article in *Nature*, 315, p. 393.
6. See the work referenced by Gaffan, D. (2005), *Science*, 309, pp. 2172–2173.
7. See Fries, P., and colleagues (2001), *Science*, 291, pp. 1650–1654.
8. This terminology derives from the idea that electrical "firing" produces a wave. The wave has peaks and valleys, so when I say firing goes up and down, the "ups" are the peaks, and the "downs" are the valleys. When the ups of one wave get in phase with those of another wave, it increases the height of the wave and, likewise, deepens the valleys.
9. http://viscog.beckman.uiuc.edu/grafs/demos/15.html

10. These ideas about memory and neglect are explained in more detail in a short review article by Gaffan (see reference in note 8).

11. See deSchotten, M. T., and colleagues (2005), *Science*, 309, pp. 2226–2228; also refer to Gaffan reference in note 8.

12. In language, cognitive work with details, such as letters in words, is almost always identified with left temporal cortex.

13. Stephan, K. E., and colleagues (2003), *Science*, 301, p. 384; also see comments on this work by McIntosh and Lobaugh on p. 322 of the same issue.

14. Hassabis, D., and colleagues (2007), *Proceedings of the National Academy of Sciences*, 104, pp. 1726–1731; also see commentary on this work by Miller, G. (2007), *Science*, 315, p. 312.

15. There is a much literature on learning and memory in medical schools. Another factor (in addition to category) believed to be important is the statistical approach (often referred to as Baysean). For a review see Elstein, A. S., and Schwarz, A. (2002), *British Medical Journal*, 324, pp. 729–732.

16. A pediatrician whom I know well made the following comment about attention. "Out of 100 students who see me for school failure, at least 99 present with the complaint (by teacher, parent, and or student) of attention failure. It appears that no matter what goes wrong, a failing student will always fail to attend. To me, this makes attention the most complex of all the functions of mind when looking at education. It touches almost every conceivable cause of school failure."

17. Scope on a rope is a hand-held microscope for children studying science. It emerged from the work of Dr. Cindy Henk at LSU; see http://www.scopeona rope.lsu.edu/

18. Zull, J. E. (2002), *The Art of Changing the Brain*, Stylus, Sterling, VA, pp. 13–29.

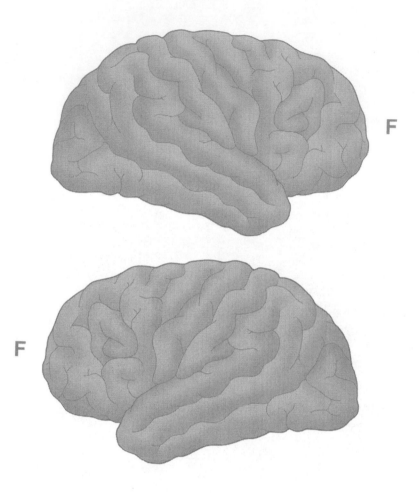

The shading of all regions of the cortex shown here is meant to imply engagement of entire cerebral cortex proposed by application of experiences and education methods described in this chapter. Lateral view of both hemispheres. A medial view would also be shaded.

9

PURPOSE AND PRINCIPLES
FOR EDUCATING

Organizing Knowledge and Serving the Learner

Learning involves the nurturing of nature.

—Joseph LeDoux

My father was a Baptist preacher, and made his living by his skill with language. As children, we always heard grammatically correct English. And, at least three times a week, we sang hymns in church, many of which we knew by heart. Most were constructed of correct and sometimes complex English sentences and phrases.

My mother did not go to college, but read the Bible often and committed large portions of it to memory. Also, she would often read novels aloud to our large family as we all sat enraptured on the living room floor on Sunday afternoons. This was another rich source of moving and effective English prose.

Thus, from our earliest childhood, my siblings and I learned correct usage of the English language and developed good vocabularies. In school, I found reading and other language assignments to be trivial. In fact, my language skills were superior to those of some of the teachers.

Therefore, I was surprised to find that my ninth grade English class was quite difficult. The teacher talked about the parts of speech and diagramming sentences, which I found slightly interesting at first but which quickly became tiresome. I had difficulty remembering the meaning of terms like preposition *or* article, *and I couldn't see the point. After all, the only reason for language was to be used, and I knew how to use it. I didn't need rules; I just knew what sounded right.*

I began to get bad grades in English. In fact, at the end of that year I got a D in the class. I can truthfully say I didn't care, and I don't think my parents did either. They may have been puzzled, but it didn't seem to worry them. In fact, my father was much more interested in my typing grade. He had learned to type as an adult, using only two fingers, and since he typed all his sermons, he could see the value of "touch" typing. He believed we should learn this skill while we were young; it is hard to learn new things when you get older.

That was what school was for: to learn things that would help you in your real life—the sooner, the better!

What is the purpose of education? As educators, what do we want to achieve? What do we *need* to achieve, in our time and place?

My father's response to those questions, while still important, now seems inadequate. A great deal has changed in the intervening years; the world is more complex. And, in many ways, society expects far more of "education" than it did in the past. But despite this complexity, the core of what my parents believed still applies. We must keep our eye on how things are changing and attempt to prepare learners for the future (for example, by teaching them to type). At the same time, it is important to stay alert to differences that make some things irrelevant for some learners.

In the following sections, we develop an idea for the purpose of education, appropriate to our time and place.

Our Time

Two factors strongly influence our thinking about the purpose of education in our time. One is the need to prepare learners for what has been called "lifelong learning." It is widely believed that, in the future, individuals will change their professions often during their lifetime. I have seen estimates as high as a dozen employment changes through a working lifetime. These changes will require facility in adapting and learning new skills; we will need to learn about learning. Effective education will provide insight into human learning, and that insight will become an "applied science." We will learn how to apply those insights.

Progress in cognitive science and neuroscience can eventually make a significant contribution to this goal. Some aspects of this contribution will be technical, but they will also lead to changes in perspective. These changes may not be obvious at first but, in retrospect, I can see them in myself. As my understanding of the human brain has grown, I have become much more "learner focused." My perspective now has the learner, rather than the educator, at its center. I have reached that point as I have consciously tried to develop experiences that I believe will influence the learner's brain and mind.

A second factor that has influenced education is technology. The changes it has brought and will continue to bring are apparent and pervasive. We are accustomed to accessing information in seconds; this expediency is a huge time saver in obtaining information. Technology also makes mental tasks easier. We use it to calculate, to find the right word, to find our location on the planet, and to plan our trips around the planet.

The challenge that faces us now is to blend the growing insights about human learning with the power of technology. This is a goal of education in our time.

A Single Purpose

It is actually fortunate that our understanding of learning and our sophisticated technological tools have appeared more or less simultaneously. This offers an opportunity to combine them so that they serve each other and, perhaps, ultimately lead to dramatic synergy between them. Cognitive science will give us insight into comprehension and manipulation, and technology will provide speed and power. This complementary circumstance must play a major role in helping us define the purpose of education in our time.

My proposal is that the purpose of education, now and in the future, should be to *put all learners on the path from brain to mind.* Now that we have begun to define some of the central features of this path, we should turn our attention to the task of training new teachers. Eventually, these new teachers will lead their own students, including both children and parents, onto that path.

We should be clear. The challenge is not to increase the amount of information available or to make that information easier to access—technology can do that. Rather, it is to focus on understandings and actions based on those understandings. We need to go *slower,* not faster, deeper, or wider. From novelty in the newborn to wisdom in the aging, our goal should be concept, not content.

The Approach

It is a challenge to identify a primary purpose in education, and there are more challenges ahead. Even if we agree on this purpose, we may not know how to achieve it. It is good to acknowledge the need for a change of purpose, but more complicated to know how to accomplish the change. As they say, "The devil is in the details."

To confront one of those devilish details, I have divided the overall challenge into two main themes. The first theme focuses on creating, explaining, and illustrating a specific method of educational planning and practice based on the nature of the brain rather than on specific subjects. The second theme focuses on the individual learner. It is about the development, or growth, of an individual's mental capabilities. This growth includes processes that are based on both "nature" and "nurture"; their commonality derives from the fact that they are about the learner himself or herself.

I refer to these two themes as "content-focused" and "learner-focused." An example of the content-focused theme is the way we explored visual knowledge, particularly in chapter 4. We described two aspects of visual information: (1) that which provides insight into category (the *what*), and (2) that which provides information about relationship (the *where*). These aspects are a property of the knowledge itself—its *content*. Generally, this content is not subject to change. It is constant, a property of physical reality. For example, the physical structure of a chair is the same today as it was yesterday.

The learner-focused theme draws our attention to *differences* in individuals and how they *change*. The individual interacts with the content, and that interaction changes the individual's mind, qualitatively and quantitatively. An example is the notion of "windows" for learning specific topics or mastering skills. It can be debated whether such windows exist, but, assuming for the moment they do, the change is the closing of the window for a learner. Such change can dictate modification of our educational plans over time. Educators may need to focus more on individuals, their differences, and how they change, rather than on the group.

This "divide and conquer approach" is just that, an approach. I am only suggesting ideas for dealing with these two challenges. These suggestions could lead to a more specific and detailed program in the future.

Constancies

Throughout this book, a great deal of the discussion has focused on change and difference. Now I want to shift gears and focus on some things that don't change. It will help you to recognize this major change in direction; it may actually be a relief!

There are specific aspects and functions of the brain that remain the same in all individuals throughout a lifetime. I call these aspects "constancies." It is this fact that leads LeDoux (quotation at the beginning of this chapter) to say: "Learning involves the nurturing of nature." The things that don't change come from nature, and those that do, from nurture. Nature provides the general structure and functions of a brain, but nurture turns it into a mind. The scaffolding of the brain (nature) defines the arena in which change happens through experience (nurture).

One aspect of this view requires further explanation. Note that neither term—nature or nurture—implies virtue or lack of virtue. Just because something originates in nature does not imply that it is good or bad. It just is. Neither is nurture necessarily associated with virtue. Even though nurturing implies "caring" or "caring for," the general meaning of the term in biology is disconnected from such subjective attributes. Nurturing is experience. Whatever happens, good or bad, is part of nurturing.

This view comes from the broader context of evolution through natural selection. Darwin's theory attributes change to random events, not to purposeful ones. As the saying goes, "Things happen." In biology, those things are not guided by anything. Nature does not know purpose. Whatever happens to an individual, whatever changes, must survive in competition with what has already happened—what *is*. If, by chance, these purposeless changes enhance survival, the changes also survive. Through this process, qualities that we feel are good or bad, beautiful or ugly, faster or slower, etc., arise.

The term "learning" can also be ambiguous in this way. As stated in earlier chapters, the biological perspective of learning is also neutral. Even though we most often feel instinctively that learning is good, that instinct is misleading. Learning is not necessarily associated with virtue. We can learn good things, and we can learn bad things.

Nature and Constancy

When we begin to think about the process of evolution through natural selection, it may be difficult to imagine constancy. Change is an essential aspect of all life, and it was change that drove evolution, ultimately leading to the powerful human mind. In this long view, everything changes all the time. But that is a very long view—too long!

It is true that evolution is about change, but that change occurs so slowly that it has no meaning for individual humans. Significant genetic change only happens over many generations. If the time span of a human generation is 20 years, then 200 generations is a time span of 4,000 years, roughly the time elapsed since invention of a fairly sophisticated system of writing. Thus, there is very little reason to expect significant change in the skills and capabilities of the human brain over a hundred or even several hundred years. Biological constancy will be the norm over many generations.

If we are right, and little or no heritable change in brain cortex is expected soon, it follows that difference between the brains of different species will remain the same for all members of those species, and for all their normal offspring. I implied this constancy in earlier chapters when I discussed the division of labor among different parts of the brain. The most basic functions of different regions of cortex (sensory, motor, and integrative) are, have been, and will be present in each individual. Likewise, the separation of "what" and "where" in the front integrative and back integrative cortex is constant; it is found in all humans and many primates.

This is not to say that we are all of equal ability. For example, even though some of us are "good at" math and others less so, we all still retain the power of symbolizing. And while some of us are very creative and others less so, we all have working memory and ability to predict. The skills and capabilities are constant, but the differences in individuals remain.

A brain without these constancies and differences would not belong to our species.

Differences Are Constant

Constancy implies that the *differences* in the brain of different species are also constant. Let's look at specific differences in the cortex of two animals that seem very similar. This will help us think about the differences between human cortex and that of other animals in general, and may even give us ideas about what kinds of educational goals we might set for development of human minds.

The figure on page 235 compares the distribution of cortex in the brain of a rat and a related animal, the tree shrew.[1] This distribution is always the same for each species, with small variations. The differences between the rat and the tree shrew are small but, if we look carefully, it is apparent that the amount of cortex devoted to specific functions (S for somatosensory, M for motor, A for association, Au for auditory, V for visual, Ol for olfactory) is not the same. This is because the regions of cortex most important for survival are present in greater amounts than are less important regions.

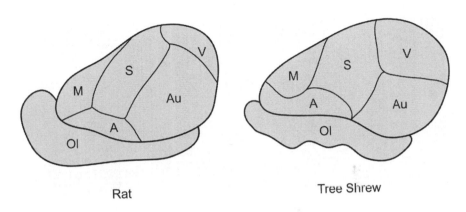

Rat   Tree Shrew

For example, we can argue that the visual cortex (V) in the tree shrew is larger than that of the rat because vision contributes more to survival in the tree shrew; good vision is helpful when you live high off the ground. Rats do not climb trees, and their vision is obscured by grass and other objects on the ground. In this case, a more powerful auditory sense does more to enhance survival. Indeed, the rat has more auditory cortex than the tree shrew.

These biological characteristics are a constant in the brains of these species, and we can anticipate that this will be true for each in the foreseeable future. If we wanted to do research on the minds of rats and tree shrews, we could count on these differences for many generations.

The cortex differences in these animals are relatively small; those that separate our species from others are more dramatic. As we discussed in chapter 4, people have much more integration (association) cortex, and proportionally much smaller amounts of auditory and olfactory cortex, than the rat or tree shrew. The result is that the human organism has great powers of integrating information, of thinking and predicting. Our survival as a species undoubtedly depended on having these major regions of integrative cortex.

Constancies in Integrative Cortex: Eight-Point Strategy

Many of the high-level functions of the human mind arise in the integrative cortex. I have created the figure below to summarize the functions we have discussed in previous chapters. The image on the left represents regions of cortex that lie underneath those top regions. You can visualize this physical structure by mentally sliding the "TOP" over so it lies on top of the "BOTTOM."

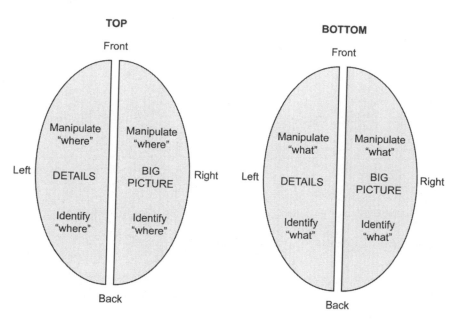

Integrative Cortex

In both views, we see right and left hemispheres as well as front and back cortex. As shown, and consistent with what was discussed in earlier chapters, an important function of back regions of integrative cortex is to identify the "what" and "where" of *received* information. On the other hand, the front regions of integrative cortex, as shown, are involved in *manipulating* the "what" and "where" information to plan (create) future actions. Finally, the drawing indicates the difference between right and left hemisphere that we discussed earlier. The right hemisphere is about the "big picture" and the left about "details." Putting these together, we can identify eight broad functions of integrative cortex. For example, in the top-right regions of back integrative cortex I have assigned the function *identify elements of "where" in the big picture*. This means that this region of cortex is responsible for analyzing the spatial arrangement of the major elements that have been perceived in the sensory cortex. In a landscape painting, this would be the relative location of the sea, the trees, the mountains, and other major aspects of the painting. In the bottom-left regions of integrative front cortex, the function is *manipulate the details to change the category content (the "what")*. In our landscape painting, this might be adding a small bird at a precise place in the sky, or changing the tint of green for a specific tree or grassy area. In this way, we arrive at the following capabilities of nature's integrative cortex:

1. identify (perceive) the parts (categories) found in the big picture;
2. manipulate the parts of big picture;
3. perceive the parts of details;
4. manipulate the parts of details;
5. perceive the relationships (arrangement) in big picture;
6. manipulate the relationships in big picture;
7. perceive the relationships of the details; and
8. manipulate the relationships of the details.

In addition to these eight capabilities, we could add the capabilities of sensory and motor cortices. However, I have linked those cortical regions more to "brain" than to "mind" (see chapter 2). The integrative cortex is most responsible for producing a creating and problem-solving mind.

An Assignment to Engage the Integrative Cortex

To illustrate how we might use these eight regions of integrative cortex in a specific school assignment, I use the example of a book report. This is not to say that book reports are different from other assignments, or to suggest that teachers should use them.[2] It is simply an example that illustrates one way educators might use the eight regions of integrative cortex in a practical assignment. For that purpose, I have divided the assignment into eight parts, each of which engages a different region of integrative cortex. In addition, the parts are subdivided into two groups of four. The first four are projects for study and analysis of the book, and the second four are for actually constructing the book report.

Study and Analysis

1. Identify the characters, places, and times for the story (identify, details, category: back, lower, left).
2. Identify the themes or moral of the story (big picture, category, identify: back, lower, right).
3. Identify overall organization of the book—beginning, middle, end (big picture, relationships, identify: back, upper, right).
4. Identify key specific events, changes, people, places (specific, relationships, identify: back, upper, left).

Create and Write

1. Create a title and theme for a review of the book (big picture, category, create: front, lower, right).
2. Create overall organization of your review (big picture, relationships, create: front, upper, right).
3. Create a list of specific points for your review (details, category, create: front, lower, left).
4. Create your review, written in logical sequence and with correct grammar (details, relationship, create: front, upper, left).

This example is for a specific assignment in a specific subject. My purpose in presenting it here is simply to illustrate application of the ideas we discussed earlier. However, I believe it can also serve as a challenge for application in your own subject. Perhaps you are already trying to specifically identify aspects of your subject that can be labeled "big picture" or "relationships" and so forth. If not, I encourage you to try. Only when we can apply ideas to our own specific situations—when we actively test them—do we begin to grasp them more fully.

An important virtue of this approach is that it applies to any subject. It is not necessary to discard teaching the traditional subjects to try it. In fact, applying this approach in a specific subject will enhance educators' appreciation and comprehension, not only of their own field, but also of the entire curriculum. We may find ourselves inventing new and different kinds of assignments based on this approach. Just thinking about examples of (1) big picture, (2) details, (3) identify, (4) manipulate, (5) category, and (6) relationship in subjects like math, social studies, and others is very catalytic. The traditional subjects (curriculum) can serve as *vehicles* for developing deeper insight.

These vehicles take us further along the journey toward mind. They can help us learn and use *every* subject and solve *every* kind of problem.

Time: A Constant Battle

We might not consider the issue of time to be a constancy, as described above, but it certainly is a constant concern in education. So perhaps this is a good place to discuss the time pressure associated with implementing new approaches to education.

The ideas we have been discussing can become time-consuming. In education, as in any serious undertaking, good work takes time. This realization may draw us up short. Where will we find the time? Are the potential gains in comprehension worth it?

This desire for quality education is one important factor in the time consideration, but there is another important one—the tendency to add topics and subjects to curricula or other educational plans without any compensating reductions. We aren't necessarily good editors when it comes to education. Often it seems that, just when we have perfected key aspects of our practice, they become obsolete. We should remove them, but it is hard to turn our back on something that has taken so much energy and devotion. It is hard to be heartless. Nevertheless, it behooves us to become better editors.

A second important realization is that we may address this challenge with the hoped-for marriage with technology that I spoke of earlier. We have computers, Google, the Web, electronic messaging, and multitasking already, but now we need to develop new applications that facilitate the approaches I am suggesting.

Of course, the claim that "I don't have the time" may not be as compelling as it seems at first. New things are often confusing and intimidating, but it may be that the feared time losses will not actually be as great as imagined. As we become more comfortable with the eight-part approach, even just getting used to the terminology, the time challenge may become less daunting.

Getting started is always the most difficult challenge.

Speed Limit

Occasional breakthroughs do happen, and we may find ourselves moving faster while at the same time improving quality. But that cannot be predicted or arranged, and we shouldn't count on it. In fact, the safer assumption is that comprehension and understanding *cannot* be accelerated. We are far better off cultivating patience and paying attention to the details that are always part of quality. Initially, depth is more important than speed. There is no greater waste of time than taking shortcuts.

There are neuroscientific reasons why I suggest that it is difficult to accelerate deepening education. These reasons are related to both the nature and size of integrative cortex in the human species. For the first, we should remember that these regions of cortex are the most heavily engaged in the process of reflection. To a great extent, this process involves formation, recall, consolidation, and reconsolidation of memory. This memory processing is not directly under conscious control, and very often important insights appear by chance. The best we can do may be to increase the odds that it will occur.

A second aspect of integrative cortex that slows reflection is its physical size. These regions are the largest of all the cortical regions, containing far more neurons than the others. Depth of understanding and comprehension involves discovery of synapses and neuronal networks within this huge number of neurons.

My argument is that, no matter how fast we can get information, the speed limit of the cognitive brain is the time-limiting factor. We can't go faster than the slowest step. Learning cannot go faster than is permitted by brain structure and chemistry—by nature.

Danger of Speeding

One expression of our impatience and desire to learn faster is evidenced by parents' efforts to accelerate their babies' learning. I am suspicious of this, especially as it applies to language skills. As noted in chapter 6, I have observed an overreliance on language in my own students. They do not seem to have the images they need to actually understand the language they use. The research quoted in that chapter supports that suspicion.[3]

It seems important to remind you that, as I discussed in chapter 6, the development of images through direct experience ultimately leads to the growth of symbolism—language—to describe those images. It can be a disservice to children to begin stressing the symbolic system before the images are developed.

Babies learn language directly through experience and instinctive parceling of the phonemic structure it contains. The time frame for this process probably depends on each individual child's environment and experiences and on the nature of the specific language itself. My argument is that we should trust this natural process of development through experience. We can provide an environment that stimulates sensory and motor cortex in nonspecific and broad ways, but efforts to direct a baby's mind toward specific academic goals such as numbers or language are probably misdirected and may even be harmful.

To deal with our impatience and concern about language development, we might focus more on *preparing* the brain to learn specific things, rather than on moving directly to particular academic subjects. We can't speed up the brain by putting in a new gear, but we can provide varied experiences that will support development. Examples of that were discussed in chapter 7, where we focused on forming implicit memories. It is important to remember that the brain is an organ of *self*-development, and it is that process we should consider when preparing a mind to learn. We do not want our babies to become faster machines, but rather to develop into reflective, analytical, thinking adults.

Speed does not create comprehension.[4] Fast learning can mean fast forgetting.

Exceptions to Constancy

I have stated that there are objective aspects of knowledge that are constant; the form of a particular chair is an example. Such constancies lead us to make general predictions in education, but we should be alert to exceptions.

A great deal of our predicting originates from experience. It is simply remembering forward, as discussed in chapter 8. Very often this works, and when it does, it seems trivial. For example, a decade or two ago, it became apparent that computers would be needed in school classrooms and probably at home. Educators had enough experience to make that prediction; it was obvious.

But other predictions may not be so successful. For centuries we have used mathematic equations to solve science problems. It seems trivial to predict that this will remain the same, if not forever, at least for centuries. However, I recently read about Wolfram's ideas on the future of science.[5] He claims that we will see dramatic change because of computers. Even mathematical equations will not be the useful tools they are today. The study of nature will proceed through use of simple computer programs and the interactions between these programs, rather than through the idealized models represented in mathematical equations.

How will we prepare students for this? Should we stop teaching mathematics, or stop using it to describe natural phenomena? If so, when should we stop? Certainly not now! We wouldn't know how to replace it.

The best we can do is to remain alert and watch for unexpected change.

The Second Theme: Focusing on the Learner

To review very briefly, the constancies we have discussed divide themselves into three categories: (1) the objective structures and processes in the *physical world* itself; (2) the structures and connections in the normal *human brain* that are derived from nature; and (3) the brain *processes* that lead to change, such as the way connections are modified and the time involved in those modifications.

These are things we all share. They are our common heritage as members of the human species. They represent a reliable foundation that supports us in achieving the purpose of education, the development of the mind. They don't come with a guarantee, but at a minimum, they provide us with ideas for experimentation and educational innovation.

Now we explore our second theme: change in the learner. This change will draw us into considerations of the earliest child development, beginning from birth; changes in the child through enrichment of experiences; changes in complexity and efficiency in the adult years; and, ultimately, the process of aging in adults.

The focus will be change and plasticity.

From Birth

In general, change in the cerebral cortex is greatest in the first year of life outside the womb. During this time, the number of cortical synapses increases dramatically. Depending on the region of cortex, this increase is on the order of five- to 20-fold. Also, depending on the cortical region, it can peak as early as a year or continue for perhaps two to three years. Following the peak, synapse numbers begin to drop off slowly, and continue a slow decline throughout life.

We can't directly observe this change in the brain, but we become dramatically aware of it in our daily experience with a new baby. For example, we see evidence of changes in auditory cortex during the first six to eight months as babies begin to identify the natural breaks in sound in their "native" language. Neuroscience research has unequivocally linked this change to change in synapses and connections in the auditory cortex, but the function of the overall function of this region does not change. It *remains* auditory.

We can also identify "windows" that suggest change during this time. An interesting example of this is face recognition in humans and other species. If babies are exposed to faces of different species (chimpanzees, for example) up to age 1 or so, they can learn to tell one individual chimp from another, and the children will retain that ability as they grow older. But if exposure to chimp faces begins when children are older than one year, this recognition skill is less robust and may not develop at all. It seems that a "face recognition" window may be closing.[6]

In dramatic situations such as brain damage, some of the constancies we discussed earlier may be somewhat modified. For example, in the visually impaired, the visual cortex can be preempted for use in the auditory function. Increased sharpness of hearing becomes apparent, and the earlier the loss of sight, the greater the auditory change.[7]

Very early experience is most likely to influence such changes, and, generally speaking, the later we encounter something, the less likely we are to learn from it. We may have long suspected this, but that suspicion is now supported by cognitive and neuroscience research. Generally, the most significant capabilities of the human mind are already developed by the time a child enters school. And the people who influence development of the child the most are those who surround the new baby, the family. Arguably, they are the most important educators.

This does not necessarily mean that schools cannot influence the early, preschool years. In fact, in the future it may well be that schools have more programs and plans for direct interaction with families, starting from birth. Existing programs such as Head Start may support such early intervention under special conditions, but it could become the norm as our understanding of these very early experiences increases. Early education may become even "earlier." It could use expert teachers whose specialty is early development, and their students would be family members. Rather than preschool children, it would be parents and siblings who go to school-before-school.

That would integrate school and community life.[8]

Enrichment

What might educators who specialize in early development teach family members with a new baby? The answer to this question will change as we learn more, but there is a general theme that has been known for more than a decade: "enrichment." Animal research has repeatedly demonstrated development of a thicker cortex with more neuronal branching when the very early environment is cognitively and socially enriched with toys, exercise apparatus, a variety of physical structures, colors, and playmates. Furthermore, baby animals of other species (non-human), raised in such enriched environments become more creative and active in play and tend to learn more quickly than normal. We now understand that this is most likely due to increased neuron firing triggered by such a wide variety of sensory experiences, since neurons that fire frequently tend to branch more often.

Enrichment works because it provides complex and varied stimulation of neurons. The sensory systems are the vehicle for internalization of experience. Such experience stimulates growth of more complex networks of sensory neurons and presents more complex challenges and opportunities that then engage front integrative cortex. This increased complexity expands the possibility of effective problem solving and creative thought—development of mind.

Rich experience during childhood can help us successfully meet new challenges later in life. The opportunity to design and create experiences for babies gives parents and educators great influence in development of the mind. In particular, effective enrichment includes challenges and problems. Experiences of this sort stimulate those areas of the brain that are naturally used more when we encounter such challenges.

However, this influence carries danger as well as opportunity. Experiences are not always under our control or well designed. For example, we may invent challenges that are too great and may internalize frustration. Irrational or unpredictable experiences may meet the requirement of complexity, but also have long-lasting negative outcomes. We need to develop good judgment in using this power over developing minds, and we will need further research and guidance from early childhood experts. Eventually we will have more research to guide us, first in the home and, as the child develops, in school. Establishment of the very early child development expert as part of the school system would be a positive step in that direction.

We must think carefully about our babies' experiences.

Revisiting Windows

There is the possibility that neuronal change eventually may lead to closing or narrowing *windows* for learning. Few would dispute the belief that, in general, learning can become more difficult with age. Frequently, we worry about getting too old to learn much at all. The windows may close completely.

This concern has led to the concept of the "critical period" for learning certain things. This concept implies that the "period" begins at birth or shortly thereafter, but that there is a defined age beyond which learning becomes much more difficult or even impossible. It has also been thought that a specific critical period may be different for different brain functions—for example, learning language compared to learning faces.

No doubt, this is a serious concern; hence, the term "critical." However, I believe it has been overemphasized. Except as a result of disease or accident, it is unlikely that at some specific age our ability to learn a particular subject or skill will be suddenly eliminated. And even though our ability to learn decreases through biological aging, it is not true that we can do nothing to counteract it.

Let me expand on this good news. Agreed, as we get older, learning becomes more difficult. However, I am unaware of any research suggesting that there are precise cutoffs. Specific examples of possible critical periods vary greatly with different individuals, different experiences, and different species. For example, possibly the most dramatic example of a critical period for vision was discovered in cats[9], but later work showed that the effect was not obvious in ferrets.

With humans, a significant amount of research has been done on learning a second language. The window seems to begin closing generally around adolescence, but the precise time frame differs widely among individuals, ranging over the entire second decade of life. A dramatic loss in our ability to learn after a certain age, in the absence of disease or physical damage, has never been demonstrated.

More good news: Continuing research suggests that learning need not be dramatically reduced with aging. There are biological processes that are part of natural aging, but that does not mean that things are beyond our control. Quite the opposite! In fact, research continues to create more optimism for retaining or regaining learning skills, and even memories, in humans and other animals.[10] In addition, the actual growth of *new neurons*, described in chapter 8, is greater than normal in older rats that are learning how to navigate a maze, or that learned how when they were young.[11]

Whenever examined, it appears that the habit of learning new things helps retain the ability to learn. By intent and practice, individual members of the human species can extend their ability to learn during ageing and conceivably even eliminate any personal critical period for learning.

Agent of Change

Reduction in the capacity to learn during aging is highly variable, and differs significantly among and within individuals. For example, we may lose our ability to memorize a new song, but retain our ability to improve our golf game. Also, for each individual, loss might occur quite early or quite late or, more likely, at unpredictable times. We are, nonetheless, making progress in understanding factors that lead to aging-related changes in neurological function and, thus, in learning.

One such factor depends on a biological phenomenon that has been known for over a century: *myelination.* In this process, axons and dendrites[12] become coated with a layer of insulating material called myelin. This does not happen with all brain cells. The process is more extensive in the axons of neurons that send signals over long distances in the body, or that are part of very heavily used pathways in specific regions of cortex. Also from childhood until well into middle age, myelination proceeds slowly throughout much of the nervous system, including the brain.

Myelin acts as insulation, reducing potential short-circuiting of neuronal firing. It also speeds up the transmission of signals along axons. For several decades, neuroscientists paid relatively little attention to myelin since it seemed to be inert—simply insulation. However, in the last few years we have learned that it is not inert, but rather plays an important role in neuronal change that occurs through dendritic branching.

Myelin appears to be an agent of change.

Myelin and Change

How does myelin influence change in the brain?

A partial answer is "myelin can inhibit plasticity." It reduces the neuron branching process that leads to potential new synapses.[13]

However, you will recall that neuron branching is one of the results of frequent neuron firing, so we have a competition; activity stimulates branching, and myelin reduces it. But this competition is not a completely fair one. The effect of activity on branching is direct, whereas the effect of myelin is more diffuse. The latter depends on non-neuronal cells in the brain—a type of cell that is different from the neuron. And the effect of electrical stimulation on myelination is not directed specifically at active neurons, but rather makes itself felt in what we might call the "neighborhood" of those neurons. In addition, the intense signaling linked to formation of long-term memory (described in chapter 7) activates cellular processes that block the myelination system. Activity generates growth and change while slowing myelination.

This is good for learning. New challenges stimulate new neuron networks to branch and slows their myelination. New and rich experiences remain the best prescription for retaining our ability to learn as we age.

Myelin and Cortex: An Overview of Change

I have brought myelin to your attention because it seems to be part of the story of aging and cortical change. The cerebral cortex is mostly (but not completely) unmyelinated at birth, but becomes increasingly myelinated over time. This progression is shown in the illustration below, which was constructed by Flechsig more than a century ago.[14] The darkest areas are those that myelinate very early in life; the intermediate areas become myelinated to a great extent during adolescence; and the lightest areas are much more slowly myelinated but show continual change, extending into mid-life and beyond. The figure on page 248 shows a surface view of the left hemisphere, and the bottom view is a representation of its inner surface.

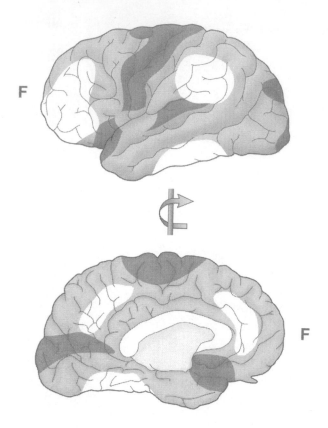

The areas of cortex involved in this change can be viewed in light of the functional understandings we have achieved since Flechsig's time. Myelin first appears in the most fundamental and earliest-functioning cortical regions, the sensory and motor regions. These are cortical areas that babies use first as they begin life inside and then outside outside the womb. With time, myelination extends beyond those areas, reaching deeper and deeper regions of integrative cortex. However, it seems that the central, or deepest, regions of integrative cortex remain unmyelinated.

Myelination, then, comes into our story about development of the mind. First, if the firing patterns associated with skills and knowledge that have worked effectively throughout our life become myelinated, they may well remain that way. As far as we know, once myelinated, always myelinated, except in cases where disease intervenes. As long as we repeatedly fire those patterns, that is, repeat behaviors and practice things we believe to be wise, they will remain myelinated. In theory, we can stabilize our wisdom.

A second possibility for development of the mind is related to the deep unmyelinated regions of integrative cortex. These provide us with the opportunity for new branching and new synapses, since the lack of myelination suggests that the habitual firing patterns of neurons in those regions are not fixed. They are available for change, and may be most likely to be recruited when our experiences are novel, creative, and speculative. New learning can proceed, new branches can form, and new connections can better develop when unmyelinated regions of cortex are open and remain open.

These advantages are available as long as we choose the right kind of experiences. By "right" I mean those experiences that go with wisdom, that are new and rich, and that lead to branching and keep these regions from myelination.

They are in reserve, ready to use when wisdom is needed, and ready to become new parts of our ever-developing mind.

A Different Kind of Change

Throughout this book, the process of learning through experience has been explained as neuronal change characterized by branching and synapse alterations and retained by memory. This is a neuronal theory of learning and retaining information. At one time there was an additional belief, what I will call the DNA theory. That theory said that information is found in DNA, so learning involved change in DNA.

In the history of biology, the DNA theory of learning was discarded half a century ago. But, as is often the case with history, recently the story has changed. DNA is back in the picture. We have now discovered that, although our DNA is faithfully copied generation after generation, not all of it is necessarily used. And the regulation of how it is used can be influenced by our experience. Some experiences actually block use of some parts of the DNA. The information is still there, but it cannot be expressed.

Biologists in prior decades absolutely would have rejected the idea that experience can influence DNA in this way, but this concept is now widely accepted. There are two mechanisms for learning: change in neuronal networks and change in DNA.

Maybe we will discover more, in new, yet-to-be-written, histories.

Epigenetics

It is important to realize that this change does not alter our theory that learning emerges from experience; it just broadens the impact of experience. Not only does experience alter synapses directly, it also alters DNA. There are now many examples of this phenomenon beyond learning. In fact, it is so significant that a new term has been invented to describe it: *epigenetics*. The use of the prefix *epi* is meant to convey the idea that there is something above, or influencing, genetics.[15]

We do not discuss epigenetics in detail here, but there is one important example to consider since it is related to learning behavior in the young and may well have future implications for child education in humans. The phenomenon of maternal nurturing in young rats is that licking and grooming her pups (mother's experience) can be learned by the pups. This in itself is not a surprise. What does surprise us is that this learning is not based on mimicry or neuronal network memory, but rather on the modification of DNA expression. It is epigenetic. Not only can the pups learn the behavior, they can *pass it on genetically* when they mature and have their own litters.

The physical cause of this learning is complex, but it is at least partly traceable to chemical events that occur in the mother when she licks and grooms her offspring. Those changes are related to the hormone oxytocin and its receptors in the amygdala. We discussed this hormone in chapter 3 and identified it as a key to positive emotion and reward. This makes the research even more interesting, since the same system is found in our own species. Ultimately, research in this field may open up highly important new insights into child learning, development, and education.

Experience and Gender

These fascinating studies of epigenetics also led to new findings regarding gender that may influence education in the future. It turns out that increases in oxytocin actions are stimulated by estrogen, which naturally changes in the mother during the later stages of pregnancy. Maternal behaviors are transmitted from generation to generation directly by the impact of experience on oxytocin receptors in the limbic areas of the brain. These neurological changes last throughout the animal's lifetime.

With regard to gender, then, later research showed that the changes in oxytocin receptors caused by grooming differ between male and female pups.

There were positive effects for both genders. The females increased their maternal behaviors in caring for the pups, and the male pups showed reduced anxiety and fear. However, the male pups developed *lower* levels of oxytocin receptors if they were groomed, while receptors for another hormone, vasopressin, increased. In some ways, vasopressin is the opposite of oxytocin; it triggers defense of the home territory through aggressive behaviors attacking invaders. It is also involved in competition for a female, and both these behaviors are essential to the reproductive process.

Thus, the brain responses of males and females to the same experience (licking and grooming) are significantly different, but *together* they contain the wide repertoire of behaviors needed for survival of both individuals and the species as a whole.[16] The female retains the supportive, nurturing behaviors, and the male retains the protective behaviors.

This research is in an early stage, but it is already affecting our ideas about two very important subjects in development: the influence of gender on behavior, and the *boundary* (or lack of boundary) between biological change and change due to experience. Ultimately, these new perspectives raise the possibility that we may begin to better understand differences between males and females in our own species, and to apply that knowledge to learning and education.

Plasticity and Intelligence

Following the theme of biological change through experience, I conclude this chapter by drawing attention to one of the few studies of cortical change that extends over the period characteristic of the school years. This study involved 300 children ages 6 to 18. MRI measurements of cortical thickness were obtained at least twice for each child during these years. The goal was to detect any trends over time, and to unveil any changes in specific regions of cortex that might provide new insights into maturation and development of adult thinking.

A key result of this study is shown in the figure on page 252. These data show the thickness of cerebral cortex for three groups of children (1 = normal intelligence, 2 = above normal intelligence, and 3 = superior intelligence) over the 12 years of the study. Remarkably, the cortex of children of superior intelligence started out significantly thinner than that of the other two groups. However, during the first five to six years of the study, there was a dramatic increase in thickness with that group (superior), while the other two groups did not change dramatically. And in the last six to seven years of the study, cortical thickness decreased steadily for all three groups, ending up at essentially the same point.[17]

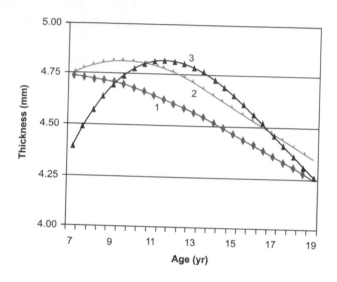

This work suggests that it may not be the thickness that matters, but rather the dynamicity. As the authors of this study conclude, "[C]hildren are not cleverer solely by having more or less grey matter (cortex) at any one age. Rather, intelligence is related to *dynamic* properties of cortical maturation."

It's the change that matters.

Where Is the Change?

The cortical changes shown above were observed in most cortical regions, but were most apparent in right front integrative cortex. In the terminology we have used, this region of cortex can be identified with the manipulation of *relationships in the big picture.* Thus, this research provides a great opportunity for both theoretical discussion and direct experimentation about development of the young mind. Providing specific kinds of challenges might well stimulate cortical change in the area that is most important in creating, problem solving, and predicting. We don't yet know whether these cortical changes are the *result* of enrichment, but it seems safe to say that experience does play a role. In fact, in the study described above, it was also noted that socioeconomic status of the family correlated with intelligence of the children, while biological factors such as gender or handedness did not. Of course, it could be that socioeconomic status provides more opportunities for enrichment of childhood experience, or vice versa. We do not know the causative relationships in this complex dynamic among social, economic, and biological factors.

Further research will begin to unravel these issues, but in the meantime it seems safe to say that education will be most effective when it consists of enriched experiences requiring adaptability and action.

Thinning

These studies are of great interest generally, but the thinning of the cortex may be particularly provocative. It does not seem surprising that cortical thickness increases at first in the superior intelligence group. The explanation for that would be more cortical neuronal branching, driven by the increased challenges and complexity children face as they approach puberty.

However, the subsequent thinning of cortex in all groups suggests something else. In earlier chapters we discussed the finding that activity of motor neurons actually reduces dramatically during learning, especially when perfecting an action or skill. Thus, the thinning of cortex may imply that as children become more skilled at dealing with challenges, they begin to discard ineffective or relatively less important neuronal pathways. This is "learning by losing," or pruning, which is described in *The Art of Changing the Brain*, and in chapter 2 of this book. Ultimately, it seems likely that both increased branching and decreased branching are dynamically associated with the cortical changes evident in the graph above. Both are needed for learning, and both are important for intelligence.

Growth of Mind

The central theme of this chapter is neuronal change. We looked for those things that change within the lifetime of an individual and those that do not. We considered that the former rests on the latter—a foundation for change. We looked at change in cognition as well as in emotion and temperament.

We encountered several specific aspects of change that suggest ideas about development and curriculum. And we left loose ends begging to be tied.

Those loose ends consist of the multitude of ideas for our journey from brain to mind. Some of those ideas are more important than others, and nearly all of them can benefit from clarification and integration into a big picture. This is the goal of the final chapter: I attempt an analysis of the journey from brain to mind in terms of the individual—the self.

I try to weave all these threads about the brain into the whole cloth of mind.

Notes

1. With permission from Nolte, J. (2002), *The Human Brain* (5th ed.), Mosby, St. Louis, MO, p. 538.

2. Some teachers who read this example informed me that book reports are not assigned as frequently as was once the case, but it still seems to be a good example. Maybe if book reports were assigned this way, they would be more useful in the future.

3. See note 6 in chapter 6.

4. However, it may well be that comprehension produces speed. Cognitive research implies that when experts have a cognitive framework supporting the details of their expertise, memory of new details can be established almost instantaneously.

5. Wolfram, S. (2002), *A New Kind of Science*, Wolfram Media Inc., Champaign, IL.

6. Pascallis, O., and colleagues (2002), *Science*, 296, pp. 1321–1323.

7. Gougoux, F., et al, (2004), *Nature*, 230, p. 309.

8. A program somewhat like this has been initiated by the Mandel School of Applied Social Sciences at Case Western Reserve in Cleveland, OH.

9. Hubel, D. H., and Weisel, T. N. (1963), *Journal of Neurophysiology*, 26, pp. 994–1002.

10. Fischer, A., and colleagues (2007), *Nature*, 447, pp. 178–182; also see review article by Sweatt, J. D., p. 151, in the same issue.

11. Gould, E. and colleagues, (1999), *Nature Neuroscience*, vol 2, pp 260–265

12. Generally, myelination is more common with axons and less so with dendrites. However, dendrite myelination has been demonstrated more recently and more extensively that was recognized earlier.

13. Wang, K. C., and colleagues (2002) *Nature*, 417, pp. 941–944.

14. Flechsig, P. (1886), *Gehirn und Steele*, Veit, Leipzig, Germany; see also Gross, C. G. (1998), *Brain Vision Memory, Tales of the History of Neuroscience*, MIT Press, Cambridge, MA, p. 74.

15. Two highly active areas of research on epigenetics (in addition to the nurturing work) are learning by place cells in the hippocampus and the biology of autism. A useful website for study of the nurturing process is http://learn.genetics.utah.edu/content/epigenetics/.

16. Two references describe the research on which these conclusions are based: Champagne, F., et al. (2001), *Proceedings of the National Academy of Science* (USA), 98, pp. 12735–12741; Francis, D. D., et al. (2002), *Journal of Neuroendocrinology*, 14, pp. 349–353.

17. Shaw, P., et al. (2006), *Nature*, 440, pp. 476–480.

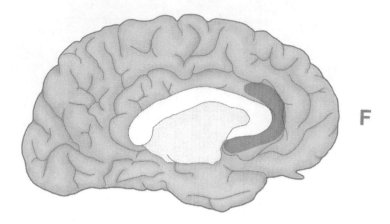

F

Region of limbic cortex known as the "anterior cingulate." This region is implicated in self-awareness, and makes connections between brain areas involved in cognition, and other areas involved in emotion.

IO

THE CONNECTING THREAD

Metacognition and the Integrated Mind

How wonderful, how very wonderful the operations of time, and the changes of the human
mind!

—Jane Austen, *Mansfield Park*

*My family had just moved from one town in Michigan to another, and
I enrolled in a new school. I was in first grade, and to this day it seems
like everything about school began in that first-grade class.*

*Two key events happened that year: I learned to read, and I learned
to play softball. From those events my mind began to expand, and even
today I use memories of that time period to help me solve problems and
trust my mind, both in and out of school.*

*In my first memory of reading, I am sitting in the back row of the
class, watching the teacher make marks on the blackboard. The marks
were the letters of the alphabet, and for the first time, I consciously realized that they were connected to the sounds of words. I began to copy
what the teacher was doing. As I did that, I began to understand reading and put it all together: I began to read.*

*But that was my secret. The teacher didn't know and I didn't tell
her. I kept quiet in the back row with the other students whose last
names started with Z.*

*In the next memory, my teacher is dividing the class into reading
groups: the lions and the butterflies. The strong readers were the lions,
and the weak ones were the butterflies. Suddenly I realized that she
thought I was a butterfly! Of course, she would, because I was keeping
quiet, but I was still very upset. My self-image had changed. I viewed
myself as a strong reader, a lion!*

257

I was determined to show off my reading skills. I had no doubt that I was one of the best readers in the class, and I consciously looked for ways to establish that fact. I raised my hand, volunteering to read.

Sure enough, the next day, I was moved from the butterflies to the lions. It was a moment of pure joy. My reading improved by leaps and bounds. The world of facts and stories opened up to me. I put things together: first letters, then words, then ideas, then plots, then entire books.

What about softball? That was not at all like school. It was a game played outdoors, and it involved throwing, catching, and hitting. Yet, in a strange way, it was still about reading. In softball you had to put things together, just like reading. I could see that to be a lion when playing ball I would have to learn the parts of hitting, the parts of catching, and the parts of throwing. Even more important, I had to do them. No one would know what a softball lion I was unless I showed them.

What worked in school also worked outside of school.

This story is about the growth of my own mind, and it illustrates many of the ideas found in preceding chapters. The story also draws attention to the notion that self-awareness plays a key role in development of the mind. Even at a very young age, I was aware of the possibility that I could control my own learning. I could try out my own ideas about successful learning, and I could even apply those ideas to different challenges.

This awareness is a thread that winds its way throughout this book. The notion that understanding the basis for change from brain to mind can lead to conscious application of that knowledge is inherent in every chapter of this book. In fact, looking back in this direct and conscious way exposes an overview of the journey toward mind that was not previously apparent. The thread of awareness begins to reveal the "whole cloth" of the mind.

That whole cloth appears in each individual throughout his or her unique experiential lifetime. It does not depend on school or formal education, although both make contributions in important but unpredictable ways. The threads of all our individual experiences are woven together, each one making its unique contribution to the final fabric.

Awareness of both the threads and the fabric is of great importance in the journey toward mind.

Metacognition

In many ways, a learner's awareness and insight about development of his or her own mind is the ultimate and most powerful objective of education; not just thinking, but thinking about our own thinking. It is when we begin to comprehend our own thought that we can sense progress in our journey toward mind. This comprehension may be our highest and most complex mental capability.

The term *metacognition* is often used in discussions and descriptions of this self-examination process. The prefix *meta* comes from the Greek, meaning *beyond*. Its application can be illustrated with the concept of abstraction. For example, if we produce abstractions as discussed in chapter 8, but then discuss and generalize about the process and mental work that led to those abstractions, we are going "beyond abstraction." We are aware of our own thinking process, and consciously focused on developing an overarching perspective on it.

Here is how we will use the term in this chapter. First, we will think of it from the perspective of the *individual* learner, focusing on our own metacognition. Metacognition is something we do for ourselves. No one can provide metacognition for another person. Second, it is a conscious process. The goal is to become *aware* of what we assume, think, and believe, and how we use that awareness in our mental activities. Third, metacognition uses certain aspects of what has been called the *executive* function of the brain. Those aspects include but are not necessarily limited to making choices, planning, and intentional memory recall. The executive element is found in *initiating* thinking about experiences. It is a *decision* to support and continue the journey toward mind.

Becoming metacognitive, however, is not an endpoint. As I suggested earlier, the notion of endings, or finish lines, in our journey is not necessarily useful. Although life ultimately ends, the journey is open-ended. It always offers opportunity. We should think of it not as an objective but as a state of mind. Gaining a metacognitive state of mind offers greater possibilities for experiencing the joy of learning than, perhaps, any of the other objectives or goals discussed so far.

But this state of mind is an opening, not an ending. It is mental growth and expansion.

*   *   *

The Journey: Redux

Later in this chapter we will turn back to the brain and discuss the regions of cortex that seem to be involved in metacognition. Before that, it may be helpful to revisit our journey from this metacognitive perspective. I will do that in the next few pages. We will follow the sequence proposed in chapters 2–9 (*random action → discovery → joy → intentional action → integration → images → symbol → forming memories → predicting → experiential change*), asking whether we can find inherent metacognitive features, or see new ways to enhance or encourage them. We will not only discover the metacognitive process inherent in those chapters, but also make suggestions about how to facilitate metacognition development and success at each of these stages.

We will ask whether we can follow the thread and, if so, how do we do it?

Where the Thread Begins: Random Action

To begin this revisiting, we go back to chapter 2. As we discussed there, the earliest stage of learning begins in the womb. As a baby begins to move, twist, and kick, these unplanned and spontaneous actions produce physical experiences that have the potential to produce cognitive understandings later on. We remain unaware of this early in life, but the associations are there, nonetheless.

Its relevance here is that learning by this random process actually continues throughout life. As a newborn the baby may randomly turn her head in the crib, leading to new discoveries about her environment, but the same thing happens with adults. Just walking through a park and randomly moving our head and eyes can lead to perceptions of new aspects of the park. For example, we may see a large tree we never noticed before.

Any purposeful action, such as our walk in the woods, has elements that seem random. The environment surrounds us with potential sensory experience. This kind of experience may not reach our consciousness, but it can reach the sensory cortex of our brain. We can gain knowledge without awareness.[1]

Our question now is, "Is metacognition related to random action?"

If random action generates new knowledge of which we are unaware, the challenge of metacognition is to become aware of at least some of this knowledge—to recognize knowledge of our knowledge. To become aware we will have to search. It is like a treasure hunt where we don't know exactly what the treasure is, but we believe it is out there: a search for the unknown. We have a conscious belief that our random actions have, over time, led to experiences and knowledge of which we are unaware. There are things to be discovered within our own minds.

If we believe there is hidden treasure, and we believe it is worth finding, the next step may well be a decision to initiate a search. But initiation requires a plan of some sort. How are we going to search? The answer to this question is highly individual. It will be based on our conscious knowledge derived from experience. We may turn to reflection, waiting for an idea to arise. Or we may try to help out by asking questions. What did I encounter today? Did I find any surprises? Any mysteries? What ideas did I get? We may have a discussion with our mate or partner about the day, keep a diary or journal, or develop other ways to stimulate reflection. It seems that there is no particular formula or general instructions guaranteed to produce meta-cognition, but reflection is always at the heart of it.

In fact, all this analysis of metacognition is metacognitive in itself. It is individual, it is conscious, and it involves continued executive direction guided by decisions and choices. It is the use of the conscious mind to discover the unconscious.

Discovery: Keeping Track of the Thread

Discovery is an essential point along the thread. It is necessary if random action is to lead to metacognition. In fact, discovery is the ultimate goal. We want to experience the conversion of unconscious sensory experience into conscious awareness of a meaning, concept, or relationship.

Perhaps the central aspect of discovery is *ownership*. When we discover something, we start believing that we own it. We can see clear examples of this throughout human history. For example, in exploration of the "new world" by Europeans, whenever the "explorer" realized that a particular geographic location had not been previously known in Europe, he would plant the flag of his country in the soil of the "new" country. He claimed ownership.

Ownership is a powerful force in human experience. As children, we fight over ownership. It's mine! No, it's mine! Wars are fought over ownership. And ownership is part of metacognition. We know when something is ours; our ownership is known to us. Recognizing this sense of ownership is part of metacognition.

Discovery is part of the bridge from unconscious to conscious. Random, thoughtless, unconscious actions lead us to new experiences, and when those experiences are intense, we become conscious of them through the attention processes described in preceding chapter 8. The awareness of discovery, and how it transpires, is another metacognitive process.

Joy

Action and discovery produce joy. This brain connection (the thread?) between the basal ganglia, reward, and action was described in chapter 3. And, as I said above, that joy is at least partially related to ownership. Acquiring new ideas, knowledge, or skills makes us happy. The feeling of joy is something we want to experience. Thus, metacognition is its own reward. We want the cognition so we can have the joy, and having the joy makes us aware of the cognition. Metacognition and joy are packaged together.

As I claimed in *The Art of Changing the Brain*, another aspect of the joy is our sense of movement, or progress. If we have a goal, something we desire, and we are moving closer to it, the movement is joyful. I believe this is true of both physical and mental movement. Our mental perception of progress and the joy it brings comes from our perception of actual physical movement and progress—again, the mental derives from the physical. We can lump random action, discovery, and joy together as the foundation of metacognition. They support all the other elements of mind that we have been discussing in this book.

Completing actions, actually reaching a goal, also produces joy. We will try hard to get what we want, be it an object, a person, or an idea. This can be subconscious, but if we succeed in drawing it into our consciousness, as I suggested above with random action, it becomes more powerful. It is a step toward metacognition.

Intentional Action

As our metacognitive experience grows, our awareness grows. We begin to recognize the world outside our mind, including behaviors and actions of other people. That awareness influences our own goals and actions. Thus, as we mature, we progress from random, unconscious, actions to intentional actions. *Action → discovery → joy* still works, but the actions become more intentional. We choose to do things that have a purpose, and fulfillment of such purposes, as well as progress toward them, triggers our internal reward system: the "joy system." This, in turn, increases our awareness, and so the link between intentional action and emotion becomes established. (Of course, the same thing is true with intentional actions that lead to unsatisfactory, even painful, outcomes).

These connections with the emotion system become more and more common as our awareness increases. Metacognition is now the tool we use to produce more cognition. More than the outcome, metacognition now provides the mechanism by which we can obtain discovery and joy.

An important aspect of intentional action is mimicry (chapter 2 again). We see behaviors and actions that we know or think will make us happy, and we copy them. We have learned how to activate our internal joy machinery through exploring and reaching goals, so we set specific goals and intentionally undertake exploration.

Integration

Moving on in this review of earlier chapters, we find the thread becoming clearer. We know what we want to accomplish and how we are going to do it. Development of the mind accelerates. We begin to see the world as a conglomeration of parts, some fitted together to make complete wholes, and others incomplete and frustrating. We are always trying to convert the latter into the former.

As in my story at the beginning of this chapter, we begin to consciously manipulate the parts and assemble them in precise ways, dictated by comprehension. We begin to integrate experiences and objects in order to achieve specific goals. We begin to ask ourselves questions: "What are the parts?" "How can I put them together?" "What do I know, and what do I need to learn?"

In chapter 4, I divided this capability into two elements, based primarily on our understanding of perceptive capability of the brain. One is to bring the smallest details together in a way that can only represent specific objects, events, and ideas. We perceive those integrated details in the unique way characteristic of precisely "what" they represent. This also means we know what they do *not* represent. We establish boundaries and categories.

The second way we comprehend our experience is by recognizing relationships of parts to each other, in space. In chapter 4 we spoke of this process as determining "where" things and events are. Often, this capability is not so demanding of detail. We may sense things on the periphery, even out of focus, but the fact that they are where they are is central to our understanding.

Now, we can see the metacognitive potential of this "what" and "where" arrangement. When we become aware of these two aspects of perception, we can make an executive decision to focus on each one, as we reflect on experiences. For example, we can first focus on the exact nature of something we perceive; let's say a person at a basketball game. Attending to specific details, we realize that the person is a girl cheerleader, not a player. Then, noticing where the cheerleader is, let's say in the back row of the crowd, we suddenly realize that she is actually not involved in this game; where she is gives us more accurate and extensive information.

Awareness of this way to analyze experiences, and consciously using it, can lead us beyond our initial understandings—beyond our cognition.

Patterns: Vehicles for Metacognition

Following the thread now leads us to chapter 5. Electrical firing patterns in the brain can be viewed as vehicles for metacognition. When these vehicles transport one pattern to another, the combination is a new pattern that carries new meanings. For example, when the pattern that represents our image of a neuron merges with the pattern that represents the image of a neocortex, the new pattern gives us understanding of the neuronal network. When the pattern of a melody merges with the pattern of a rhythm, we have a song. Recognizing the melody and the rhythm leads to the emotion of recognition, and thus to the rest of the song. We become aware of our understanding. It is this unending flow of patterns and combinations of patterns that is the root of comprehension and creativity.

In the human brain, these patterns arise primarily from vision, sound, language, and points of pressure throughout the body (touch and body position). Thoughts and memories arise when those patterns fire. The primary pattern can be cued by the firing of a small fragment of the total pattern, triggered either by experience or memory. Part of our concept of mind involves layers of patterns that cue each other, triggering new patterns that come to represent thoughts and insight.

To function as a vehicle in this way, patterns must be strong enough to make us aware of them. They must be able to compete with other patterns in our mind. They must also be transferable from one region of cortex to another, say from back cortex to front cortex as proposed in *The Art of Changing the Brain*, or through mirror neurons as described in chapter 2 of this book.

We can be made aware of our patterns if someone asks about them: "What are you thinking?" In our model of the brain, one way we can answer that kind of question is to directly identify an image or partial image in our mind. Another way is to have language scripts and structures that are linked to such visual images; language that cues our images. A third way is to recognize how our body is feeling, otherwise known as "body language." And a fourth way is through neurons that connect our emotions with our cognition. How do we feel about the cheerleader at the game? Do we care?

Getting answers to those and other questions enhances metacognition.

Symbolic Processes

The thread now leads to chapter 6. The conscious use of symbolic systems (language, numbers, musical notes) to explain, and possibly more important, to manipulate the patterns we just discussed, seems to be one of the clearest expressions of metacognition. The invention of symbolic systems was necessary because the brain itself has no inherent system or code that can serve such a function. So far as we know, the data inherent in all experiences is recorded directly as sensory input. It is not converted to meanings through a system such as the genetic code or the Morse code. In the absence of a "brain code," we invented others.

We use these symbolic systems to explain and describe the world, our experiences, our memories, and our feelings. The neuronal patterns for all this are originally vague and complex, but through use of clear and invariable symbols, we may be able to convey the patterns to others. We may, for example, hear a word (a symbol) that sounds familiar, but we cannot get a clear image. Let's say the word is "boy." That is no problem, but the specific boy doesn't show up in our image. So we look for additional symbols. Let's say "little" and "pony." Now our image becomes more complete. Remember the little boy on the pony? The image now includes additional symbols that greatly increase its clarity.

The only way we can even discuss the meaning of metacognition is through our symbolic systems. Our understanding itself is based on them. By communicating with ourselves using a precise symbolic system such as language or numbers, we regenerate the firing patterns that originated from a concrete visual or auditory experience. (See chapters 5 and 6 for the model of this relationship between images and symbols.) The language gives us a back door to the pattern. If we want an image of metacognition, we will have to use that back door to first access the firing pattern that represents "cognition," and then move that pattern into a second layer—cognition of cognition.

Forming Memories

None of these cognitive or metacognitive functions of the mind can work without the phenomenon of memory. In order to consciously manipulate and integrate thoughts and symbols, we must remember them. This is where our thread seems to lead. To make memories useful, we must form them and recall them. That is what led us to have two chapters, one on memory formation (chapter 7), and one on memory recall (chapter 8).

Memories are forming all the time in our experience, but the things we find memorable differ. We form new memories based on old ones, but those old memories are where the individual differences lie. If we remain aware of our prior experiences, we will be more likely to know what will be memorable in our new experiences. The memorable aspects of any specific experience are likely to be different for each individual simply because of prior knowledge. We can know what new things are likely to be memorable if we remind ourselves of what we already remember. This is a metacognitive approach to forming memories.

Even if our prior experiences are similar to those of other people, the way we remember them can still be very different. I remember different details of sports events than my friends, even though we all enjoy and watch the same games. This seems to be primarily accidental. The things we pay attention to at each moment of a game can differ for each of us. We are each forming our own train of memory based on what we happened to notice earlier. That train may be accidentally interrupted at any point, which often leads to forming a new memory. The interruptions are not planned, but expecting them can be part of our own plan. It can be part of our metacognition about forming memories.

The dynamic and flowing nature of memory discussed in chapter 7 is also a key element in understanding the formation of memories. Memory formation, consolidation, and reconsolidation with time are continuous. We should expect specific memories to change anytime we talk about them. If nothing else, the memories we talk about may very well include the talking when we reconsolidate them. The reconsolidated memory is changed since it now includes the brain activity derived from the talking itself. Our memories of experiences must flow, because our experiences flow.

Perhaps the most important aspect of forming memories is the strong link between cognition and emotion. It almost seems black and white. If an experience is emotional, we will seek to understand it. If it is not, we won't. The emotion systems in the brain are intimately involved with attention. Things that stir our emotion get attention. This is one way we become aware of our experiences, and when we are aware we remember. We will form more and longer lasting memories when the memory includes neuronal pathways to the emotion structures such as the amygdala, nucleus accumbens, and hypothalamus. If those connections are missing, the memory may be missing too.

Awareness of the importance of emotion, and reminding ourselves of it, is a key metacognitive strategy for enhancing memory formation.

Using Memories

To the extent that it engages awareness, control, and intent, the ability to recall and use our memories is inherently a metacognitive skill. These topics and other related ones are discussed in chapter 8. The thread continues. Although the exact word does not appear there, in many ways that chapter is primarily about metacognition. It is about the awareness of and access to our personal cognitions.

The fundamental challenge for metacognition is intentionally recalling memories that are useful when confronting a new challenge. This cannot be forced, but there are specific approaches that can be consciously applied. Basically, these ideas represent an intentional, structured search for cues. As discussed earlier, our proposal is that cues work because their neuronal firing patterns have some overlap with that of an aspect of a memory. Possible cues include such things as category, place, subject, people, and time (as in decade, or season). These are not unique or particularly creative suggestions, but the intentional and organized approach may surprise you. Rather than hoping for a new insight, the metacognitive approach is direct, conscious, and methodological. Our minds contain memories of problems and experiences beyond what we are able to consciously recall. A method for accessing them increases the probability we will find something useful.

Another methodical way to search for useful patterns of neuronal firing is to put the challenge into language. Talk the problem through to yourself. Or, perhaps better, write about it. The permanence of writing may make it a good approach. Talk disappears into the air, but written expression stays around and gives us time to think. The value of language for recall was discussed in earlier chapters. Just our choice of words or tone of voice will contain hints for new perspectives, insights, or metaphors.

An example of this is my use of the "journey" metaphor in this book. It was working well until I suddenly remembered that journeys usually come to an end. I was disturbed by this as I did not want to imply that the development of the mind must have an end. I had used the metaphor throughout the entire book. I was stuck with it. I had a problem!

My response involved briefly writing short descriptions of journeys with different ends. I wrote "the end of the road," "the end of life" (don't want that one!), "the end of marriage" (not that either), and then I remembered a journey from my childhood. The end of this one was different. It was a journey to the top of a big hill. As it progressed, the light got brighter and brighter, and as we reached the end it opened up to unlimited new perspectives. With a sigh I smiled and wrote, "leads to the light!"

Metacognition can be methodical, but we *can't force* it. Looking back to chapter 8, you will recall several segments that describe and prescribe patience, the patience required when we are waiting for an answer. Sometimes we have to be intentionally patient. At the same time we have to remain alert. As Ellen Langer says, we have to be mindful.[2] A moment of opportunity may well occur, but we must wait. This mental drifting can be a strategy for metacognition. Our mind can drift, our focus can diminish, and we may neglect what is happening around us. But while drifting, our mind may still be searching for the right cue. It may well already be prepared to respond when a good cue shows up.

Ironically, if we attend too much, we may miss it.

Metacognition and School

Our metacognition thread led us to the classroom in chapter 9. That chapter differs from the others in that it contains specific ideas for curriculum and content in formal education. The focus remains on enhancing and supporting the journey from brain to mind, but with groups of learners rather than individuals and with specific attention to particular strategies. Each specific idea could provide the basis for a lengthy discussion of metacognition, which I will not undertake here.

This chapter, however, has a strong emphasis on developing new directions and approaches in formal education, in the future. These proposals remain to be tested, but the notion of looking ahead deserves some new attention here. It is interesting to ask whether metacognition may become a useful, perhaps essential, topic in formal schooling situations, or in other settings such as groups of learners in adult education. Might metacognition be taught like literacy or mathematics, as a subject throughout the curriculum (one appropriate to the developmental stage of learners)? At the present time, formal schooling is based on curricula designed to match the growth in student capabilities with age. This implies that we know enough about development to teach at a level that is effective as learners mature. If that is so, do we also know enough about the development of metacognition to make it a subject in the curriculum? If a school class is expected to learn certain facts each year, does that also mean that they can understand what they learn about learning each year? Can they explore their own learning, and that of their peers?

This question is meant to open the door just a crack; to give us ideas for what could lie ahead, but not to propose or describe an entire new adventure. We have come to a loose end with our thread. If we are to follow it further, we will need to anchor it firmly to specific and concrete educational structures.

Can we imagine a "curriculum for learning?" Or courses, entitled "Metacognition?"

*   *   *

An Accidental Experiment

We are at the end of our search for metacognition in earlier chapters, As I promised, I will now turn to discussion of the brain and neurological processes in metacognition.

This is a new part of the chapter, but still our central idea is the same. Our focus is the self—the individual. Realizing that each of us reaches metacognitive goals by different routes on a different time scale prompts specific questions. Are there explicit areas of the brain involved as we recognize specific aspects of our self? If so, what functions can we attribute to those areas? Can we stitch those functions together to create ideas about our own identity and how we understand that identity? How can we apply the notion of metacognition to understanding our own personal and unique learning and knowledge?

In exploring these questions, let's consider what I call an "accidental experiment" that occurred nearly 200 years ago. It was accidental in the sense that the experiment itself was, indeed, an accident; it derived from a mistake that no one would ever make intentionally. It is also accidental in the sense that the outcome of the accident generated thoughts and speculations that could never have been predicted.

The accident involved a man named Phineas Gage. He was a workman in the construction of Vermont's Rutland and Burlington railroad in the early 19th century. His job was to blast out cuts and tunnels through the rugged stone cliffs where the railway would lie when completed. The blasting involved drilling holes approximately three feet deep and one inch in diameter into the rock, pouring blasting powder into the holes, tamping the powder down into the hole with a steel rod, and then lighting the powder to blast out large hunks of granite. On the fateful day, the powder exploded while being tamped, and the rod blew out of its hole, striking Phineas under his right cheekbone, rocketing up through his brain, out of his skull, and landing 85 feet away.

Phineas was knocked unconscious by the accident, but unexpectedly and shockingly, woke up in a few minutes. He was treated by a skillful physician and, even more surprising, after some weeks he was able to leave the hospital. At first, he even retained his cognitive abilities such as reading and calculation, but he then began to behave abnormally in ways described below by his physician:

The equilibrium or balance, so to speak, between his intellectual faculties and animal propensities, seems to have been destroyed. He is fitful, irreverent, indulging at times in the grossest profanity (which was not previously his custom), manifesting but little deference for his fellows, impatient of restraint or advice when it conflicts with his desires, at times pertinaciously obstinate, yet capricious and vacillating, devising many plans of future operations, which are no sooner arranged than they are abandoned in turn for others appearing more feasible. A child in his intellectual capacity and manifestations, he has the animal passions of a strong man. Previous to his injury, although untrained in the schools, he possessed a well-balanced mind, and was looked upon by those who knew him as a shrewd, smart businessman, very energetic and persistent in executing all his plans of operation. In this regard his mind was radically changed, so decidedly that his friends and acquaintances said he was "no longer Gage."

Notice: "He was no longer Gage." He was no longer *himself.*[3]

Metacognition, Gage, and his Brain

I suspect we are all metacognitive to some extent. We think about our thoughts and plan our plans. Some of us do this more than others. Understanding our selves varies, both in extent and in focus. In the case of Phineas Gage, certain aspects of this capability seem to have disappeared completely after the accident. His previously "well-balanced" and "shrewd" mind had vanished. Its "balance between intellectual facilities and animal propensities was destroyed." He was dramatically changed.

Perhaps the more crucial point is that Gage apparently *did not know* he was not himself. He was unaware of his own mind. He did not—it seems, he could not—explain his own behaviors. He had lost a great deal of his metacognitive ability.

This accident has fascinated neuroscientists and neurosurgeons since it happened, but a direct investigation of the actual brain damage was never considered until recent decades. Then, because his gravesite was known, it was realized that Gage's skull was still available for examination. The famous skull was recovered and the damage analyzed to determine exactly what regions of his brain had been destroyed. This analysis pointed to the anterior cingulate (both right and left) and, to a lesser extent, some other frontal and prefrontal cortical regions.[4]

For several decades, these regions of the brain have been implicated in what has been called the "executive" functions—a kind of control center for issuing internal directions and making choices. This would be a natural candidate as a center for metacognition. Thus, following the study of Gage and his brain, a great deal of research continued to implicate the anterior cingulate and other linked frontal cortex regions in metacognitive functions and in being heavily engaged in identification of the "self." Among other examples, this work includes studies of executive attention[5], self-regulation[6], contributions to behavior[7], and self-reflective thought[8]. In most cases the anterior region of cingulate cortex was most consistently activated, but in others the posterior regions also was engaged.[9] These regions of cortex are part of what is called the limbic lobe, shown at the beginning of this chapter. Of course, the "anterior" region is that which is closest to the front.

Great Excitement in the Anterior Cingulate

The location of the anterior cingulate in the brain is ideal for establishing a bridge between emotion and cognitive centers of the brain. This was recognized when Gage's skull was studied, and has been confirmed by the research reports referenced here as well as by many others. At the time of this writing, it does not seem an exaggeration to say that the anterior cingulate cortex might well be the subject of the most fascinating area of cognitive neuroscience research ever. I will briefly discuss the work of Allman and his colleagues to illustrate this assertion.[10]

A key Allman paper is titled, *The Anterior Cingulate Cortex: The Evolution of an Interface between Emotion and Cognition.* The work described leads the authors to make the following statements: (1) "We propose that the anterior cingulate cortex is a (evolutionarily new) specialization of the neocortex"; (2) "Functions central to intelligent behavior, that is emotional self-control, focused problem solving, error recognition, and adaptive responses to changing conditions, are juxtaposed with the emotions in this structure"; (3) "The anterior cingulate cortex contains a class of spindle shaped neurons that are found only in humans and great apes"; (4) "The spindle cells appear to be widely connected with diverse parts of the brain, and may have a role in the coordination essential in developing the capacity to focus on different problems"; (5) "Furthermore, they (spindle cells) emerge postnatally, and their survival (following birth) may be enhanced or reduced by environmental conditions of enrichment or stress, thus potentially influencing adult competence or dysfunction in emotional self-control or problem-solving."

In other research papers, discovery of spindle cells in dolphins and elephants, both species known to possess some aspects of human intelligence. Furthermore, in all these species, the spindle cells are exceptionally large and appear to have a potential for connecting distant regions of cortex (regions other than anterior cingulate) with one another. That is, they may serve an integrative function, bringing information from sensory and motor regions as well as emotion together for processing—what we might call *intelligence*.

Anterior cingulate cortex and its spindle cells are ideal for metacognition.

An Anterior Cingulate Fable

To bring this all together, here is a fairy tale of the anterior cingulate.

> Once upon a time, about 15–20 million years ago, some species were struggling for survival, more than others. In particular, these included the ancestors of apes, elephants, whales, dolphins, and other strange creatures that would eventually become Homo sapiens. I will call them the "struggling species—SS." At least some regions of neocortex had now evolved in the brains of these SS. In addition, they possessed the much more ancient emotion systems that were essential for survival using speed, strength, aggression, and escape. And they continued to reproduce, driven by ancient and essential behaviors and attractive emotions
>
> The struggle came from the fact that the SS were not very fast, or strong, or nasty. They could sense danger or threats through their emotion systems, but it didn't do them much good when they couldn't escape or fight. So they struggled!
>
> However, our friends the SS did have a good bit of neocortex, and so did their babies. That relatively new invention allowed the SS to map out their world, and probably also to remember the maps. They might even have had memories of where danger lurked, or what kinds of other living species were dangerous, strong, or fast. If that were so, it was possible that they could make plans for escape or tricking the potential enemy!
>
> But they had a problem: They had both emotion systems and cognitive systems, but the two systems were not well-connected to each other. So the SS experienced fear, but didn't know what to

do or when to do it. They also had at least primitive maps of their environment, but did not link those maps to their emotions.

Meantime, new babies were constantly being born in the SS, and eventually, in a few individual animals, the spindle cells grew to greater length than in others. This normal genetic variation led to a few new babies that grew quite large spindle cells after birth, and some of those cells occasionally were large enough to connect the emotion structures to the neocortex.

This was a big deal. When the occasional new baby had really large spindle cells, the cognitive areas of cortex began to talk to the emotion areas of the brain, and vice versa. Those messages allowed that baby to identify danger, feel fear, and develop a plan of escape using the neocortex. Those individuals survived longer and passed on that gene for spindle cell growth to their babies. And so it went. Bit by bit the large spindle cells in the anterior cingulate were found in more and more of the offspring, and those species began to compete effectively with the others. They struggled less.

Eventually they became the very smart animals they are today.[11]

Message From the Spindle Cell

We might call the spindle cell a *metacognition* cell. In addition to their location in the anterior cingulate and the previous research linking this area of the brain to metacognition, the linkage of the cognitive to the emotional is itself a powerful aspect of the metacognitive process. For metacognition *we need to know what we think and how we feel about it; inversely, we must know what we feel and what we think about that.* Metacognition is inherently an integrative process, blending thought and emotion into a unique combination for each of us.

The linkage between emotion and cognition is a powerful tool for understanding the self. Not only is communication facilitated, so is memory. Memories have their factual content and their emotional content. If they are linked through this bridge of the anterior cingulate, then damage to the bridge will create trouble. This biological illustration strongly supports the idea that education requires such a bridge. If we lose the connection, we may revert back to mental capabilities characteristic of our postulated evolutionary ancestors.

To go "beyond cognition," we add emotion. The spindle cells may take us there.

Experiential Change

At the beginning of this chapter I quoted Jane Austen: "How wonderful, how very wonderful the operations of time, and the changes of the human mind!" I chose this quote because I find myself continually reflecting on change and its role in learning. The optimistic and wonderful idea that change emerges from the "operations of time" prompts us to ask what those "operations" are.

We can say that the answer to that question is "experience." But that is unsatisfying because "experience" is too broad a term, and leaves too many unanswered questions. In chapters 2, and 9, however, I describe two somewhat more specific types of experience that have been shown to change the brain, and they ultimately show themselves as changes in the mind. First, there are experiences that increase knowledge and complexity. This change produces an increase in thickness or density of cortex, which is the result of increased branching of cortical neurons; this is an increase in "connectivity, indeed, in connectability." Ultimately, it is associated with deepening and extension of knowledge.

The second type of change leads to reduction in cortical thickness and engagement of fewer neurons, which enhances efficiency. This is learning by elimination of unnecessary complexity. It can occur both by inhibition of specific synapse activity, or by reduction of the actual number of connections. The experiences that lead to this kind of learning are based on practice and self-analysis. On metacognition. When learning this way, we repeat specific challenges, and intentionally search for un-essential parts of our mental processes; the parts that were originally highly complex and inefficient. Learning a skill is an example of this kind of change. Effective educators can recognize inefficient approaches of learners, and help learners stay off unnecessary detours and break bad habits.

Increased complexity is part of Austen's wonderful change, but so is efficiency.

Beginning Metacognition

At what age should we begin to focus on increased complexity and efficiency in formal schooling? In our book we began early. The first stage, random action—discovery—joy, occurs when we are very young. (But not only when we are young.) It might even make sense to perceive this early development as a different category than the one that characterizes mentally conscious children and adults. Perhaps only when our experience is rich enough and complex enough should we expect thinking about thinking. However, I am not sure of this. My own experience suggests that metacognition can develop in young children. At least it seems possible that it did for me.

The story at the beginning of this chapter suggests at least the beginnings of metacognition when I was in first grade. I became aware of the idea of breaking things into their parts. I was aware that thinking that way helped me read better and might eventually help me hit the ball better. I didn't label this "thinking," but it seems to me that I was aware of it, and was applying it. I was doing more than learning; I was *thinking* about learning.

You may have examples of metacognition in yourself or others, as a child. These examples might include things like learning to win at cards by analyzing your own way of thinking, or listening to a parent read a story, and realizing that adventure stories engage you because they make you worried.

If we look, we may find metacognition everywhere and anytime.

If Not Time, What?

If metacognition does not necessarily depend on age, upon what else might it depend?

This book is organized based on a possible answer to this question. That answer is that metacognition depends on the nature of our experiences. If development proceeds along the path I have laid out, then it is important that all the stages I described take place. Not that the sequence must be linear, as we discussed in chapter 1, but that each aspect of cognitive growth we have discussed takes place and makes it contributions to the overall picture. If some don't occur, development of the mind may be slowed or interrupted. The process is unified and synergistic, so that all aspects of the journey supports and enhances the others. Each stage depends on others, in a sort of pyramid, as shown below.

The logic of this book is the logic of this pyramid. Metacognition is weakened in the absence of the experiences that support it. On the other hand it may develop early in life if the necessary foundation exists.

The figure on page 277 is not as an answer or explanation, but a way to encourage an interesting discussion. It is basically a review of the book, and

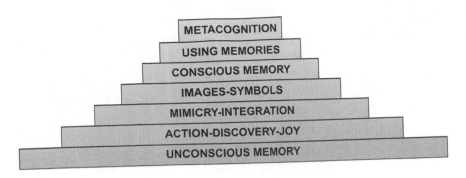

it clearly illustrates the importance of each aspect of the journey as a foundation for the others. It suggests a theory of the mind as a whole. If any stage is missing, the entire structure suffers. For example, if the development of the symbolic systems is incomplete or absent, it becomes impossible to get the most out of the cognitive processes that depend on use of our conscious memories. Or, if we miss the discovery phase and its related joys, there is bound to be a negative impact on the emotional and motivational elements of learning in general.

In addition, in constructing the pyramid I combined some aspects of the journey that were discussed separately in earlier chapters. For example, in chapter 2 I link action closely with discovery, and discovery with joy. Listing them together is an intentional effort to suggest unity. Not that we don't discover things that are negative or even dangerous, but rather that joy is most likely to occur with discovery, and discovery with action.

I have also linked *mimicry* with *integration*, and *images* with *symbols*. The rationale for these combinations can also be found in earlier chapters. To summarize, mimicry is an integrative process in which we merge our perceptions, gathered through the sensory systems, with our notions of our self. We take ownership of our perceptions by mimicking them. And, as I stressed in chapter 6, our symbolic systems allow us to describe our images. The images are highly complex patterns, so the use of symbols to describe them is of great—possibly essential—value for comprehension.

The Integrated Mind

For certain purposes, the pyramid model is useful. It illustrates the development theme and the dependence of specific aspects on support of others. It is a new way of looking at the journey. However, it suffers from the limits imposed by the complexity of the topic. As with all the metaphors and models that preceded it in earlier chapters (the journey, a light [at various points], the thread and its cloth), the pyramid fails to illustrate the living complexity of a human mind. In fact, it gives a misleading and somewhat disturbing impression of separation of layers, and lack of interaction between the implied functions. This is not at all like a mind.

To address that shortcoming, I have constructed a model that includes such interactions. This model, illustrated in the figure below, also includes specific brain areas rather than implying them. It is more of a model and less of a metaphor.

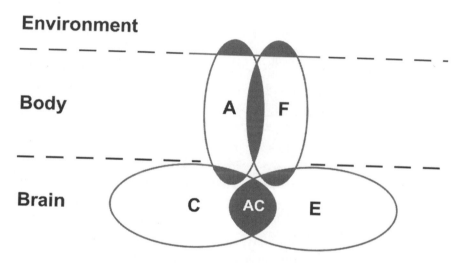

The first aspect of our model is the concept of three layers, or compartments: Environment, Body, and Brain. The basic idea is inspired by a paper written by my neuroscience colleagues Hillel Chiel and Randy Beer, entitled "The Brain Has a Body: Adaptive Behavior Emerges From Interactions of Nervous System, Body, and Environment."[12]

In the overall model, the three layers all contribute to mind. It is an integrative model, and not limited to just the brain. Integration is indicated by the overlapping regions in the model. It is important to note that the overlap is not directional. In each region of overlap, the interaction is bidirectional; it goes both ways. This is a key, even essential, feature of integration, as I discuss in chapter 4.

With those general features in mind (no pun intended), let's examine the model. A good place to begin is the overlap region labeled **AC** (**anterior cingulate**). As we discussed, this is the area of cortex that contains the spindle cells, and it is strategically situated to provide for interaction between other regions of cortex (labeled **C**), and emotion structures (labeled **E**). I have provided the Wikipedia identification of those areas in the endnotes.[13] They are all regions in the brain and, as noted above, they are extensive.

The **C** and **E** regions of the brain both give and receive information to the body. The cortical brain areas both sense and generate actions (**A**) in the form of movements and behaviors. The emotion areas of the brain generate feelings (**F**) in the body. The actions and feelings influence each other, as indicated in the overlap. Thus, our model provides for integration of cognition, emotion, actions and feelings throughout the brain and the body.

The remaining feature of this model is the role given to the environment. A major aspect of this impact is information and memory about objects or experiences that activate any element of our sensory systems: things we see, hear, and touch; that is, that originate outside the body (in the environment). The second part of this environmental impact is mediated through our actions and our motor brain. Our body senses, and our brain knows, what we do and the impact of what we do. As discussed in earlier chapters, it is the motor system that provides our ability to alter the environment. For example, we see some litter lying on the walkway, (knowledge of environment), and we go over to pick it up (changing features of the environment). Finally, both the sensory and motor elements are influenced by our cognitive abilities and our emotional reactions (and vice versa).

The model integrates cognition, emotion, action, feelings, sensory experience, and motor experience, in the human organism interacting with the environment. It is a holistic concept, a "big picture" for what we call the mind. And included in this picture we find a key aspect of metacognition: self-knowledge.

γνῶθι σεαυτόν *gnōthi seauton*

"Know thyself." In contrast to the Greek, the English words appear simple. However, in reality, actually knowing ourselves, the Greek comes closer. Self-knowledge is complicated.

In classical history Socrates is often given credit for being the first, or among the first, educators to recommend self-knowledge to his students. Of course, we will never know "the first," but this kind of thinking can be found at other places around the same time. For example, the philosophy of *Vedanta* emerged in India.[14] Vedanta is based on the concept of connectedness between all beings, and between the various aspects of human personality and behavior.

The connectedness inherent in our proposed model of the mind is reminiscent of these ancient ideas. The model also meshes well with more modern psychology concepts which divide self-knowledge into three categories: *cognitive, affective,* and *executive*.[15] In our efforts to know ourselves, we analyze our reasoning, our emotions, and our decision making. Likewise, in our model of the integrated mind, reason and emotion are at the core at each level: brain, body, and environment. And, although the third element, *executive*, is not explicit in our brain model, it is implicit in the form of action. The inclination to plan, select, and carry out actions is a characteristic aspect of executive behaviors.

Our model of the integrated mind is a generalization, of course. It comes from our effort to define a category (the mind) rather than a specific instance (a mind). Individual minds differ from one another, producing specific behaviors and thought. As I have said earlier, the self emerges from the individual mind. We are each different; we are our *selves*.

One of the ways we differ is the extent to which we are metacognitive. Some of us are naturally more inclined to metacognition than others. We have a different mental "style" if you will. But even those of us who are not naturally so inclined can intentionally turn our minds inward.

Each of us can choose to gain more self-knowledge. That is part of our journey, too.

The Parts and the Whole

The unifying aspect of our model, and of Vedanta, contrasts with the categorization that emerges from modern brain research. Today we tend to break things into component parts. I have done the same thing here. Perhaps this is a natural outcome of modern research methods that are geared toward identifying different brain compartments, or modules. These methods are designed to identify specific cortical regions that become more active when a certain behavior occurs. Their very premise is that such areas exist and function at least somewhat independently.

This perspective may be challenged in the future as we develop methods that are designed to discover connectedness rather than separation. But the notion of modules will not disappear quickly. It is widespread and I use it myself throughout our book. However, if you look back through earlier chapters, you may notice that there is also an intentional and persistent emphasis on connectedness.

Our model of the mind certainly stresses connection. It tends to unify rather than divide. It stresses overlap of brain *structures*, rather than divisions between them, and this structural overlap leads to extensive overlap between different brain *functions*. This is particularly apparent with cognition and emotion. Virtually all aspects of cognition influence emotion, and vice versa.

This connectedness is a fundamental idea emerging from our book-long discussion of the journey toward mind. In contrast, it can be argued that the brain is more about separation of functions than about connections. Thus, developing connections is central to the journey. Looking at individual functions of specific domains has brought us inexorably toward a model of the mind that features connections. Our future understandings about the mind must have that feature. New insights will emerge as we come to understand and pay attention to this key concept.

The Future in the Past

We are coming to the end of our book, but to me, it seems that the journey has just begun. It has been amazing—a joy. Personally, I hope I will continue moving, finding new paths, and reaching new destinations. But I suspect I will also find a lot that looks familiar. There will be some revisiting, but from a different perspective. As seems to often be the case, looking ahead brings us back to beginnings. So to begin our ending, I suggest that we look back to the way we started our book. Let's revisit *The Great Transformation* of chapter 2.

Remarkably, I find metacognition back there. I openly attempted to get my readers to think about their own learning. The last few pages of that earlier chapter urges us to think about our own actions, and their connections to our own minds. Raising the idea of metacognition was not a conscious approach on my part. I did not even think of it, and did not use the term when I wrote those pages. But the concept is there.

Another thing that struck me in this revisiting is the fact that we never explained *The Great Transformation*. I defined it, but never explained how it works. The reason for this was (is) that we don't actually know how it works. In spite of all the topics and ideas about the mind throughout the entire book, you will not find a satisfying physical or neuronal explanation of this very first one. The question it poses is "how does the mind change its received information, into conscious and appropriate actions?" How does it change data into movements? And the answer still remains a mystery.

I am not saying that there aren't any theories that attempt to explain this mystery. And I am not saying that it is the only mystery. In fact, our book is full of mysteries—and of theories! But the phenomenon of the great transformation is one of the major mysteries.

Many books still to write and experiments to be done.

Looking for More Light

Our book, and our minds, are both spiraling (not circling) along. That spiral takes us around to places that seem familiar, but we have a different perspective. Things look different from this new perspective, but they are still clouded. It is as though we are peering into a new corner of a dark closet. We can direct a light into that corner, but the closet remains dark and mysterious. We just know more about the corner.

The mysteries of mind still challenge the greatest thinkers and scholars. It seems that, at times, the frustration may be too great to bear. There is the temptation to explain everything in one fell swoop. All our knowledge about the nature of matter and energy seems inadequate. In our frustration we find "mind mysteries" becoming entangled with other mysteries; ones that have little to do with the brain or the mind. New ideas in philosophy, physics, or mathematics can creep in: such things as chaos theory, quantum theory, or even proposals about new forms of matter and/or energy. It is intimidating for all of us.

So, I want to close with a bit of cheerleading. Personally, I do not believe we will need to go to such lengths in our exploration of the mind. And we should not be intimidated. The greatest success will come when we turn the light back on and continue our exploration.

It all comes down to light. And that is good news since the mind itself is a source of light. We must continue our self- examination, our metacognition. Each of us has that choice. We may not be able to predict what we will find or when we will find it, but it is the process that matters. As long as we choose to continue it we will have new light—not only from outside ourselves but from within.

As the Buddha says: We will *find our own light.*

Notes

1. Unconscious, or "implicit," memory is discussed more extensively in *The Art of Changing the Brain*, chapter 5.

2. Langer, E. (1990), *Mindfulness*, Perseus Books, Cambridge, MA.

3. http://en.wikipedia.org/wiki/Phineas_Gage#Brain_damage_eand_mental_changes

4. Damasio, H., et al. (1994), *Science*, 264, pp. 1102–1105.

5. Fernandez-Duque, D., et al. (2000), *Consciousness and Cognition*, 9, pp. 288–307.

6. Posner, M. I., et al. (2007), *Cognitive, Affective and Behavioral Neuroscience*, 7, pp. 391–395.

7. Devenski, O., Morrell, M. J., and Vogt, B. A. (1995), *Brain*, 118, pp. 279–306.

8. Johnson, C., et al. (2002), *Brain*, 125, pp. 1808–1814.

9. Johnson, M. K., et al. (2009), Oxford Journals, *Social Cognitive and Affective Neuroscience*, 4, pp. 313–327.

10. Allman, J. M., et al. (2010), *Proceedings of the New York Academy of Sciences*, 935, pp. 107ff. Allman is the leader of this research group at the California Institute of Technology. As such he is not the first author in all publications. This group was not the first to discover the spindle neuron, but the earliest reports of this unusual structure appeared in 1925. This report came from the work of Von Economo, and now spindle cells are commonly called Von Economo neurons.

11. I do not intend to claim that the anterior cingulate provides the only route to intelligence. Parrots with a brain the size of a walnut behave in ways that seem to demonstrate planning, emotional bonding, and other aspects of human intelligence. However, while it is not certain, even small brains may well contain structures that provide pathways between cognition and emotion—regardless of size.

12. Chiel, H. J. and Beer, R. D. (1997), *Trends in Neurological Science*, 20, pp. 553–556.

13. The top dorsal part of the ACC is connected with the front and back cortex as well as the motor system and the frontal eye fields, making it a central station for

processing top-down and bottom-up stimuli and assigning appropriate control to other areas in the brain. By contrast, the ventral part of the ACC is connected with emotion structures (amygdala, nucleus accumbens, hypothalamus, and anterior insula) and is involved in assessing the salience of emotion and motivational information; see Bush, G., Luu, P., and Posner, M. I. (2000), *Trends in Cognitive Science,* 4, pp. 215–222.

14. http://en.wikipedia.org/wiki/Self-knowledge
15. http://en.wikipedia.org/wiki/Self-knowledge_(psychology)

EPILOGUE

In the introduction for this book, I told the story of my experience with technology at Heathrow Airport. That experience had a significant impact on my thinking, but I have said little about it up to now. It would have been off the point; this book really isn't about technology.

It is, however, driven by the reality that computers and the Web are now, and will continue to be, a major factor in educational change for the next decades. That reality lies restlessly beneath the surface of educational theory and practice around the world. It has been called a "disruptive innovation." Some predict that by the end of this decade, more than half of all public high school classes in the United States will be taught on the Internet. The "disruption" will be characterized by disappearance of both *successful* and *less successful* established institutions and practices.[1]

The loss of less successful schools and educators might not be a tragedy, but what about losing the successful ones, too? How can that happen? The explanation is that even when educators begin to change and adapt to technology, the actual magnitude of the change is far too limited. Those changes tend to focus on "improvements," fitting technology into existing systems and philosophies. But, the claim goes on, what will be necessary is more dramatic than improvement; *the entire system must change.*

This argument has influenced me in two ways. My Heathrow story demonstrates one of these ways. I am serious about my worry that heavy educational reliance on technology may actually threaten the things we value most about the mind—literally. And even if the threat is not as great as I fear, I find it impossible to ignore. This predicament is a little like that of global warming. We may not be sure whether the coming change will do severe damage, but it might! And the damage could be irreversible. We don't want irreversible damage to developing minds. That possibility alone is enough to keep us from ignoring it. Just hoping for the best won't do.

The second way this disruptive aspect of educational technology influences us sounds like the first. The same urge to get going is there, but not for the same reason. In addition to concern or urgency, I find myself motivated simply by the possibilities, the opportunities. The conditions are ripe for change, driven not by worry or fear, but by opportunity.

The technology is here. We can use it now, and we are. But we must guard against forgetting the main objective. Technology is not central; learning is. Technology is only a tool. It is available now, but before we develop new applications, we must ask how learning works. Then we can see what technological tools will make it work better. Now, in 2011, we have the opportunity to bring both knowledge of the mind and technology into existing schools, together.

*   *   *

The situation is not ideal, however. The technology train has already left the station. It is underway, but may be headed toward the wrong destination. So what can we do? Addressing this question is the main objective of this epilogue.

To begin, notice that I don't consider myself a Luddite. I won't be smashing any computers. My approach to the problem does not involve protests or campaigns or strikes. Rather, I will try to develop constructive and practical ideas. In fact, simply *recognizing* the challenge may be as important as any specific suggestion that follows. Often, awareness is the most compelling aspect of change.

Assuming I have your attention, then, let's begin with the greatest pressure driving us toward using new and more powerful technology in education (and elsewhere). That pressure comes, and has come in the past, from the continual increase in speed and power of computers. This focus is based mainly on the belief that the goal of education is to get more information, faster. I noticed this several years ago at a time when I was just beginning to study the learning research and to think seriously about education. Even then, I was uneasy about this trend, having always been an advocate of reflection in the learning process. In my experience, learning was deeper and longer-lasting if I went slowly. Speed was not an ally. Neither complexity nor efficiency could be obtained quickly. Like good wine, the mind requires time.

As you now know, my belief is that, first and foremost, learning is about action. That is why "action" is the central theme at the beginning of this book. Getting information does not equal learning. We have to use it. Take action! In the past, I have often expressed this belief by challenging early adaptors of new educational software to ask themselves: "What does it ask the user *to do*?" The more things we try to do, the more we will learn. However, that message was often resisted, even when the answer to the question was "nothing." This defect was often thought to be minor, something to come back to later, if ever. Even when taken seriously, the actual inclusion of action in learning seemed to be too time-consuming. The excitement produced by immediacy overcame serious effort to take a more deliberative path. "This program is so neat and so fast that I just can't wait," is the claim.

At this point, then, I urge you to ask yourself the "action question." It is essential if the goal is to build the mind. You can do this even if the train is moving along. It is practical.

*   *   *

"Ease of use" is another reason that technology is moving ahead so quickly. It is easy to stay on this technology train, never asking about learning. I am not saying that educational applications should be difficult, but I do believe that other things are more important. However, it is almost impossible to resist this "easy way." If we are going to put first things first, some change will be necessary. Now, almost subconsciously, our first question about a technical change is something like, "Is it hard?" or "Is it complicated?" We may need to break this habit.

It won't be easy. Almost all popular changes in technology make thing easier. For example, as I described in the introduction, it was easier for *HAL* to lead me to the rental car return at Heathrow Airport than to figure it out using my own mind. But easy things don't necessarily exercise the mind. An essential aspect of learning is challenge. Without it we lose the joy. Lack of challenge means little reward for success. Yes, it felt good to find our destination, relieving our tension and worry, but we weren't kidding ourselves. It wasn't because we had overcome some meaningful challenge and were proud of ourselves. We hadn't and we weren't.

Assuming that ease of use will save us time, maybe educational users of new technology could use the time they gain for improving educational practice. For example, we might work on some or all of the elements in our pyramid of the mind (chapter 10) to make progress in the journey. This approach can be called "join them." Stay on the technology train, but use the time differently. Instead of just resting while technology does the work, go to work together with the technology experts. Not only can we join them, but we also may "enrich them."

*   *   *

One aspect of the brain, learning theory, and knowledge is that it is about the living person. About people. This social element is of great importance in effective learning. People remember their experience with others more than any delivery method or isolated searches. This is one reason why retention of the *class* in educational practice is important for at least a portion of the day. Isolated and intense work is also of great value, so any technology or Web application should seek a balance of individual and group assignments and programs.

This is a strength of technology, as evidenced by the explosion of "social use" applications such as Facebook, Twitter, and texting. If our cell phone is nearby, it is almost impossible not to check and recheck it, no matter what else we are doing. Another example is the apparent appeal of responding to voices, rather than text. I am told that, given a choice, most of us prefer to respond to a recorded request rather than a written one.

This social nature of technology is the opposite of what some predicted a decade ago. At that time the image was one of isolated individuals hunched over their keyboards. It seems certain that this concern is still valid in some cases, but the natural social instincts of our species remain important and powerful. I mention this here because it illustrates the potential for more integration of both group work and isolated work. Both are important in development of the mind.

*   *   *

I could write more in this vein, but you see how it goes. Even though technology has a head start, ultimately it is trumped by education for development of the mind. Be it action, integration, image, symbols, memory, school, or metacognition, every destination in the journey from brain to mind can make technology the slave, instead of the reverse. We should expect new technical advances that will help us meet the objectives we have discovered here. But now that we understand more about the journey, we can point technology in the right direction. The cart has been ahead of the horse for too long.

Note

1. Christensen, C., Johnson, C., and Horn, M. (2008), *Disrupting Class: How Disruptive Innovation Will Change the Way the World Learns*, McGraw-Hill, New York, NY.